PERSONAL INSOLVENCY IN THE 21ST CENTURY

Since 1979 the world has witnessed a remarkable cycle of personal insolvency law reform. Changes in capitalist economies, financial crises and political interest groups all contributed to this cycle of reform. This book examines the role of interest groups and distinct narratives in shaping reform in different countries while drawing attention to the role of timing, path dependency and unintended consequences in the development of personal insolvency law.

The book presents case studies of personal insolvency law in the US, France, Sweden, and England and Wales. It then analyses how, following the Great Recession of 2008, international financial institutions paid greater attention to the significance of household debt in contributing to financial instability and the role of individual insolvency law in providing a fresh start. Personal insolvency law reform became part of EU responses to the eurozone crisis and the EU has proposed harmonisation of individual insolvency law to promote entrepreneurialism. This book examines the extent to which these developments represent an emerging international commonsense about personal insolvency and its relationship to neo-liberalism. Finally, this book discusses whether the international emergence of individual personal insolvency law represents a progressive step or a band-aid for the costs of neo-liberal policies, where a significant number of people live.

Personal Insolvency in the 21st Century

A Comparative Analysis of the US and Europe

Iain Ramsay

•HART•

OXFORD • LONDON • NEW YORK • NEW DELHI • SYDNEY

HART PUBLISHING
Bloomsbury Publishing Plc
Kemp House, Chawley Park, Cumnor Hill, Oxford, OX2 9PH, UK

First published in Great Britain 2017

First published in hardback, 2017
Paperback edition, 2019

A catalogue record for this book is available from the British Library.

Library of Congress Cataloging-in-Publication Data

Names: Ramsay, Iain, author.

Title: Personal insolvency in the 21st century : a comparative analysis of the US and Europe / Iain Ramsay.

Description: Portland, Oregon : Hart Publishing, 2017. | Includes bibliographical references and index.

Identifiers: LCCN 2016058794 (print) | LCCN 2016059674 (ebook) | ISBN 9781849468091 (hardback : alk. paper) | ISBN 9781509900992 (Epub)

Subjects: LCSH : Bankruptcy—Europe. | Bankruptcy—United States. | Debtor and creditor

Classification: LCC K1375 .R36 2017 (print) | LCC K1375 (ebook) | DDC 346.407/8—dc23

LC record available at https://lccn.loc.gov/2016058794

ISBN: HB: 978-1-84946-809-1
PB: 978-1-50993-217-7
ePDF: 978-1-50990-098-5
ePub: 978-1-50990-099-2

Typeset by Compuscript Ltd, Shannon

PREFACE AND ACKNOWLEDGEMENTS

I am extremely grateful to the Leverhulme Trust for a Research Fellowship in 2014 which provided me with the time to engage in the research on this book and also visit the US and Sweden.

In the US, Leslie O'Neill, Librarian at the University of Pennsylvania, provided much assistance in accessing the National Bankruptcy Archives in the Biddle law library. I also profited from discussions with bankruptcy judges and a US Federal Trustee. I have learnt much from the many US scholars who have participated over the years in the Law & Society Collaborative Research Network on household debt and consumer bankruptcy, in particular the late Jean Braucher. Bill Whitford initiated the comparative socio-legal study of consumer bankruptcy at the international Law and Society meeting in Glasgow in 1996 and I have benefited much from his insights, support and friendship. Johanna Niemi, my other co-author on earlier books on this topic, generously read the manuscript, providing very helpful comments. I also owe an intellectual debt to the many European scholars with whom I have discussed personal insolvency and to Jason Kilborn's trailblazing studies of European personal insolvency systems. Conversations with Joseph Spooner illuminated many issues.

In Sweden several individuals and groups assisted in my research. These included Annina Persson, Richard Ahlström, Anne-Sophie Henrikson, and Vilhelm Nordenanckar of the Swedish Consumer Protection Agency. I had useful meetings with officials at the KFM (*Kronofogdemyndigheten*, known colloquially as the *Kronofogden*), the Swedish Business and Credit Information Agency (UCAB), and the Swedish Bankers Association. I also met with several debt counsellors who provided valuable background information.

In France I benefited from discussions with officials at the Bank of France, a major consumer lender and consumer interest group.

The Insolvency Service in England and Wales were helpful in providing data on the various English insolvency remedies.

I would like to thank Jeremmy Okonjo, and Indre Dapkeviciute for research assistance, the latter providing a valuable background paper on 'bankruptcy tourism'.

The title of the book 'personal insolvency' is intended to indicate a broader scope than consumer bankruptcy. Insolvency and bankruptcy have technically distinct legal meanings in some jurisdictions but this is not a technical legal text and I use the terms insolvency and bankruptcy interchangeably throughout the text.

Chapter 4 is a substantially revised and updated version of my article 'A Tale of Two Debtors: Responding to the Shock of Over-Indebtedness in France and England—A Story from the *Trente Piteuses*' (2012) 75 *MLR* 212. Some ideas developed in Chapters 1 and 4 were sketched in an article appearing in a special issue of the *Temple University Law Review* honouring Bill Whitford entitled 'U.S. Exceptionalism, Historical Institutionalism and the Comparative Study of Consumer Bankruptcy Law' (2015) 87 *Temple L Rev* 947.

An upsurge of research on credit, debt and insolvency has occurred since the Great Recession of 2008. The study of personal insolvency has also increased but there remain many important questions about its social and economic role. I hope that this book will stimulate others to probe this important area of law.

Finally, thanks to Toni Williams for reading and commenting on chapters, notwithstanding heavy administrative duties, and for unending encouragement without which I doubt that this book would have been completed.

I am aware that comparative studies are inevitably somewhat superficial and that there will be errors in my interpretations of the laws of the different jurisdictions discussed in the text. None of the above should be implicated in these errors.

Tom Adams at Hart Publishing was extremely efficient in the production of the text and thanks to Ceri Warner and Janet MacMillan for copyediting.

Eliot College
University of Kent
January 2017

CONTENTS

1

The Rise of Personal Insolvency Law

I. Introduction

In 1883, TH Farrer, an eminent English civil servant and one of the architects of the Bankruptcy Act 1883, wrote:

> A further point of great interest is the question of making some proceeding analogous to bankruptcy applicable to the case of workmen who have little or nothing but their weekly wages so that they may in the case of insolvency be able at moderate cost and on reasonable terms, to obtain their discharge and so that the sentence of imprisonment which county court judges now inflict for willful non-payment of small debts may be reduced within the smallest compass.[1]

The answer to Farrer's question was the administration order, introduced in Joseph Chamberlain's 1883 Bankruptcy and Insolvency Act and subsequently described as the 'poor man's bankruptcy'. This permitted an individual to repay a portion of debts over a period of years and then write off any balance remaining. The administration order had a chequered career[2] in the twentieth century, influencing reforms in the United States (US) in the 1930s,[3] European reforms in the 1980s, but limping into twenty-first-century England and Wales as other mechanisms for writing down debt emerged.

In 2013, specialists from the International Monetary Fund (IMF), reflecting on their experience of advising and influencing European governments on the adoption of new personal insolvency laws in the wake of the eurozone crisis, described an emerging European model of personal insolvency as a repayment plan of three to five years with a discharge of remaining debt at the end of this period.[4] This continuity in ideas about personal insolvency relief contrasts with the massive change in the role of household debt in the economy, and its triggering of the Great Recession in 2008. Moreover the poor man's bankruptcy had become

[1] TH Farrer, *The State in Its Relation to Trade* (London, Macmillan and Co, 1883) 35–36. The discussion of bankruptcy was in a chapter entitled 'General Limits of the State on Contractual Obligations'.

[2] See discussion below, ch 4.

[3] See discussion below, ch 3.

[4] See Y Liu and C Rosenberg, *Dealing with Private Debt Distress in the Wake of the European Financial Crisis: A Review of the Economics and Legal Toolbox* (Washington DC, International Monetary Fund, 2013).

the poor person's bankruptcy as women now represented the majority of users.[5] The IMF concluded in 2012 that recessions triggered by large increases in household debt could result in slower economic recovery than those triggered by other events.[6] Swift and effective insolvency procedures during a recession to reduce the household debt overhang could therefore have a valuable macro-economic effect by restoring consumer demand in the economy, an argument developed systematically by economists Atif Mian and Amir Sufi in their bestselling analysis of the 2008 recession, *House of Debt*.[7] In 2013, the World Bank published a report on personal insolvency, justifying the introduction of a personal insolvency discharge in terms of reducing lost productivity and costs to families and communities, while creating incentives for responsible lending and accounting practices, and allocating the risk of losses to those in the best position to spread those risks.[8] The European Union (EU) proposes greater harmonisation of personal insolvency law as part of the development of an integrated credit and capital market.[9] In the early part of the twenty-first century, personal insolvency law had become a significant market institution and ground rule of credit markets.

This book analyses the political and institutional development of personal insolvency law since 1979 in the US and Europe, while recognising that states entered this period with distinct regulatory institutions and historical baggage which helps with understanding differences in approach to personal insolvency law. The period since 1979 is remarkable for the introduction and reform of individual insolvency systems throughout Europe and other parts of the world (see Table 1.1) and increased use of these systems by over-indebted individuals.[10] This period follows the enactment of the Bankruptcy Reform Act 1978 in the US, the election of Margaret Thatcher in the United Kingdom (UK) in 1979, the increasing influence of neo-liberalism, and the growth of household debt as a driver of the economy[11]

[5] See ch 3 section VI.

[6] IMF, *World Economic Outlook* (Washington DC, IMF, 2012) 91. See also F Bornhorst and M Arranz, 'Growth and Importance of Sequencing Debt Reductions Across Sectors' in M Schindler and others (eds), *Jobs and Growth: Supporting the European Recovery* (Washington DC, International Monetary Fund, 2014) ch 2. The Bank of England concluded in 2014 that 'there is evidence that high levels of household debt have been associated with deeper downturns and more protracted recoveries in the United Kingdom'. See P Bunn and M Rostom, 'Household Debt and Spending' (2014) 3 *Bank of England Quarterly Bulletin* 304.

[7] A Mian and A Sufi, *House of Debt: How They (and You) Caused the Great Recession, and How We Can Prevent It from Happening Again* (Chicago, University of Chicago Press, 2015).

[8] See J Kilborn, J Garrido, C Booth, J Niemi, and I Ramsay, *World Bank Report on the Treatment of the Insolvency of Natural Persons* (Washington DC, World Bank, 2013); see also JM Garrido, 'The Role of Personal Insolvency Law in Economic Development' (2013) 5 *The World Bank Legal Review* 111. Garrido notes that the 'association between insolvency law and economic development is frequently overlooked … An effective personal insolvency law regime provides solutions for indebted persons while attaining broader goals for inclusive economic development.'

[9] See ch 6, 111.

[10] See Figure 3.3 in ch 3 for the rise in per 1,000 capita filings in England and Wales and Canada between 1987 and 2012.

[11] See for example C Crouch, 'Privatised Keynesianism: An Unacknowledged Policy Regime' (2009) 11 *The British Journal of Politics & International Relations* 382, 382; A Barba and M Pivetti, 'Rising

in many countries, in some acting as a substitute for stagnant wages.[12] The household debt-to-income ratio in the UK rose from 90 to 160 per cent between 1987 and 2007.[13] Increased inequality developed in many states[14] and more financial failure occurred during this period than any previous historical period.[15] Capitalism was being transformed.[16]

Table 1.1: Personal Insolvency and Debt Adjustment—Dates of Significant Legislative Change in European Jurisdictions and US since 1978

Austria	1993
Belgium	1997, 2005, 2009
Cyprus	2015
Czech Republic	2006, 2008
Denmark	1984, 2000, 2005, 2010
England and Wales	1986, 1990 (not in force), 2002, 2007, 2015
Estonia	2003, 2010
Finland	1992, 2015
France	1989, 1995, 1998, 2003, 2010, 2014
Germany	1994 (in force 1999), 2001, 2013
Greece	2010, 2013, 2015
Hungary	2015
Ireland	1988, 2012, 2015
Italy	2012
Latvia	2007, 2009, 2010, 2013

(continued)

Household Debt: Its Causes and Macroeconomic Implications—a Long-Period Analysis' (2009) 33 *Cambridge Journal of Economics* 113, 113; RG Rajan, *Fault Lines: How Hidden Fractures Still Threaten the World Economy* (Princeton, Princeton University Press, 2010). 'Cynical as it may seem, easy credit has been used as a palliative throughout history by governments that are unable to address the deeper anxieties of the middle class directly', ibid 8–9; W Streeck, *Buying Time: The Delayed Crisis of Democratic Capitalism* (London, Verso Books, 2014) 32–46. For an overview of studies see B Kus, 'Sociology of Debt States, Credit Markets, and Indebted Citizens' (2015) 9(3) *Sociology Compass* 212. See further discussion below at section III.

12 See below, section III.

13 See P Bunn and M Rostom, 'Household Debt and Spending in the UK', Bank of England Staff Working Paper no 554 (London, Bank of England, 2015) 1.

14 See discussion in T Piketty, *Capital in the Twenty-First Century* (Cambridge Mass, Harvard, 2014); B Milanovic, *Global Inequality: A New Approach for the Age of Globalization* (Cambridge Mass, Harvard, 2016).

15 See C Kindelberger and P Aliber, *Manias, Panics and Crashes: A History of Financial Crises* (Hoboken NJ, Wiley, 2005) 15. See also CM Reinhart and K Rogoff, *This Time is Different: Eight Centuries of Financial Folly* (Princeton, Princeton University Press, 2009).

16 Probably the best and most prescient analysis of these transformations can be found in M Castells, *The Information Age: Economy, Society and Culture* (Oxford, Blackwell, 1998).

Table 1.1: *(Continued)*

Lithuania	2013
Luxembourg	2000, 2013
Netherlands	1998, 2007, 2008
Norway	1992
Poland	2009, 2014
Portugal	2004, 2012
Romania	2015
Russia	2015
Scotland	1985, 1993, 2002, 2007, 2010, 2014
Slovakia	2004, 2006, 2011
Slovenia	2007, 2015
Spain	2013, 2015
Sweden	1994, 2007, 2011
US	1978, 1984, 1994, 2005

Source: Author

Personal insolvency systems can be divided initially into 'old' and 'new' systems. Old systems, primarily in the common law countries, recognised from the mid-nineteenth century the possibility of an individual non-trader using the bankruptcy system to discharge debts.[17] These systems became dominated by consumers rather than businesses at different periods: in the 1930s in the US;[18] by 1971 in Canada;[19] and only in the late 1990s in England and Wales.[20] Continental Europe is a site of 'new' personal insolvency systems in states that, previous to the 1980s, had not recognised the possibility of individual non-traders discharging their debts.

Two forms of personal insolvency now exist in Europe and the US. 'Straight' liquidation bankruptcy is when an individual gives up non-exempt assets for a discharge of most unsecured debts after a period ranging from a few months in the US to three to five years in several jurisdictions.[21] The second approach envisages repayment by an individual of a proportion of their debts in return for receiving

[17] The trader requirement for bankruptcy was abolished in England and Wales in 1861.
[18] See below, ch 2.
[19] See Office of Superintendent of Bankruptcy, Canada, Annual Report, 1971 noting 3,647 and 3,045 consumer and business bankruptcies respectively and see discussion of consumer bankrupts in *Report of the Study Committee on Bankruptcy and Insolvency Legislation* (Tassé Report) (Ottawa, Government of Canada, 1970) at para 2.1.13 indicating that 'the plight of the consumer or wage-earner debtor is one of the most important problems that must be faced in the field of bankruptcy in Canada'.
[20] See below, ch 3, Figure 3.2.
[21] Canada, 9 months; UK 12 months; Australia, New Zealand, 3 years. The EU Commission proposes a period of 3 years for 'honest entrepreneurs'. See discussion below, ch 6.

a discharge of the remainder after, typically, three to five years. The US, Canada, and the UK have both alternatives, while the repayment model is the dominant European model. That consumers should make an income contribution where possible rather than use straight bankruptcy is a dominant contemporary theme. Controversial is how much income or how great an attempt at payment should be made by a debtor as the price of a discharge. Liberal access to straight bankruptcy with a relatively swift discharge is increasingly a 'suppressed political alternative' for consumers, even in those jurisdictions such as England and Wales where it is available to consumers.[22]

The introduction of debt relief mechanisms in Europe followed the period of credit and capital liberalisation of the 1980s. Two 'critical junctures'[23] occurred. The first was in the late 1980s and 1990s, and included a banking crisis in the Nordic countries, a mini sub-prime crisis in France, and Germany's adjustment to reunification, all of which resulted in a first wave of debt adjustment laws, in some cases intended to be temporary (France), in others layered on to an existing business bankruptcy reform (Germany). The US model of Chapter 13—the income repayment chapter of the US Bankruptcy Code—the English administration order, and an earlier Danish reform influenced these reforms.[24] In all continental EU countries the US idea of a straight discharge for debtors was considered and rejected and significant periods of debt repayment were required before the possibility of a discharge. In France the original objective of the law was that individuals would repay all debts over time. These reforms experienced initial negative feedback about the institutional processes adopted and the ability of individuals to access relief. In France the courts were overloaded. In Germany and Sweden many debtors went through a fruitless attempt at a voluntary settlement before being able to access judicial debt relief. In all countries many individuals had no repayment capacity and few assets. Reforms addressing these process issues were often driven by concerns about reducing judicial costs. Other aspects, such as increasing access and reducing the waiting period before discharge, proved more intractable to change, resulting in phenomena such as zero-repayment plans while individuals waited for a discharge. During the 2000s, new EU Member States in central and Eastern Europe adopted insolvency legislation, often following the less than optimal German model.[25]

[22] See discussion below, ch 3.

[23] A 'critical juncture' is a period of 'contingency during which the usual constraints on action are lifted or eased.' J Mahoney and KA Thelen (eds), *Explaining Institutional Change: Ambiguity, Agency, and Power* (Cambridge, Cambridge University Press, 2010).

[24] Jason Kilborn has provided valuable accounts in English of the development of these systems. See eg J Kilborn, *Comparative Consumer Bankruptcy* (Durham NC, North Carolina Press, 2007); J Kilborn, 'Twenty Five Years of Consumer Bankruptcy in Continental Europe: Internalizing Negative Externalities and Humanizing Justice in Denmark' (2009) 18 *International Insolvency Review* 155.

[25] For a trenchant critique of the operation of the German law in the 2000s by one of the few systematic empirical studies of the German system see W Backert, D Brock, and K Maischatz, 'Bankruptcy in Germany: Filing Rates and the People Behind the Numbers' in J Niemi, I Ramsay, and WC Whitford (eds), *Consumer Credit, Debt and Bankruptcy: Comparative and International Perspectives*

The Great Recession and subsequent eurozone crisis are the second critical juncture. In the US the issue of writing down mortgage balances in bankruptcy, a response to the foreclosure crisis, was raised but defeated in Congress.[26] The troika (EU Commission, IMF, and European Central Bank) and the European Semester (the annual cycle of economic policy guidance and surveillance) required or strongly recommended the introduction and revision of corporate and individual insolvency laws in several countries, including Spain, Portugal and Greece, either as a condition of bailouts or under the new EU monitoring of the stability pacts.[27] In Ireland, reforms were underway but the international institutions influenced modifications to the original proposals.[28] Since international standards did not exist for personal insolvency,[29] and little systematic empirical study existed of consumer insolvency schemes in Europe, the international agencies were forced to make policy 'on the hoof' as they went along.[30] The Great Recession stimulated a rethinking of the role of household debt regulation and individual bankruptcy in the European project of achieving an integrated credit and capital market.

Significant differences continue to exist within the European systems and between these systems and the US system in terms of access criteria, institutional frameworks, discharge conditions and the financing of systems. This book began as a study in comparative public policy in an attempt to explain these differences. Part of the answer for existing differences lies simply in timing rather than deep-seated cultural differences between countries. Although Anglo-Saxon systems were not designed for consumers, and the discharge was a mechanism for obtaining debtor cooperation,[31] these systems could be converted to consumer use, sometimes by enterprising private intermediaries, without the high political costs of legislative reform. This low-visibility method of bringing about change often resulted in subsequent legislative acceptance of the practices that seemed

(Oxford, Hart Publishing, 2009). They note that many debtors have no repayment capacity: 'It has to be questioned whether there is much sense in a six-year-long period of good conduct (*Wohlverhalten*) before discharge from remaining debts is allowed. Why should people be kept under financial "probation" when there is no recognizable output for creditors and there is evidence of poor quality of life for debtors?'

[26] See below, ch 2 section V.A.

[27] See below, ch 6.

[28] For discussion of the Irish reform process see J Spooner, 'Long Overdue: What the Belated Reform of Irish Personal Insolvency Law Tells Us about Comparative Consumer Bankruptcy' (2012) 86 *American Bankruptcy Law Journal* 243: J Spooner, 'Sympathy for the Debtor? The Modernization of Irish Personal Insolvency Law' (2012) 25(7) *Insolvency Intelligence* 97.

[29] In contrast to corporate insolvency, where the United Nations Commission on International Trade Law (UNCITRAL) Guidelines are used by the international agencies to assess countries insolvency laws.

[30] Susan Block-Lieb expresses it nicely as 'shooting from the hip'. S Block-Lieb, 'Austerity, Debt Overhang, and the Design of International Standards on Sovereign, Corporate, and Consumer Debt Restructuring' (2015) 22 *Indiana Journal of Global Legal Studies* 487.

[31] See J McCoid II, 'Discharge. The Most Important Development in Bankruptcy History' (1996) 70(1) *American Bankruptcy Law Journal* 163.

to be meeting a social need. David Moss and Gibbs Johnson note the relatively unplanned rise of individual insolvency law in the US, commenting that 'at least since the beginning of the twentieth century students of consumer bankruptcy have found it to be a bewildering institution. No-one it appears ever intended to create it.'[32] In contrast, introducing a 'right not to pay one's debts'[33] in countries such as France and Sweden in the late 1980s entailed the high political costs of successfully introducing legislative change in the face of a powerful financial lobby. It is not surprising that the initial attempts to do so were hedged in by significant controls on access or the possibilities for discharge of debt.

Chapters two to five examine changing personal insolvency law and policy in the US, England and Wales, France, and Sweden, and outline the relevant political interests, the political and institutional context, and the role of narratives in framing policy choices in each country. These countries were chosen for several reasons. First, the US credit and bankruptcy system often serves as an international model to be either emulated or avoided. It influenced initial European reforms[34] in the 1990s and, more recently, European policymakers and think tanks argue that the US has recovered more swiftly than the EU states from the recession because of its liberal bankruptcy laws that permit a fresh start.[35] I therefore consider US bankruptcy law in a longer historical frame to illustrate the continuing conflicts within the US over the terms on which individuals should be able to discharge debts. England and Wales has, notwithstanding its similar legal origins, followed a different trajectory from the US in personal insolvency. France has developed a unique system to manage over-indebtedness, which is sometimes held up as an international model for developing countries,[36] and Sweden represents a personal insolvency system within a Scandinavian model of capitalism and social welfare.

Existing literature identifies distinct classifications of personal insolvency systems. Nordic countries are associated with a 'welfarist' perspective, while the French over-indebtedness system is conceptualised as consumer protection and

[32] D Moss and G Johnson, 'The Rise of Consumer Bankruptcy: Evolution, Revolution or Both' (1999) 73 *American Bankruptcy Law Journal* 311.

[33] I take the phrase from the title of Ripert's article in the 1930s. See G Ripert, '*Le droit de ne pas payer ses dettes*' (1936) *Dalloz, Recueil Hebdomadaire Chronique* 57.

[34] See N Huls, 'American Influence on European Consumer Bankruptcy Law' (1992) 15 *Journal of Consumer Policy* 125, 135–37.

[35] V Jourova (Director General, Justice), 'Insolvency Law in Europe—Giving People and Businesses a Second Chance' (speech at the Conference on 'Insolvency law in Europe: current trends and future perspectives', Jurmala, Latvia, 23 April 2015) http://ec.europa.eu/commission/2014-2019/jourova/announcements/insolvency-law-europe-giving-people-and-businesses-second-chance_en: '[I]n the U.S. the average debt discharge period is less than one year, while in most EU countries it's between five and seven years. There is evidence which shows that shorter discharge periods allowed U.S. households to recover more quickly from the crisis.' See also G Steinhauser and M Dalton, 'Lingering Bad Debts Stifle European Recovery' *Wall St Journal* (New York, 31 January 2013).

[36] For example, influencing reform proposals in Brazil and see Consumers International, *Model Law on Family Insolvency for Latin America and the Caribbean* (2011), www.consumersinternational.org/media/880320/a%20model%20law%20on%20family%20insolvency%20for%20latin%20america%20and%20the%20caribbean.pdf.

the US system as market regulation.[37] These images are helpful but may not capture the contemporary reality of these systems. Thus chapter five indicates that Sweden does not represent a social welfare approach to debt relief, for example, but is, rather, a tough creditor-oriented system. Jan Heuer has provided an empirically based classification of the underlying normative structure of individual insolvency laws. The 'market model' (US, Canada) provides a swift discharge, allocating market risks to creditors as superior risk-bearers and ensuring the re-entry of the debtor to the credit market. The 'restrictions model' (England and Wales, Scotland, Australia, New Zealand) has similarities to the market model but includes significant restrictions on debtors as a mechanism of public protection. The 'liability model' (Germany, Austria) emphasises the individual responsibility of debtors for repayment. Finally, the 'mercy model' (Denmark, Finland, Norway, Sweden, France) represents needs-based systems where the nature and scope of relief offered debtors is significantly dependent on the discretionary decisions of bureaucratic decision makers.[38]

Heuer's classification underlines the normative ideas underlying the different systems carried into effect, for example in Germany, with the requirement of the repayment period before discharge, the integration of debt counsellors into the system to teach consumers the proper norms of credit behaviour, and the obligation to search for work during the repayment period. This approach smacks of the influence of German ordoliberal ideas of the responsible citizen.[39] These normative ideas may also reflect political interests. The initial German legislation represented agreement between the German banks and debt counsellors on the importance of the period of good behaviour before the possibility of discharge.

The differences between insolvency systems reflect historical contingency and the influence of political interest groups and ideas. The German example of the confluence between ideas and political interest groups suggests that we should be cautious of attributing the current German system to cultural causes. The differences between European regimes raises the question of the extent to which these systems may be converging, with both the internationalisation of household credit and as a consequence of the Great Recession of 2008. Chapter six moves the analysis, therefore, to the international level and discusses the emergence of an international 'common sense' about personal insolvency in the wake of the Great Recession, as international and regional actors paid greater attention to the role

[37] See J Niemi, 'Collective or Individual? Constructions of Debtors and Creditors in Consumer Bankruptcy' in J Niemi, I Ramsay, and W Whitford (eds), *Consumer Bankruptcy in Global Perspective* (Oxford, Hart Publishing, 2003) 41–60.

[38] See J Heuer, 'Social Inclusion and Exclusion in European Consumer Bankruptcy Systems' (on file with author) and J Heuer, 'Private Überschuldung und Sozialpolitik: Varianten der staatlichen Regulierung von Verbraucherinsolvenz und Rechtschuldbefreiung' (2015) 61(3) *Zeitschrift für Sozialreform* 315.

[39] See the discussion of ordoliberalism in M Foucault, *The Birth of Bio-Politics, Lectures at the College of France* 1978–79 (A Davidson (ed), trans G Burchell) (Basingstoke, Palgrave Macmillan, 2010) 81 where the state, according to Ludwig Erhard, establishes 'both the freedom and responsibility of the citizens'.

of household debt in contributing to financial instability and prolonging debt-fuelled recessions. Writers claim that a transnational legal order[40] of corporate insolvency norms has now spread throughout the world. I do not make such a broad claim but do suggest a common set of ideas emerging through 'good practices' and 'cross-country experience'. The troika and European Semester imposed insolvency reforms on some countries and the EU promotes harmonisation of insolvency norms as an element of the ground rules of an integrated retail credit market. The historical trader/non-trader distinction surfaces again in contemporary EU proposals with a liberal discharge promoted for entrepreneurs but a more cautious approach adopted towards consumers.

Finally, chapter seven poses the question of whether the development of personal insolvency law since the early 1980s represents a progressive step. This might seem an odd question since most writers conceptualise personal insolvency law as providing relief from hardship. It represents part of a social safety net, a socially provided insurance,[41] and perhaps a last-gasp addition to other social protections.[42] The World Bank argues that providing a fresh start for debtors in personal insolvency may increase productivity and promote entrepreneurialism and economic stability. However, finding reliable evidence demonstrating the contribution of insolvency law to these objectives is not easy and is a task compounded by the difficulties of longitudinal study of bankrupts and obtaining a reliable counterfactual control population. Studies have questioned whether individuals do obtain a fresh start[43] and US studies have questioned the benefits of Chapter 13—the

[40] Gregory Shaffer defines transnational legal ordering as 'the transnational production of legal norms and institutional forms in particular fields and their migration across borders regardless of whether they address transnational activities or purely national ones'. G Shaffer (ed), *Transnational Legal Ordering and State Change* (Cambridge, Cambridge University Press, 2013) 6–7. See below, ch 6.

[41] Elizabeth Warren and Jay Westbrook argue that 'the genius of the Western democracies has been maintaining the lively edge of capitalism while preserving social stability and productivity through various devices that contain the market's inevitable shocks to individuals and communities. Bankruptcy is an integral part of that machinery.' See E Warren and JL Westbrook, *The Law of Debtors and Creditors: Text, Cases, and Problems* (New York, Aspen Law & Business, 2006) 353–54.

[42] See discussion of the relationship between regulatory private law protections (such as insolvency) and the welfare state in H Haber, 'Regulation as Social Policy: Home Evictions and Repossessions in the UK and Sweden' (2015) 93(3) *Public Administration* 806.

[43] See eg E Cohen-Cole, B Duygan-Bump, and J Montoriol-Garriga, 'Who Gets Credit after Bankruptcy and Why? An Information Channel' (2013) 37 *Journal of Banking & Finance* 5101 (limited debt availability after bankruptcy). See also S Han and G Li, 'Household Borrowing after Personal Bankruptcy' (2011) 43 *Journal of Money, Credit and Banking* 491; S Han and W Li, 'Fresh Start or Head Start? The Effects of Filing for Personal Bankruptcy on Work Effort' (2007) 31 *Journal of Financial Services Research* 123. For a study on the limited effects of Swedish restructuring law see R Ahlström, S Edström, and M Savemark, 'Is Debt Relief Rehabilitative? An Evaluation of Debt Relieved Persons' Health, Life Quality and Personal Finances Three Years after Conducted Debt Relief' 2014:15 (Stockholm, The Swedish Consumer Agency, 2014); R Ahlström, S Edström, and M Savemark, 'Over-Indebtedness as a Risk Factor for Inequality in Health and Life Quality among Swedes—A Survey of Debts, Health and Living Conditions among Over-indebted Households in Sweden' (Stockholm, The Swedish Consumer Agency, 2014); R Ahlström, 'The Costs to Society of Over-indebtedness

repayment model—for many homeowners, but a recent econometric study claims that it is beneficial in mitigating the consequences of financial distress.[44]

A darker vision of insolvency law is that it performs both a disciplining and legitimating function in a debt-driven neo-liberal economy, depoliticising class conflict between debtors and finance capital. Within this vision, consumer debt is a secondary form of exploitation of the surplus population, which staves off rather than solves the problems of falling rates of productivity and stagnant wages. The higher levels of default within this system confers a disciplining role on personal insolvency law which individualises failure, concealing its class dimensions. Within this view, the history of US bankruptcy law since 1978 is one of financial interests promoting measures to discipline debtors through means testing and required counselling.[45] The US Bankruptcy Abuse Prevention and Consumer Protection Act of 2005 (BAPCPA) of 2005 represents within this narrative the power of the financial lobby to restrict access to bankruptcy and increase corporate profits.

Susanne Soederberg's analysis highlights the contrasting characterisations of insolvency law as social control and individual empowerment. Whichever perspective is adopted, class issues are significant. Unequal access to debt relief is a political powder keg. In 1883, the English[46] administration order was intended to address the criticism that bankruptcy and a discharge of debts was only available to the middle classes while working-class debtors suffered imprisonment for debt. During the recent eurozone crisis, political movements organised around mass write downs of debt in Spain and Greece. The European Central Bank (ECB) in 2015 recognised the issues of political legitimacy raised by the existence of different standards of debt restructuring for corporate and individual debtors. The availability of personal insolvency law was 'important to ensure that the political appetite for resolving less socially sensitive NPE portfolios is not undermined'.[47]

in Sweden—Loss of Production, Health Care Expenditures, Sick-Leave and Disability Pensions' (The Swedish National Audit Office, 2015). I discuss further these issues in ch 6, in particular the relationship between insolvency laws and entrepreneurialism, in the context of EU proposals for a Directive to harmonise insolvency law.

[44] See eg K Porter, 'The Pretend Solution: An Empirical Study of Bankruptcy Outcomes' (2011) 90 *Texas Law Review* 103; S Green, P Patel, K Porter, 'Cracking the Code: An Empirical Analysis of Consumer Bankruptcy Outcomes' (https://papers.ssrn.com/sol3/papers.cfm?abstract_id=2839060) noting at 1 that 'study after study … has found that only about one-third of consumers who enter chapter 13 complete their repayment plans and therefore receive a discharge'; cf W Dobbie and J Song, 'Debt Relief and Debtor Outcomes: Measuring the Effects of Consumer Bankruptcy Protection' (2014) 105 *American Economic Review* 1272.

[45] See eg S Soederberg, *Debtfare States and the Poverty Industry: Money, Discipline and the Surplus Population* (London, Routledge, 2014) 49, 86–87, 95–97. See discussion below, ch 7.

[46] Reference to England includes England and Wales. Scotland has its own bankruptcy and insolvency laws.

[47] ECB, *Financial Stability Review* (Frankfurt, ECB, May 2015) 148.

II. Explanations for Stability and Change in Personal Insolvency Law

Explanations of the development of personal insolvency laws include functionalism, the idea that legal changes respond to the needs of a society,[48] interest group analyses,[49] national cultural values,[50] or 'legal origins', which argues that the French civil law jurisdiction and the common law jurisdictions exhibit different styles of legal regulation.[51] These approaches provide important insights and I draw on them throughout the book. An interest group perspective highlights the role of financial interests as long-term repeat players who can shape personal insolvency law in arenas of both 'quiet' and 'loud' politics,[52] as well as through the market. Appeals to national culture or legal origins draw attention to the role of history and ideas in shaping the law, and a tendency to turn to existing institutions to solve new problems. Cultural explanations may, however, underplay historical conflicts, the role of political interest groups in promoting particular ideas, and the instrumental use of cultural arguments, images and myths.[53] Culture tends to provide a toolkit[54] of arguments in political debates over bankruptcy rather than a set of binding constraints.

Contemporary personal insolvency laws are not the outcome of a single political conflict, and a comparative study of their stability and change is a study of politics over time.[55] I draw, therefore, on aspects of historical institutionalism[56]

[48] See I Ramsay, 'Functionalism and Political Economy in the Comparative Study of Consumer Insolvency: An Unfinished Story from England and Wales' (2006) 7 *Theoretical Inquiries in Law* 625, 645–64. For a systematic analysis and critique of functionalism see R Michaels, 'The Functional Method of Comparative Law' in M Reimann and R Zimmermann (eds), *The Oxford Handbook of Comparative Law*, 1st edn (Oxford, Oxford University Press, 2006).

[49] These have often drawn on public choice analysis. For work on the US system see EA Posner, 'The Political Economy of the Bankruptcy Reform Act of 1978' (1997) 96 *Michigan Law Review* 47; DA Skeel, *Debt's Dominion: A History of Bankruptcy Law in America* (Princeton, Princeton University Press 2014) 14, 15. For Canada see I Ramsay, 'Interest Groups and the Reform of Canadian Consumer Bankruptcy Law' (2003) 53 *University of Toronto Law Journal* 379.

[50] See N Martin, 'The Role of History and Culture in Developing Bankruptcy and Insolvency Systems: The Perils of Legal Transplantation' (2005) 28 *Boston College International and Comparative Law Review* 1.

[51] R La Porta, F Lopez-de-Silanes, and A Shleifer, 'The Economic Consequences of Legal Origins' (2008) 46 *Journal of Economic Literature* 285.

[52] P Culpepper, *Quiet Politics and Business Power Corporate Control in Europe and Japan* (Cambridge, Cambridge University Press, 2011).

[53] See discussion in J Spooner, 'Fresh Start or Stalemate?' European insolvency law reform and the politics of household debt' (2013) 21(3) *European Review of Private Law* 747.

[54] P DiMaggio, 'Culture and Cognition' (1997) 23 *Annual Review of Sociology* 263.

[55] P Pierson, *Politics in Time: History, Institutions, and Social Analysis*, 1st edn (Princeton, Princeton University Press, 2004).

[56] Historical institutionalism covers a broad range of writing. Influential texts include: Pierson, ibid; J Mahoney, D Rueschemeyer, and KA Thelen (eds), 'How Institutions Evolve: Insights from Comparative Historical Analysis' in J Mahoney and D Rueschemeyer (eds), *Comparative Historical*

which conceptualises policy changes as resulting from both exogenous (societal changes) and endogenous forces, steering a middle path between views of law as an autonomous institution or an unrefined functionalism. This approach is useful for understanding personal insolvency law, which is both a highly technical subject with its own internal dynamics and professional corps, and also is an area affected by socio-economic and political change, party politics and public values such as promise keeping, personal responsibility and relief of hardship. The chapters on individual countries highlight the role of different interest groups and narratives operating within different institutional frameworks. These institutional differences include the role of parliaments, government bureaucracies, expert committees and courts in creating and developing the law. The institutional fragmentation of US politics, with its many veto points, makes 'big bang' changes difficult.[57] It is not easy to displace existing legislation. This contrasts with the 'elective dictatorship' of the UK parliamentary model, and the important role of technocracies in France and Sweden.[58] The US legislative structure may permit more opportunities for interest group provisions, and the decentralised implementation of the US Bankruptcy Code allows for experimentation and learning. The persistence of 'local legal culture' is one example.[59]

The timing of change may be significant. I have already mentioned the significance of the early abolition of the trader criterion for insolvency in many common law jurisdictions. Path dependency[60] suggests that relatively contingent historical

Analysis in the Social Sciences (Cambridge, Cambridge University Press, 2000); W Streeck and K Thelen, 'Introduction: Institutional Change in Advanced Political Economies' in W Streeck and K Thelen (eds), *Beyond Continuity: Institutional Change in Advanced Political Economies* (Oxford, Oxford University Press, 2005); J Mahoney and K Thelen, *Explaining Institutional Change: Ambiguity, Agency, and Power* (Cambridge, Cambridge University Press, 2010). A useful outline of the different varieties of institutionalism is provided in VA Schmidt, 'Taking Ideas and Discourse Seriously: Explaining Change through Discursive Institutionalism as the Fourth "New Institutionalism"' (2010) 2 *European Political Science Review* 1. Examples of applications by legal scholars include OA Hathaway, 'Path Dependence in the Law: The Course and Pattern of Legal Change in a Common Law System' (2001) 86 *The Iowa Law Review*; J Bell, 'Path Dependence and Legal Development' (2012) 87 *Tulane Law Review* 787.

[57] The Bankruptcy Reform Act 1978 was enacted 10 years after the creation of the Bankruptcy Reform Commission and the BAPCPA 10 years after creation of the National Bankruptcy Review Commission. For chronological histories of these enactments see KN Klee, 'Legislative History of the New Bankruptcy Code' (1980) 54 *American Bankruptcy Law Journal* 275. For BAPCPA, see S Jensen, 'A Legislative History of the Bankruptcy Abuse Prevention and Consumer Protection Act of 2005' (2005) 79 *American Bankruptcy Law Journal* 485.

[58] See S Steinmo, *The Evolution of Modern States: Sweden, Japan, and the United States* (Cambridge, Cambridge University Press, 2010); M Prasad, *The Politics of Free Markets: The Rise of Neoliberal Economic Policies in Britain, France, Germany, and the United States* (London, University of Chicago Press, 2006) 238–39. And see discussion below, ch 4.

[59] See TA Sullivan, E Warren, and JL Westbrook, 'Persistence of Local Legal Culture: Twenty Years of Evidence from the Federal Bankruptcy Courts' (1994) 17 *Harvard Journal of Law & Public Policy* 801. The persistence of state differences in the use of Chapter 13 and Chapter 7 suggests that learning may be modest.

[60] For an excellent discussion of this concept see Pierson, *Politics in Time* (n 55) 44–53.

choices may have long-term and unintended effects[61] resulting in an institutional structure that may be difficult to change.[62]

A critical juncture may provide an opportunity for change agents or policy entrepreneurs to provide new diagnoses of a policy area and promote an agenda for change. The Great Recession of 2008 represented such a juncture and its impact on personal insolvency law is examined in chapter six. Critical junctures may not only be exogenous events such as a severe economic downturn, but also may arise from a puzzle about existing explanations of social phenomena—for example, why do bankruptcies continue to increase during an apparently buoyant economic period? These events provide opportunities for policy actors to provide new diagnoses and agenda for change.

Reference to critical junctures suggests a picture of stability punctuated by dramatic change. However, a study of the law in action often highlights the many low-visibility realms of change and sites of political conflict over personal insolvency norms as different groups promote particular practices and interpretations. Even if we focus initially on the law in books, many important changes in insolvency law are introduced not through primary legislation but through circulars, court rules, protocols and guidelines.[63] Table 1.1, which documents primary legislation, underestimates therefore the continuing adjustments and changes to insolvency law. This is often the arena of quiet politics, a seemingly technical low-visibility

[61] David Skeel drew on path dependency when arguing that US consumer bankruptcy law, with its early rejection of English 'officialism' in 1898, and reliance on courts, set in train the need for lawyers and judges in the administration of bankruptcy. The subsequent opposition of these groups to an administrative system increased the costs of political attempts in the 1930s during the New Deal, and again in the 1960s, to substitute an administrative model based on the English Official Receiver model. If the 1898 US Bankruptcy Act had been first introduced in the 1930s an administrative model might have been adopted. 'The best way to appreciate how U.S. bankruptcy law could have taken a very different look is to consider a simple counterfactual. Suppose the nation had continued without a federal bankruptcy law into the twentieth century. If federal bankruptcy had remained precarious into the New Deal, Congress might have dealt with insolvency issues quite differently … Each of the other strands [of the New Deal safety net] is administrative rather than judicial in nature. It does not take too great a leap of imagination to speculate that New Deal lawmakers, if they had been writing on a clean slate, might well have crafted an administrative bankruptcy system.' Skeel, *Debt's Dominion* (n 49) 100.

[62] The 'dead weight of previous institutional choices' may limit the subsequent room to manoeuver. JS Hacker, *The Divided Welfare State: The Battle Over Public and Private Social Benefits in the United States* (Cambridge, Cambridge University Press, 2002) 54.

[63] The implementation of legislation may itself be dependent on executive decrees, which provide a potential veto point. See discussion below in ch 3 section III about the failure of the executive to implement legislation reforming the administration order in England and Wales. This low visibility of decision-making can sometimes mislead. Thus, two political scientists claimed that England had revised its consumer bankruptcy law in 1990 with the passage of s 13 of the Courts and Legal Services Act which permitted discharge of debts after a three-year administration order. See W Schelkle, 'A Crisis of What? Mortgage Credit Markets and the Social Policy of Promoting Homeownership in the United States and in Europe' (2012) 40 *Politics & Society* 59; G Trumbull, *Strength in Numbers: The Political Power of Weak Interests* (Cambridge, Harvard University Press, 2012). But although the Bill for the Act was enacted by Parliament, s 13 has never been brought into force. This veto had a major impact on the balance of public and private repayment alternatives in England and Wales.

world of little interest to politicians and the public.[64] Implementation by courts and officials may convert a law from its original purpose or frustrate its objectives. The hostility of many US bankruptcy judges to provisions of the 2005 BAPCPA amendments, fuelled by the failure of Congress to consult them on its passage, may have contributed to the failure of some provisions to achieve their objective.[65] Private actors and intermediaries may achieve substantial change in individual personal insolvency law through inventive 'conversions'[66] of laws to serve unintended objectives. Entrepreneurial accountants converted the individual voluntary arrangement (IVA) in England and Wales, intended to provide relief for company directors, into a mass-produced consumer remedy.[67] Groups may also undermine intended legislative objectives, as finance companies did for the 'fresh start' in the US in the 1950s and 1960s.[68] This study of the role of private actors in the conversion of law illustrates the limits of institutional design. Bankruptcy legislation in the US has favoured repeatedly the idea of Chapter 13 repayment plans for consumers, but only with modest success.[69]

Institutionalists have developed a useful vocabulary of 'conversion', 'drifting',[70] and 'layering' to describe political strategies of change and stasis.[71] I have already mentioned the significance of conversion. Drifting is the politics of inaction and in chapter three is illustrated by English developments. Layering 'the addition of new rules which do not displace existing rules but operate on top of or alongside existing rules and policies', may 'alter or compromise' an existing institution.[72] Layering may occur because of the high political costs of direct legislative repeal.[73] It may reflect a political strategy to undermine existing law by adding an exception that over time provides a precedent for a more direct displacement of existing law. The 'substantial abuse' amendment introduced by financial interests in the 1984 US bankruptcy reform legitimated the idea that a significant group of individuals

[64] See my discussion in I Ramsay, 'Interest Groups and the Politics of Consumer Bankruptcy Reform in Canada' (2003) 53 *University of Toronto Law Journal* 379, 412–18 and the discussion of the development of the individual voluntary arrangement protocol in England and Wales in ch 3 section V.A.

[65] See discussion of the failure of the serial filing provisions in ch 3 (at n 151).

[66] 'Conversion' describes a situation where the rules remain the same but are interpreted or implemented differently by actors who 'actively exploit the inherent ambiguities of the institutions'. Mahoney and Thelen, *Explaining Institutional Change* (n 56) 17.

[67] See below, ch 3 section IV.

[68] See below, ch 2 section III.

[69] See generally, ch 2 section III.

[70] Mahoney and Thelen, *Explaining Institutional Change* (n 56) 17: '*Drift* occurs when rules remain formally the same but their impact changes as a result of changes in external conditions (citing JS Hacker, 'Policy Drift: The Hidden Politics of US Welfare State Retrenchment' in W Streeck and K Thelen (eds), *Beyond Continuity: Institutional Change in Advanced Political Economies*, 1st edn (Oxford, Oxford University Press, 2005). When actors choose not to respond to such environmental changes, their very inaction can cause change in the impact of the institution.'

[71] Hacker states that these are often 'covert strategies that political actors adopt when trying to transform embedded policy commitments': ibid 16.

[72] See Mahoney and Thelen, *Explaining Institutional Change* (n 56) 15.

[73] See below, ch 2 section IV, concerning the strategy of financial interests in the US after the Bankruptcy Reform Act 1978.

were abusing bankruptcy and assisted in developing the personal responsibility agenda that dominated the 2005 amendments. Layering may also result simply in contradictions within a statute. This may be said to have been the consequence, in 2002, of the English layering of an entrepreneurialism agenda onto a statute encrusted with the historical, quasi-criminal status of bankruptcy.

Terence Halliday and Bruce Carruthers draw on both institutional insights and sociolegal studies to propose a cyclical theory of legal change that they describe as 'recursivity'.[74] This theory claims that much lawmaking goes through cycles. New laws often contain ambiguous and contradictory provisions that result in unintended consequences, conflicting interpretations and creative compliance, generating a further round of reform that ultimately results in a settling of the law on a new equilibrium. These cycles of reform may often be triggered by scandals or crises. Halliday and Carruthers point to US corporate bankruptcy law as an example with recursive episodes during the 1890s, 1930s and late 1970s. Applying their analysis to the development of international corporate bankruptcy norms after the Asian financial crisis, they conclude that this process of change is one of 'trial and error', 'innovation and adaptation', and 'learning from experience'. While convergence may exist at a level of global principles, much variation continues at the level of local implementation and the law in action.[75]

Halliday and Carruther's analysis might seem applicable to personal insolvency law with a cycle of reforms in Europe beginning in the 1980s, with states initially 'muddling through' with partially effective laws being adjusted over time, sometimes by courts, or legislatures, in other cases by private intermediaries. The Great Recession triggered a further cycle of reforms with the movement towards a new European equilibrium of individual insolvency law norms, with substantial variations in implementation and detail.

Significant differences exist, however, between the dynamics of corporate and individual insolvency development. Cross-border issues are of less significance in individual insolvency, notwithstanding the existence of 'bankruptcy tourism'.[76] In corporate insolvency law, a small group of global actors promoted the internationalisation of a modified US (Chapter 11) rescue culture based on a shared narrative of the importance of corporate insolvency to economic development and international financial stability. A similar group with a shared agenda does not exist in individual insolvency law and no country has a strong interest in internationalising its individual insolvency law. English lawyers and policymakers may be keen to make London an attractive forum for corporate restructuring, but not one for EU citizens seeking to take advantage of the liberal bankruptcy discharge in England.

[74] See T Halliday and B Carruthers, *Bankrupt: Global Lawmaking and Systemic Financial Crisis* (Palo Alto, Stanford University Press, 2010) 15–32; and see the initial development of this approach in T Halliday and B Carruthers, 'The Recursivity of Law: Global Norm-Making and National Lawmaking in the Globalization of Corporate Insolvency Regimes' (2007) 112 *American Journal of Sociology* 1135.

[75] ibid 33–35.

[76] See discussion below, ch 6 section V.

A corporate rescue model can be portrayed as making everyone better off, including creditors and the wider community, whereas individual insolvency law represents primarily a modest redistribution from creditor to debtor. Since it is also often portrayed as a redistribution from one group of consumers (those who pay their debts) to another (those who do not), personal insolvency law reform is often controversial, a hot potato best left to national actors to sort out.

A. The Role of Narratives in Personal Insolvency Policy

Narratives provide a framework of ideas about the goals of a policy, the nature of the problem addressed, and the most appropriate instruments to achieve these goals.[77] Narratives are important in agenda setting, cementing political coalitions (for example, debt counsellors and creditors agree on overspending as the cause of over-indebtedness), and giving meaning to the work of bureaucracies and actors in a bankruptcy system.[78] Actors within a bankruptcy system—judges, accountants, lawyers, advice bureaux—develop 'social constructions' of bankrupts, narratives about debtors and the appropriate use of the bankruptcy process.[79] These actors often contribute to bankruptcy policymaking and so their constructions of debtors may be influential.[80] Since the public may have relatively little knowledge of bankruptcy or bankrupts, interest groups, policy entrepreneurs, and academic 'model mongers' have an incentive to promote particular narratives. Critical junctures (the Great Recession) may provide opportunities for changing diagnoses and policy prescriptions. Large increases in bankruptcy filings provided opportunities for financial interests in the US to promote narratives of bankruptcy abuse and the idea of 'lifestyle insolvencies' as part of a political campaign to reduce access to bankruptcy. The sound bite of the $400 'bankruptcy tax' was created and cited in US and UK legislative debates even though it had little empirical support.[81] Similarly, the UK banks and some professionals promoted an image of debtors 'living beyond their means' in the 2000s.[82] The Great Recession globalised issues

[77] See PA Hall, 'Policy Paradigms, Social Learning, and the State: The Case of Economic Policymaking in Britain' (1993) 25 *Comparative Politics* 275.

[78] See M Blyth, *Great Transformations: Economic Ideas and Institutional Change in the Twentieth Century* (Cambridge, Cambridge University Press, 2002); see also Schmidt, 'Taking Ideas and Discourse Seriously' (n 56).

[79] P Rock, *Making People Pay* (London, Routledge, 1973); J Braucher, D Cohen, and RM Lawless, 'Race, Attorney Influence, and Bankruptcy Chapter Choice' (2012) 9 *Journal of Empirical Legal Studies* 393; I Ramsay, *Debtors and Creditors—A Socio-Legal Perspective* (Abingdon, Butterworths Law, 1986).

[80] Their constructions may also have practical consequences in steering individuals to particular solutions. Studies in the US indicate racial stereotyping of debtors by lawyers in decisions whether to channel individuals to Chapter 7 or 13.

[81] See E Warren, 'The Phantom $400' (2004) 13(2) *Journal of Bankruptcy Law and Practice* 77. For the US citations, see below, ch 2 (n 124). For the UK, see the debates on the Enterprise Act 2002 below, ch 3 section IV.

[82] See below, ch 3 section V.A.

of household debt and household insolvency with international agencies and their consultants hurriedly developing international policy scripts around personal insolvency, economic recovery and entrepreneurialism.[83] These early narratives in the construction of an international common sense of personal insolvency may have long-term influence.

Personal insolvency narratives are constructed from contrasting and conflicting ideas. These include the concepts of a fresh start, a second chance, the prevention of social exclusion, and the promotion of entrepreneurialism (responsible risk-taking). Counter-narratives include the influential *pacta sunt servanda*—the 'common sense' idea that 'one pays back one's debts' associated with the maintenance of 'good payment culture'—the control of moral hazard, and the importance of personal responsibility reflected in the slogan 'can pay, should pay'. These ideas represent the toolkit for political argument, and policymakers often claim that they have drawn a balance between the values. This may lead to quite different results in each country since it may be difficult to measure an optimal balance. In addition, central concepts such as the fresh start or financial inclusion are ambiguous. A fresh start might be interpreted as either a simple discharge of debts or the more complex idea of financial rehabilitation No unequivocal answers exist as to the scope of the fresh start, how much of an individual's human capital should be devoted to repaying creditors in an insolvency, what specific assets should be exempt from seizure, and which debts should be excluded from the fresh start. Financial inclusion might include a variety of measures ranging from a simple discharge of debts through credit counselling and employment advice to ensure an individual's full participation in society.[84]

Dominant narratives about bankruptcy reflect partly the 'storytelling power of the stakeholders'[85] who link their story to more general values in society. The success of any particular group may depend on the national context of the production of influential ideas, described by John Campbell and Ove Pedersen as a country's 'knowledge regime'—'the organizational and institutional machinery that generates data, research, policy recommendations and other ideas that influence public debate and policymaking'.[86] This includes the role of political think tanks, academic researchers, governmental advisory units and their relationship to legislatures. Changes in a knowledge regime will affect how influential ideas are produced and disseminated in policy regimes. For example, lawyers, legal academics, and judges played an influential role in consumer bankruptcy development in

[83] See below, ch 6.

[84] See D Beland, 'The Social Exclusion Discourse: Ideas and Policy Change' (2007) 35 *Policy and Politics* 123. He comments that it 'legitimizes modest policy reforms entirely compatible with moderate understandings of economic liberalism'.

[85] JF Witt, 'Narrating Bankruptcy/Narrating Risk' (2003) 98 *Northwestern University Law Review* 303.

[86] JL Campbell and OK Pedersen, *The National Origins of Policy Ideas: Knowledge Regimes in the United States, France, Germany, and Denmark* (Princeton, Princeton University Press, 2014).

the US through institutions such as the National Bankruptcy Conference[87] and the National Association of Bankruptcy Judges.[88] However this influence was disrupted after 1978 by policy entrepreneurs for creditor interests.[89] This disruption coincided with the increasing 'war of ideas' in the US in the late 1970s as the post-war consensus on policymaking broke down. Consumer bankruptcy was transformed by policy entrepreneurs from a technical issue to the political issue of addressing personal responsibility.[90] In contrast, in France the knowledge regime was dominated by state technocrats who attempted to manage a more consensual approach to policy.

A disjuncture may exist between expert knowledge of the reasons for bankruptcy and public knowledge and attitudes to bankruptcy. For example, the Association of Business Recovery Professionals (R3, the English trade association for insolvency practitioners) conducted a study on attitudes to bankruptcy in 2012 which found that 82 per cent of individuals thought that some people take advantage of the system to write off debts incurred through reckless spending, and 65 per cent of respondents thought that most individuals could avoid bankruptcy by reining in their spending behaviour.[91] This focus on individual mismanagement of finances as a cause of bankruptcy contrasts with the majority of existing empirical studies which draw attention to the importance of issues such as unemployment (see Tables 1.2 to 1.6).[92] The general public's view of the causes of bankruptcy, based on the R3 study, cannot be simply explained solely by the rise of neo-liberal ideas of personal responsibility since the 1970s. Paul Rock's small survey of Londoners' views of debtors in the late 1960s found that in response to the question 'What

[87] The National Bankruptcy Conference, established in 1932, drafted many of the provisions of the 1938 Chandler Act, and during the 1950s and 1960s annually presented to Congress proposed amendments to the Bankruptcy Act as well as commented on and opposed proposals from other sources. It was an elite group of about 50 members by the 1960s composed of practitioners, referees in bankruptcy and law professors. Testimony of Frank Kennedy, vice-president National Bankruptcy Conference, *Hearings before the Subcommittee on Bankruptcy of the Committee on the Judiciary, US Senate Second Session on SJ Res 100 A Bill to Create a Commission to Study the Bankruptcy Laws of the US* (1969) 50. See for further discussion ch 2 section III.

[88] Before the Bankruptcy Reform Act 1978, this group was known as the National Conference of Bankruptcy Referees. It also sponsored Congressional Bills. See discussion below, ch 2 section III.

[89] See E Warren, 'The Changing Politics of American Bankruptcy Reform' (1999) 37 *Osgoode Hall Law Journal* 189. John Fabian Witt refers to the importance of 'narrative entrepreneurs' in US bankruptcy history. This describes how particular groups were able to strategically shape ideas about risk and law's approach to risk-taking. See Witt, 'Narrating Bankruptcy' (n 85). John Pottow develops this theme in his analysis of the lobbying landscape surrounding the enactment of BAPCPA. JAE Pottow, 'A U.S. Perspective on the Contextual Terrain of Political Economy in Insolvency Reform' in S Ben-Ishai and A Duggan (eds), *Canadian Bankruptcy and Insolvency Law : Bill C-55, Statute c. 47 and Beyond* (Markham, LexisNexis, 2007).

[90] Pottow, ibid 386–87.

[91] See 'Personal Debt Snapshot GB population calls for tighter controls on payday loans and a tougher bankruptcy regime to curb reckless spending', available at https://www.r3.org.uk/media/documents/policy/research_reports/personal_debt_snap/R3PersonalDebtSnapshotW8_FINAL.pdf. The statistics are based on responses to the statements: '[m]ost people could avoid bankruptcy by reining in reckless spending' and '[s]ome people take advantage of bankruptcy to write off their debts that they built up through reckless spending'.

[92] In 2014, an EU study of over-indebtedness concluded that 'macroeconomic factors are among the most important causes of financial difficulties … higher unemployment levels as well as increases in unemployment were associated with an increase in all types of arrears.' Civic Consulting, *Overindebtedness of European Households: Updated Mapping of the Situation, Nature, Cause, Effects and Initiatives for Alleviating its Impact* (Brussels, 2014) 8.

would you say is the main reason for people being in debt?' 61 per cent responded 'not enough self control', 20 per cent 'too easy to get credit', and nine per cent 'poverty'.[93] The 'common sense' knowledge that one should live within one's means and pay one's debts is a powerful historical idea.[94] It provides fertile ground for interest groups that promote the idea in the media that bankrupts are irresponsible or imprudent individuals.[95] Politicians are sensitive to media images since newspaper coverage represents a form of surrogate political demand. Moving insolvency policymaking from an issue dominated by technical experts to a political arena may reduce the influence of expert narratives, suggesting that the institutional context for bankruptcy reform (expert committees, parliament) may affect the outcome.

A central question in any narrative is the reason for individuals filing for bankruptcy. Tables 1.2 to 1.6 outline causes for over-indebtedness and insolvency in England and Wales, France, Germany and the Netherlands. These data indicate the role of unemployment, credit overextension, separation and divorce, and the significance of individual business failures in those countries that permit sole proprietors to use insolvency law.[96] In the US a seminal study of consumer bankruptcy cited employment problems (67.5%), divorce (22.1%), and medical bills (19.3%) as causes of bankruptcy.[97]

[93] See P Rock, *Making People Pay* (London, Routledge, 1973) 17, Table 1.5.

[94] See the interesting discussion of the power of common sense ideas about debt in framing acceptance of the need for austerity in the UK after the financial crisis of 2008. L Stanley, '"We're Reaping what We Sowed": Everyday Crisis Narratives and Acquiescence to the Age of Austerity' (2014) 19(6) *New Political Economy* 895. See also D Graeber, *Debt: The First 5,000 Years* (New York, Melville House Publishing, 2011) 2–3, who commences his book by documenting a conversation where an individual responds to the idea of a debt amnesty for developing countries with the comment 'But', she objected as if this were self-evident, '[t]hey'd borrowed the money! Surely one has to pay one's debts.' His book concludes that the principle is 'a flagrant lie' and that only some people have to repay (391).

[95] See the discussion in ch 2 section IV.A concerning the US and ch 3 section V on the construction of English insolvents as 'binge borrowers' and the bankers' campaign to restrict entry to IVAs in 2005. Rafael Efrat noted how the *New York Times* changed in the 1960s to depicting bankrupts as irresponsible or incompetent rather than the previous typification of the bankrupt as a fraudster, with greater emphasis on the extent to which they were subject to unemployment and other changes of circumstances. R Efrat, 'The Evolution of Bankruptcy Stigma' (2006) 7 *Theoretical Inquiries in Law* 365.

[96] A recent EU-wide survey of 'stakeholders' prepared for the EU Commission concluded that macro-economic factors such as unemployment and approaches to 'money management' were important causes of over-indebtedness. 'Incapacity to deal with financial products' or 'lack of money management skills' were regarded as the most important causes of over-indebtedness by almost two-thirds of respondents. However, over-indebted households seemed to stress the importance of unemployment and changes in employment as the dominant factor. See Civic Consulting, *The Over-Indebtedness of European Households: Updated Mapping of the Situation, Nature and Causes, Effects and Initiatives for Alleviating Its Impact Final Report* (Brussels, Civic Consulting, 2013) 92–93, 162. A Swedish study of individuals experiencing debt problems identified unforeseen expenditures (54%) and illness, unemployment, death and 'similar circumstances' (32%) as the primary causes. See Swedish Enforcement Authority, *Everyone Wants to Pay Their Fair Share: Causes and Consequences of Overindebtedness* Report 2008:1B (Stockholm, Swedish Enforcement Authority, 2008) 31.

[97] See TA Sullivan, E Warren, and JL Westbrook, *The Fragile Middle Class: Americans in Debt* (New Haven, Yale University Press, 2000) Fig 1.2: 'Job-related income interruption is by far the most important cause of severe financial distress for middle class Americans.' Ibid 75. On medical debts see D Himmelstein, D Thorne, E Warren, and S Woolhandler, 'Medical Bankruptcy in the United States, 2007: Results of a National Study' (2009) 122(8) *The American Journal of Medicine* 741–46. Although this study's claim that 62% of bankruptcies in the US are caused by medical bills has been challenged, medical bills remain a significant cause of bankruptcy in the US.

Table 1.2: England and Wales, Bankruptcies by Cause of Insolvency as Recorded by the Official Receiver 2015

	Non-Trading Cases (n=11095) %	All Cases (n=14905*) %
Business related failure	—	25
Living beyond means	19	14
Relationship breakdown	16	12
Loss of employment	12	9
Illness/accident	11	8
Reduction in household income or significant reduction in bankrupt's income	24	18
Speculation	1	1
Other	17	13
Total	100	100

* In 955 cases the cause was recorded as 'unknown/non-surrender'. These cases are not included in the table.
Source: Insolvency Service, Bankruptcies by age gender and cause of insolvency 2015 (https://www.gov.uk/government/statistics/individual-insolvencies-by-location-age-and-gender-england-and-wales-2015) (last accessed 19/12/2016).

Table 1.3: France—reasons for over-indebtedness

	Reasons	2001	2004	2007	2007 (RP)
ACTIVE	Too much credit	19.4%	14.6%	13.6%	5.4%
	Poor management	7.7%	6.4%	6%	2.4%
	Housing costs	3.1%	1.2%	1.2%	0.9%
	Excess charges	2.2%	1.4%	1.3%	1%
PASSIVE	Unemployment/ job loss	26.5%	30.8%	31.8%	32%
	Separation/ divorce	15.5%	14.7%	14.7%	14.5%
	Accident/illness	9.1%	10.8%	11.3%	18.8%
	Lowered resources	6.9%	6.2%	6.2%	7.3%
	Death	2.5%	2.4%	2.5%	3.6%
	Other	7.1%	11.5%	11.4%	14.1%
	Total	100%	100%	100%	100%

Source: Bank of France, Surveys of Individuals using Overindebtedness Commissions 2001, 2004, 2007.
Note: RP= retablissement personnel.

Table 1.4: Principal causes of over-indebtedness, 2014

	%
Unemployment or degradation of employment	23
Budget constrained	17
Routine use of credit	14
Conjuncture of events	41
Intergenerational assistance	5

Source: Bank of France, *Study of Paths leading to Over-Indebtedness* (2014) 7–8, https://www.banque-france.fr/fileadmin/user_upload/banque_de_france/La_Banque_de_France/study-of-paths-leading-to-over-indebtedness.pdf.

Table 1.5: Germany—primary causes of over-indebtedness in 2014

Causes	%
Unemployment, reduced working	26.8
Separation/divorce	9.0
Sickness	7.7
Consumer behaviour	8.6
Business failure	10
Income poverty	10.5
Other	34.4
Total	100

Source: Institut für Finanz dienst leistungen (IFF), Over-indebtedness Report 2015.

Table 1.6: Netherlands: causal factors for debt adjustment in 2012

Causes	%
Divorce	22
Reduced income	58
Overspending	32
Compensatory behaviour	33
Total (N)	3830

Source: Wet Schuldsanering Natuurlijke Personen (WSNP) [Debt Restructuring for Individuals], Monitor 2012 Table 3.6.

Statistics on reasons for bankruptcy are important politically because they underpin images of bankrupts and suggest a policy response—'the story about the nature of failure always has influenced the legislative agenda'.[98] Overuse of

[98] RM Lawless and E Warren, 'The Myth of the Disappearing Business Bankruptcy' (2005) 93 *California Law Review* 743, 746. They cite, for example, B Mann, *Republic of Debtors: Bankruptcy in the Age of American Independence* (Cambridge, Harvard University Press, 2009); E Balliesen, *Navigating Failure: Bankruptcy and Commercial Society in Antebellum America* (Chapel Hill, The University of North Carolina Press, 2001); Witt, 'Narrating Bankruptcy' (n 85).

credit may suggest greater financial literacy, counselling, disciplining of debtors or restrictions on credit granting. Unemployment indicates an unfortunate situation, which may signal the need for further investigation of existing social safety nets. France provides a stark example of the political role of statistics on over-indebtedness. The statistics in Table 1.3 collected by the Bank of France highlighted the significance of the 'passively indebted consumer' subject to external changes of circumstance. This conceptualisation drove liberalisation of the over-indebtedness law and provided the possibility for a consensus between creditors and debtors since the statistics indicated that neither creditors nor debtors were responsible for over-indebtedness. However the basis for these statistics was discredited by the French National Audit Office resulting in a new official study reflected in Table 1.4. These latter statistics have been used to justify greater financial literacy initiatives, reflecting greater focus on individual failings leading to over-indebtedness. In England and Wales, the image of the 'overborrowing debtor' mentioned above seemed to be substantiated by a 2005 study which documented the reasons for individuals using an IVA, which permits an individual to repay a portion of their debts, generally over a period of five years. The authors of the study concluded that for 83 per cent of individuals, the reason for the IVA was 'expenditure in excess of income' which was interpreted as individuals living beyond their means and 'simply … not budgeting properly'.[99] Expenditure in excess of income begs the question, however, of why the expenditure was in excess of income.

The political consequences of these data suggest caution in handling them. First, the statistics are likely to represent a crude construction of the social reality of over-indebtedness. Second, a combination of factors may often exist. An individual may attempt to maintain a lifestyle after a temporary drop in income through the use of credit cards, hoping that they will be able to get back into the job market but this may result in increasing levels of debt. Will a subsequent bankruptcy in such a case be coded as 'expenditure in excess of income' or unemployment? This may depend on the views of the coder. These data are often collected by different groups (regulators, policymakers, insolvency practitioners, academics) for different purposes. The data to be coded might be based on actual statements by debtors, or the interpretation of files completed by the debtor, or an intermediary. Given the difficulty in interpreting an individual's route into bankruptcy, the data may be affected by the views or practices of those collecting the data. Robert Lawless and Elizabeth Warren demonstrated how coding practices by government officials in the US had the effect of making business bankruptcies disappear, driving a narrative that bankruptcy was primarily an affair of overspending consumers.[100]

[99] PriceWaterhouseCoopers, *Living on Tick: The 21st Century Debtor* (London, PwC, 2006) 20. See further my discussion of this study in I Ramsay, '"Wannabe WAGS" and "Credit Binges": The Construction of Overindebtedness in the UK' in Niemi, Ramsay, and Whitford, *Consumer Credit, Debt and Bankruptcy* (n 26) 85–86.

[100] Lawless and Warren, 'The Myth' (n 98).

Finally, these data often provide a sufficient but not proximate cause of filing for bankruptcy. The actual decision to access bankruptcy may depend on the particular institutional framework of bankruptcy access in a country, including the costs and the effects of legal proceedings.[101]

Data on the reasons for filing bankruptcy fuel the debate over the effects of bankruptcy liberalisation on consumer incentives, credit availability and debtor character. Economic analysis views bankruptcy as a form of consumption insurance.[102] The concept of moral hazard, when associated with insurance, suggests that individuals will take more credit risks if they are protected by the insurance of bankruptcy and be more willing to turn to insolvency relief if they face debt difficulties. Moral hazard was often invoked after the Great Recession by governments unwilling to introduce a bankruptcy discharge because of its impact on payment culture, and international institutions often identified concerns about moral hazard when implementing reforms.[103] 'Moral hazard' is a curious term since it represents, in ordinary understanding, a judgement about individual behaviour, notwithstanding economists' arguments that it is a technical concept. It functions not merely as a technical concept, however, but also has a performative effect[104] in constructing an identity for a debtor as lacking character, implying a deterioration in that character through the introduction of the bankruptcy discharge.[105] The concept does not merely describe a phenomenon, but in public debates on debt contributes to the creation of the character of the debtor.

The effects of moral hazard are difficult to measure and a distinction should be drawn between its *ex ante* and *ex post* effects. An individual's credit choices are likely to be affected by many factors, including the widespread advertising of credit products and the behaviour of other consumers. The insights of behavioural economics suggest that, in general, individual consumers are unlikely to take into account the remote likelihood of bankruptcy when taking on credit commitments[106] or increasing their borrowing. Moreover creditors have incentives to monitor and control such behaviour. This observation raises the question of the possibility of creditor moral hazard when a restrictive bankruptcy law may create incentives for reduced monitoring by firms and excessive risk-taking. Creating

[101] See discussion in RJ Mann and K Porter, 'Saving up for Bankruptcy' (2009) 98 *Georgetown Law Journal* 289.

[102] See eg B Adler, L Polak, and A Schwartz, 'Regulating Consumer Bankruptcy: A Theoretical Inquiry' (2000) 29 *The Journal of Legal Studies* 585.

[103] See below, ch 6.

[104] On the idea of performativity and the role of economics in creating rather than describing phenomena see eg D Mackenzie, F Muniesa, and L Siu, *Do Economists Make Markets? On the Performativity of Economics* (Princeton, Princeton University Press, 2007).

[105] See the discussion in T Baker, 'On the Genealogy of Moral Hazard' (1996) 75(2) *Texas Law Review* 237.

[106] See the discussion by S Schwartz, 'Personal Bankruptcy Law: A Behavioural Perspective' in Niemi, Ramsay, and Whitford, *Consumer Bankruptcy In Global Perspective* (Oxford, Hart Publishing, 2003) 68–71, arguing that consumer biases are likely to lead to an underestimation of the risks of borrowing. The classic article justifying bankruptcy discharge based on behavioural biases is T Jackson, 'The Fresh Start Policy in Bankruptcy Law' (1985) 98 *Harvard Law Review* 1393.

access barriers to discharge may promote a model of lending that profits from high levels of defaulting borrowers.[107]

Focusing on decision-making *ex post*, for example when an individual loses a job and is facing credit difficulties, we might expect an individual to weigh the costs and benefits of a bankruptcy discharge. These costs are not purely economic but include concerns for loss of reputation and stigma associated with bankruptcy which remains significant.[108] The danger here is that a policy concern for moral hazard, with its undertones of character and responsibility, may crowd out a consideration of the social benefits of a bankruptcy discharge. These benefits include relief of hardship, increased productivity, reducing the likelihood of individuals leaving the formal economy to avoid collection action, a reduction in externalities from debt to families and the state, the creation of incentives for responsible lending and accounting by creditors, and risk shifting to creditors who are generally in the best position to bear and spread the risks of non-payment.

All personal insolvency systems have mechanisms to deter moral hazard and strategic behaviour.[109] When establishing new systems states often set up unnecessarily complex or restrictive criteria for entry or exit from bankruptcy which substantially increase the transaction costs of bankruptcy and overly deter individuals from seeking relief. Sweden, for example, created very high hurdles to entry.[110] As a consequence, the average age of the Swedish debtor in the plan is in mid-50s or older, and a category of 'eternity debtor' exists on the unpaid debt register unable to access debt relief. Personal insolvency continues to carry a stigma in many countries, which may contribute to an underuse of insolvency as a solution for over-indebtedness.

III. Household Debt, Neo-liberalism, and Personal Insolvency Law

The rise in household debt in many countries since the 1980s frames this study (see Figure 1.1). Consumers rather than corporations have become an important

[107] See R Mann, 'Bankruptcy Reform and the "Sweat Box" of Credit Card Debt' (2007) *Illinois Law Review* 375.

[108] The Insolvency Service in England and Wales concluded, in their review of the Enterprise Act liberalisation of discharge procedure, that bankruptcy still carried a significant stigma. See below, ch 3 section IV. For the US, see T Sullivan, E Warren and J Westbrook, 'Less Stigma or More Financial Distress: An Empirical Analysis of the Extraordinary Increase in Bankruptcy Filings' (2006) 59 *Stanford Law Review* 213.

[109] Examples include: minimum levels of debt, qualified insolvency, bankruptcy restriction order, conditional discharge, requirements of good faith, a period of good behaviour, requirements of mandatory counselling before bankruptcy, requirement to have attempted a negotiated settlement before filing. Financial costs may act as a barrier. Failure to disclose assets or the provision of false information may result in annulment or absence of discharge.

[110] See below, ch 5.

site of profits for financial institutions, and credit a mechanism for maintaining demand in an era of stagnating wages.[111] David Harvey writes of Thatcherism engendering the growth of a 'debt culture' into 'a formerly staid British life'.[112] Critics such as Wolfgang Streeck argue that it is one technique for capitalism to 'buy time for the existing social and economic order'.[113] Even more mainstream economists fear that 'debt is dangerous'.[114]

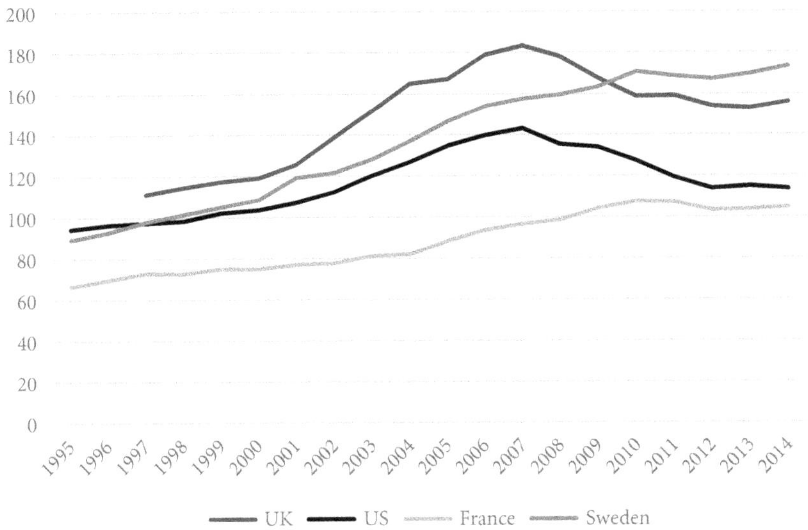

Figure 1.1: Household debt-to-income in selected European countries and US: 1995–2012 (UK from 1997)

Source: OECD National Accounts at a Glance (various years): Household Debt http://www.oecd-ilibrary.org/economics/national-accounts-at-a-glance-2015_na_glance-2015-en.

Since the crisis, a variety of studies have examined the role of household credit in the economy, but with only modest discussion of personal insolvency. Neo-liberalism remains a powerful discourse in both the US and the EU and writers point to its resilience after the Great Recession.[115] Neo-liberalism promotes freeing up markets internationally, reducing the power of labour and welfare entitlements,

[111] See sources listed in n 11.

[112] D Harvey, *A Brief History of Neoliberalism* (Oxford, Oxford University Press, 2005) 61.

[113] Streeck, *Buying Time* (n 11) 4.

[114] A Mian and A Sufi, *House of Debt* (n 7) 12; see also A Turner, Between Debt and the Devil: *Money, Credit, and Fixing Global Finance* (Princeton, Princeton University Press, 2015) 49.

[115] See T Williams, 'Continuity Not Rupture: The Persistence of Neoliberalism in the Internationalisation of Consumer Finance Regulation' in T Wilson (ed), *International Responses to Issues of Credit and Over-indebtedness in the Wake of Crisis* (Surrey, Ashgate Publishing, 2013) ch 2; P Dardot and C Laval, *The New Way of the World: On Neoliberal Society* (London, Verso Books, 2014) 2: 'Far from impairing neo-liberal policies, the crisis led to their dramatic reinforcement, in the shape of austerity plans put in place by states that were increasingly active in promoting the logic of competition in financial markets.' See also VA Schmidt and M Thatcher (eds), *Resilient Liberalism in Europe's Political Economy* (Cambridge, Cambridge University Press, 2013).

and embracing consumerism and entrepreneurialism.[116] Neo-liberalism is not, however, a return to laissez-faire. The state constitutes and structures the ground rules of markets within neo-liberalism which do not arise naturally as a spontaneous order.[117]

Neo-liberalism is increasingly a dominant rationality, associated with governance in contemporary capitalism.[118] Continental theorists link debt to forms of neo-liberal governance where individuals are required to take responsibility for managing their biography.

Maurizio Lazzarato, in *The Making of the Indebted Man: An Essay on the Neo-Liberal Condition*,[119] develops themes initiated by Foucault,[120] arguing that in contemporary society with fewer traditional 'sites of discipline', such as the factory, we have moved to a society of control[121] and that the creditor-debtor relationship is central to contemporary capitalism. The growth of a debt-dominated economy shapes the subjectivity of the indebted person so that individuals 'develop a way of life, discipline, attitudes and conduct appropriate to the "indebted man" [sic] who should learn to exploit credit markets appropriately'.[122] Credit scoring technologies and credit bureaux perform a significant sorting, channelling and disciplining role. Individuals are encouraged to check their credit score and learn how to improve their credit rating just as they might check their cholesterol level. The worldwide financial literacy and education movement[123] assists consumers to

[116] Schmidt and Thatcher, ibid 3.

[117] The transition from communism to capitalism in Eastern Europe is a stark illustration of how credit markets must be constructed involving new technologies of credit as well as changes in individuals See discussion in A Rona-Tas, 'The Rise of Consumer Credit in Postcommunist Czech Republic, Hungary, and Poland' in N Bandelj and DJ Solinger (eds), *Socialism Vanquished, Socialism Challenged* (Oxford, Oxford University Press, 2012); A Guseva and A Rona-Tas, *Plastic Money: Constructing Markets for Credit Cards in Eight Postcommunist Countries* (Stanford, Stanford University Press, 2014).

[118] Dardot and Laval conceive of neo-liberalism as 'a form of rationality' which structures not only the 'action of rulers but also the conduct of the ruled'. P Dardot and C Laval, *The New Way of the World* (n 115).

[119] M Lazzarato, *The Making of the Indebted Man: An Essay on the Neo-Liberal Condition* (Cambridge, Massachusetts Institute of Technology, 2012).

[120] See M Foucault, *The Birth of Biopolitics: Lectures at the Collège de France, 1978–79* (n 39). Individuals are invited to conceive of themselves as enterprises attempting to improve their human capital and in a constant competition with other individuals. Neo-liberalism posited a new form of homo economicus, the 'entrepreneur of the self' who must exploit their human capital, continuously adapting and searching for self-improvement, and taking responsibility for managing biographical risks. This individualisation of risk is described in the US as the 'Great Risk Shift' by Jacob Hacker. See JS Hacker, *The Great Risk Shift: The New Economic Insecurity and the Decline of the American Dream*, revised edition (Oxford, Oxford University Press, 2008).

[121] See G Deleuze, 'Postscript on the Societies of Control' (1992) 59 *October* 3. This idea of 'governmentality' where individuals experience discipline and shaping at many sites—the workplace, school—is a characteristic of neo-liberal 'governing at a distance'.

[122] Lazzarato, *The Making of the Indebted Man* (n 119) 104.

[123] See eg the relevant page on the OECD website which notes that: 'Awareness of the importance of financial education is gaining momentum among policy makers in economies the world over. The OECD and its International Network on Financial Education (INFE) provide a unique policy forum for governments to exchange views and experiences on this issue', see http://www.oecd.org/finance/

adapt to a world where they must 'live with debt'.[124] The consumer is enlisted as a regulatory subject[125] in making credit markets competitive (for example, through enhanced switching) and policing 'internalities'[126]—such as impulsiveness or myopia—which may result in over-indebtedness or obesity.[127] This is the world of the responsible borrower. Neo-liberalism is not, therefore, associated with a hedonistic consumerism, but rather the responsible consumer who manages their budget effectively.

The above ideas are not unfamiliar to historians of consumer credit. Lendol Calder argued that in the US the rise of instalment debt, which required individuals to adjust to the discipline of monthly payments, extended the discipline of the Fordist factory system to private consumption.[128] He also documents the efforts of elite opinion makers to normalise and legitimise consumer debt, for example changing its description from 'consumptive' to 'consumer' debt in the 1930s. This conscious creation of a debt culture was supported both by labour and business interests in the US. This shift in the ideology of debt was part of a more general shift to consumerism in the US. The transition to the dominance of a consumer identity was promoted by ordoliberal writers, such as Walter Lippman, to reduce class conflict between capital and labour.[129]

Contemporary neo-liberalism represents an influential background to thinking about contemporary insolvency law. All the countries considered in this book have been influenced by neo-liberal ideas, as have international institutions and the EU. But what is the role of individual insolvency in neo-liberalism? Neo-liberalism

financial-education/. For a critique see T Williams, 'Empowerment of Whom and for What? Financial Literacy Education and the New Regulation of Consumer Financial Services' (2007) 29 *Law & Policy* 226.

124 Lazzarato, *The Making of the Indebted Man* (n 119) 112: 'Learning how to "live with debt" has now been made part of certain American school curricula.' See also I Ramsay, 'Consumer Credit Society and Consumer Bankruptcy: Reflections on Credit Cards and Bankruptcy in an Informational Economy' in J Niemi-Kiesilainen, I Ramsay and WC Whitford (eds), *Consumer Bankruptcy in Global Perspective* (Oxford, Hart Publishing, 2003) 38.

125 See Williams, 'Empowerment' (n 123): D Marron, '"Informed, Educated and More Confident": Financial Capability and the Problematization of Personal Finance Consumption' (2014) 17 *Consumption Markets & Culture* 491. See discussion of this theme in N Moloney, *How to Protect Investors: Lessons from the EC and the UK* (Cambridge University Press, 2010) 47. See discussion in relation to EU in V Mak and J Braspenning, 'Errare Humanum Est: Financial Literacy in European Consumer Credit Law' (2012) 35 *Journal of Consumer Policy* 307.

126 This is in contrast to traditional economic rationale of externalities. See G Loewenstein and others, 'Can Behavioral Economics Make Us Healthier?' (2012) 344 *The British Medical Journal* 3482.

127 Margaret Atwood referred to 'Debt as the new Fat'. See M Atwood, *Payback: Debt and the Shadow Side of Wealth* (Toronto, House of Anansi Press, 2008).

128 See eg L Calder, *Financing the American Dream: A Cultural History of Consumer Credit* (Princeton, Princeton University Press, 2009). Calder drew on J Baudrillard, 'The Consumer Society', *Selected Writings* (Stanford, Stanford University Press, 2001) 81. This point was also made by David Caplovitz in the 1970s. See D Caplovitz, 'The Social Benefits and Costs of Consumer Credit' in RM Goode (ed), *Consumer Credit* (Sijthoff, Leyden, 1978).

129 See eg Lippman quoted in JQ Whitman, 'Consumerism versus Producerism: A Study in Comparative Law' (2007) 117 *Yale Law Journal* 340, 361. And see discussion of ordoliberal influence in France below, ch 4.

celebrates entrepreneurialism and chapter six discusses the extent to which encouraging entrepreneurial risk-taking through a liberal bankruptcy law has become a dominant trope in the EU's quest for innovation and growth. But the EU is also committed to a 'competitive social market economy',[130] including fighting social exclusion, which suggests wider social objectives and poses the question of how individual insolvency fits with the values of a 'social Europe'.[131] The idea of a social Europe focused initially on hard law in the area of worker rights and non-discrimination. Much social policy associated with the welfare state is within national competences, but the impact of economic integration, including freedom of movement, on social policies has resulted in greater coordination through soft law approaches.

Individual insolvency law straddles both economic and social policy, encouraging entrepreneurialism but also addressing potential social exclusion and compensating for market risks by transferring certain risks of default to creditors who are in the best position to spread these losses and monitor debtor behaviour. A swift discharge permits an individual to get back into the credit market. However, this model of a liberal individual bankruptcy discharge contrasts with a neo-liberal policy of 'responsibilisation' of the consumer. In the US, the enactment in 2005 of the BAPCPA, with its 'means test' for access, and mandatory debt counselling for bankrupts, was inspired by neo-liberal ideas of personal responsibility.[132] A tension exists within liberalism between personal insolvency law and the discharge of debts as both a site of liberation and a site of discipline.

Neo-liberalism also undercuts the distinction between consumer and producer identity through its construction of the 'entrepreneur of the self' exploiting and managing their human capital. The traditional distinction between the business risk-taker and the responsible consumer is challenged. Individuals of all social classes are faced with managing risk. More affluent individuals may embrace actively such an opportunity while lower-income individuals may have to use credit defensively to manage day-to-day uncertainties.[133]

A. False Dichotomies?—US Neo-liberalism versus EU Social Market?

A recent Swedish report on personal insolvency[134] concludes that cultural differences exist between the US and Europe in the approach to over-indebtedness.

[130] Treaty on the Functioning of the European Union (TFEU) Art 3 para 3.

[131] For a useful summary of EU social policy initiatives see C Barnard and G de Baere *Towards a European Social Union: Achievements and Possibilities under the current EU constitutional framework* (Leuven, KU Leuven Forum, 2015) https://www.kuleuven.be/euroforum/viewpic.php?LAN=E&TABLE=DOCS&ID=937 and see discussion below, ch 6.

[132] See discussion below, ch 2 section V.

[133] See N Fligstein and A Goldstein, 'The Emergence of a Finance Culture in American Households, 1998–2007' (2015) *Socio-Economic Review* 1.

[134] *An Opportunity for a Fresh Start for Serious Entrepreneurs* SOU (Statens Offentliga Utredningar/National Public Inquiry) 2014: 44. See below, ch 5.

> In the US system, writing off liabilities is regarded as an efficient way to distribute risks. Over-indebtedness is seen as a market failure—a failure of the market to assess the risks. With this approach, it is logical to regard debt restructuring as a means of efficiently tackling problems of over-indebtedness so as to enable the individual to rapidly return to the market as a consumer and borrower. It has been pointed out that in Europe over-indebtedness is regarded as a social or moral problem and that the debtor is expected to bear more of the risk.

This broad-brush cultural contrast between the US and Europe is not unusual suggesting deep differences between the US and other nations in their approaches to credit, debt and insolvency. David Skeel and Monica Prasad, for example, describe the liberal fresh start in the US as, respectively, 'unique' and 'peculiarly American'.[135] The liberal fresh start in US bankruptcy law before the enactment of the BAPCPA in 2005 seemed to 'fit' a demand-led economy[136] where consumer credit maintains demand and substitutes for social redistribution.[137] Access to credit was supported by political groups on both the political left and right in the US as a method of achieving the 'standard package' of middle-class consumption and providing workers with consumption smoothing.[138] However, high levels of credit created the danger of over-indebtedness, and bankruptcy law, although not originally designed for this purpose, performed a useful safety net function in permitting workers to return to productivity and further consumption. The US system of employment-related welfare and healthcare meant that unemployment and illness could have more dramatic effects than in those countries with public systems of healthcare and public housing benefits. This US 'open credit economy'[139] and approach to credit regulation in a minimal social welfare state contrasts with a European social model of solidarity providing a greater level of security for citizens through state regulation and redistribution. If, however, European countries are increasingly adopting the US model of the role of credit in the economy then one might, *ceteris paribus*, expect the growth of similar models of bankruptcy. The development of personal insolvency in Europe is linked to credit liberalisation

[135] Skeel, *Debt's Dominion* (n 49) 1; M Prasad, *The Land of Too Much: American Abundance and the Paradox of Poverty* (Cambridge, Harvard University Press, 2012) 183.

[136] Prasad, ibid. See also L Hyman, 'The Politics of Consumer Debt: U.S. State Policy and the Rise of Investment in Consumer Credit, 1920–2008' (2012) 644 *The ANNALS of the American Academy of Political and Social Science* 40, 40–49.

[137] See Rajan, *Fault Lines* (n 11).

[138] See G Trumbull, *Consumer Lending in France and America: credit and welfare* (Cambridge, Cambridge University Press, 2014). Trumbull argues that a coalition of political groups supported the narrative of widespread access to credit with those on the right seeing it as a bulwark against communism and labour unions supporting it as an important income-smoothing device during strikes.

[139] 'Open credit economy' was the term used by the US Bankruptcy Commission in 1970 to contrast the US system with socialist regimes. It reflected the background of the Cold War era. In its chapter on the 'Philosophy of the Bankruptcy System' the Commission noted that 'there is in the US pervasive support for the processes with which bankruptcy relates, most notably 'the open credit economy'. See *Report of the Commission of Bankruptcy Laws of the US* (Washington, Government Printer, 1973) ch 3.

since the 1980s and the subsequent crises and social costs associated with the growth of over-indebtedness.[140]

I would make three comments on the above story of US–European contrasts. First, the cultural story of the US liberal discharge policy underplays the political conflicts over the availability of bankruptcy and the relative responsibility of the debtor. The concept of personal responsibility was not only a dominant trope in the debates over the US reforms in 2005, but also was a continuing theme in earlier periods[141] and used to support restrictions on the fresh start in the US. Second, references to a 'European approach' underplay the substantial differences between European countries in approaches to credit and personal insolvency.[142] Differences in social policy between EU Member States remain as great as those between the US and Europe.[143] Authors sometimes argue that European personal insolvency procedures take a more social approach, citing the role of debt counselling in the process. However, contrary to this image, France and Sweden do not take a social welfare approach and make little attempt to integrate debt management within the welfare system. England, often characterised as a neo-liberal state, has a significant social welfare role through the large Citizens Advice network. Third, appeals to overarching cultural values may simply be an attempt to elevate the interests of a particular group. The Swedish quotation above claiming a deep cultural difference between the US and Europe may be playing a 'cultural card'[144]—a political strategy to block particular reforms by elevating one particular value—which happens to favour financial interests—into a deep cultural value. Therefore, this book rejects the story that US consumer bankruptcy law reflects an enduring cultural characteristic of the US or that there is 'an American culture of maximal consumer sovereignty and [a] European culture of maximal consumer protection'.[145] I argue in chapter two that US consumer bankruptcy law reflects conflicting values that result in a continuing debate about its role in society.

The contrast between a neo-liberal US model and a European social model also underlies the argument that the US consumer bankruptcy system is primarily a private system organised around courts and lawyers whereas European systems often involve state bureaucracies playing a more paternalistic role in managing

[140] Note that average outstanding household debt-to-income ratio in the EU countries is similar to that in the US (approximately 100%).

[141] The US Bankruptcy Commission above (n 139) noted that 'the 'moral obligation' to pay debts is widely accepted'.

[142] See below, ch 6.

[143] See eg P Baldwin, *The Narcissism of Minor Differences How Europe and America are Alike* (Oxford, Oxford University Press, 2009).

[144] Halliday and Carruthers discuss this in the context of individual state resistance to the adoption of international norms of corporate bankruptcy law. They describe 'cultural incompatibility' as a common tactic to foil international financial institutions (IFI) recommendations. This is a powerful tactic because the agencies are sensitive to the critique that they attempt to impose a 'one size fits all' approach on countries. See Halliday and Carruthers, *Bankrupt: Global Lawmaking* (n 74), 344–45.

[145] JQ Whitman, 'Consumerism versus Producerism (n 129) 383.

debtors.[146] David Skeel contrasts the English system of Official Receivers, which confers 'a pervasively governmental and administrative character' on English bankruptcy law, with the US 'judicial process' where the 'primacy of the lawyers rather than an administrator—distinguish US bankruptcy law from every other insolvency law in the world'.[147]

In fact, European countries represent a diversity of approaches, and a description of the US system as non-governmental may mislead by its implicit image of government as a Weberian top-down model of the state where political goals are established in legislation and implemented through impersonal state employees, contrasting with private regulation through lawyers and judges.[148] The US reveals, in fact, a 'loosely connected (infra)structure'[149] of judges, Chapter 13 standing trustees, court-appointed trustees and the Federal Public Trustee Service, a regulatory body with extensive monitoring powers since 2005. Lawyers also play an increasing administrative role as gatekeepers in US consumer bankruptcy. This is not a vertical Weberian bureaucracy but it represents a substantial bankruptcy infrastructure that plays an important administrative, judicial and political role. The US system demonstrates the significant 'interpenetration of public and private spheres', a further example of William Novak's argument that many historians have underestimated the role of the US state through a focus on the state as a vertical bureaucracy.

B. The Demographics of Personal Insolvency—US and Europe

Teresa Sullivan, Elizabeth Warren and Jay Westbrook concluded on the basis of a series of path-breaking empirical studies in the 1980s and 1990s that bankruptcy was primarily a middle-class phenomenon in the US (defined in terms of education, employment status and home ownership).[150] Bankruptcy in the US functioned, therefore, as a middle-class safety net, representing a pragmatic response

146 Some writers identify an evolutionary drift towards administrative processing of debtors, driven by cost concern, a recognition that individual bankruptcy cases rarely raise adversarial issues of rights, and a concern for uniform treatment of debtors. See KA Littwin, 'The Affordability Paradox: How Consumer Bankruptcy's Greatest Weakness May Account for its Surprising Success' (2011) 52 *William & Mary Law Review* 1933.

147 Skeel, *Debt's Dominion* (n 49) 38, 43.

148 See W Novak, 'The Myth of the "Weak" American State' (2008) 113 *The American Historical Review* 752, 770.

149 The phrase is taken from the Brookings Institution Report in 1971. See D Stanley and M Girth, *Bankruptcy: Problem, Process, Reform* (Washington DC, Brookings Institution, 1971) 147.

150 See T Sullivan, E Warren, and JL Westbrook, *As We Forgive Our Debtors: Bankruptcy and Consumer Credit in America* (New York, OUP, 1989); Sullivan, Warren and Westbrook, *The Fragile Middle Class* (n 97). See also, TA Sullivan, E Warren, and JL Westbrook, 'Consumer Bankruptcy in the United States: A Study of Alleged Abuse and of Local Legal Culture' (1997) 20 *Journal of Consumer Policy* 223: 'The system functions to provide middle-class debt relief.' In 2010, the Office of the Vice President of the United States, *Annual Report of the White House Task Force on the Middle Class* (Washington, Vice-President of the United States, February, 2010) drawing on a Department of Commerce report "Middle

to a high debt economy where individuals may lose jobs, have limited medical insurance or misjudge their repayment ability. This is in contrast with earlier studies that viewed bankrupts as those who were primarily poor or employed in marginal jobs.[151]

Social science research in European countries on the demographics of personal insolvency is limited. Conceptions of class may also differ between countries. Existing studies of individual insolvency have often used occupational divisions and income as measures of class. However, Pierre Bourdieu's conception of class as linked to economic, social, and cultural capital may be a more useful framework for understanding the role of individual insolvency in the twenty-first century[152] when addressing economic and social exclusion.

Some evidence exists of middle-class use of insolvency procedures by individuals in the UK[153] and Germany.[154] In France, the growth in the use by individuals of over-indebtedness commissions is linked to the growing precariousness of middle-class life and the phenomenon of *déclassement*.[155] However, French data suggest that the use of over-indebtedness commissions is more a working-class phenomenon[156] and that those who use the *rétablissement personnel* procedure, available to individuals with no capacity to repay and no assets, are in marginal jobs or outside the labour market. In Sweden, the Hedborg report in 2012 concluded that individuals registered with the Swedish enforcement authority were generally from lower-income backgrounds with debts related to public sector bills. Only 10 per cent of the 500,000 individuals registered with the authority had a mortgage. The sick and unemployed were over-represented.[157] Studies in England, Germany, France and Sweden indicate that homeowners use the process much less than in

Class in America" (Washington, U.S. Department of Commerce, Economics and Statistics Administration, January 2010) noted at 10 that '[m]iddle-class families are defined by their aspirations more than their income. The Commerce report assumes that middle-class families aspire to home ownership, a car, college education for their children, health and retirement security and occasional family vacations … Families at a wide variety of income levels aspire to be middle class and under certain circumstances can put together budgets that allow them to obtain all six items above, which are assumed to be part of a middle-class lifestyle'.

[151] See P Shuchman, 'The Average Bankrupt: A Description and Analysis of 753 Personal Bankruptcy Filings in Nine States' (1983) 88 *Commercial Law Journal* 288; P Shuchman, 'New Jersey Debtors 1982–1983: An Empirical Study' (1984) 15 *Seton Hall Law Review* 541. The Brookings Institution study of bankrupts in 1964 concluded more ambiguously that the bankrupt 'presents a picture of neither poverty nor instability'. Stanley and Girth, *Bankruptcy* (n 149) 42.

[152] See the discussion of this approach in M Savage, *Social Class in the 21st Century* (London, Pelican, 2015) 46.

[153] See I Ramsay, 'Between Neo-Liberalism and the Social Market: Approaches to Debt Adjustment and Consumer Insolvency in the EU' (2012) 35(4) *Journal of Consumer Policy* 421–41.

[154] 'Filing for bankruptcy is not an experience limited to people at the lower end of society. Nonetheless, there are some more people in lower prestige positions, like unskilled workers, and fewer people at the upper end of the distribution.' See Backert, Brock, and Maischatz, 'Bankruptcy in Germany' (n 25) 282.

[155] See discussion below, ch 4.

[156] Ibid.

[157] See ch 5.

the US. However, Greek research indicates that resort to personal insolvency is not restricted to poor households, but that significant numbers of homeowners used debt adjustment procedures, reflecting both the very high level of homeownership in that country and the possibility in Greek law of adjusting mortgage debt in insolvency.[158] In addition, in those countries that include both individual traders and non-traders in their insolvency systems, individuals who have been in trade comprise up to 20 per cent of insolvents.[159] We might conclude that, although it would be misleading to use the term 'middle class', in these European countries the use of insolvency is not restricted to the very poor but may often be drawn from the 'lower middle-class of the rich world', the primary losers from the globalisation of the world economy since the 1980s.[160]

A subset of debtors is associated with very high levels of unemployment and the receipt of social benefits. They may be using credit to supplement inadequate income and owe money to the central and local state as well as financial institutions. In France, these characteristics represent those using the *rétablissement personnel* procedure, and in England and Wales, the debt relief order, both of which provide a discharge of debts within one year. Single parents and the unemployed are often within this group with women over-represented. This group challenges the limits of insolvency law in bringing about a fresh start.

IV. Summary

Chapters two to five examine how four economically advanced states developed personal insolvency law and policy since the early 1980s and in the case of England and the US sets these changes in a longer historical context. These chapters illustrate the continuing influence of financial interests over the policy and administration of debt relief and, in England and France, the influential role of different ministries and agencies with particular agendas. These distinct institutional contexts for reform in each country often influenced the institutional framework for handling debt cases. Although policy solutions seemed initially relatively contingent, such as the role of the Bank of France in over-indebtedness management, once those solutions were in place a significant path dependency existed. Distinct narratives about debtors played particularly important roles in both France and the US in the establishment of the agenda for change. The state played an influential role in promoting these narratives in France, while financial interests promoted in the US the narrative of 'personal responsibility'.

158 See E Marsellou and Y Bassiakos, 'Bankrupt Households and Economic Crisis. Evidence from the Greek Courts' (2016) 39 *Journal of Consumer Policy* 41.

159 See eg England, Germany, Finland noted in Ramsay (n 166).

160 Milanovic, *Global Inequality* (n 14) 20.

2

US Exceptionalism?

'No country has a credit economy comparable to ours, and therefore no country has as rich and varied an experience in bankruptcy as we do have.'

Frank Kennedy, Hearings before the Subcommittee on Bankruptcy of the Committee on Judiciary US Senate Second Session on SJ Res 100 A Bill to Create a Commission to study the Bankruptcy Laws of the US (1968)

'The U.S. Code's days as a paragon may be waning.'

Elizabeth Warren, Jay Westbrook, Katherine Porter and John Pottow, *The Law of Debtors and Creditors*, 4th edn (Frederick, MD, Kluwer, 2014) 320

I. Introduction

The US consumer bankruptcy system is a continuing point of reference for European policymakers. During the 1980s, Chapter 13 of the US Bankruptcy Code was an influential model for European reformers; most European states shunned, however, the swift bankruptcy discharge available in Chapter 7. The apparent connection between the US swift fresh start and entrepreneurialism now attracts European policymakers interested in promoting growth in a sluggish eurozone. Certainly, the idea of the US fresh start has been transnationalised, but in the US this idea has been a continuing site of conflict over its meaning and scope, resulting in a consumer bankruptcy landscape that is, as Robert Frost states of the US, 'hard to see'.[1] US individual bankruptcy law does not represent a carefully planned and implemented set of policies but rather a history of conflicting narratives about debtors and the terms on which they should be permitted to discharge debts. Substantial regional variations exist in the implementation of the law, with conversions of laws by judges and practitioners, which have later sometimes been adopted in legislation. Failures of institutional design and unintended consequences are common. Neither is it a deep cultural consensus nor is it simply the reflection of interest group pressures, although creditors have influenced both the 'law in books' and the 'law in action' throughout the law's history.

[1] From the poem '*and all we call american*' by Robert Frost, *The Atlantic Monthly*, June 1951, 28–29.

The US system of administering bankruptcy also does not represent an anti-state bias when compared with European models. It is, as we shall see, only by taking a limited conception of the state that such an approach can be sustained.

The swift fresh start for a debtor, without the need for an income payment as a condition of discharge or even the requirement of insolvency as a condition of access, is a defining characteristic of US consumer bankruptcy law. Monica Prasad describes it as 'peculiarly American'[2] and David Skeel claimed in the early 2000s that the debtor-friendly US bankruptcy law was 'unique in the world'.[3] Organised around courts, the US system gives 'primacy [to] lawyers rather than an administrator'.[4] However, the enactment of the Bankruptcy Abuse and Consumer Protection Act of 2005 has limited the fresh start, and the US consumer bankruptcy system could be increasingly characterised as an 'administrative' system of processing.[5]

Nathalie Martin summarises the claim that a liberal bankruptcy law is part of US economic and social culture:

> [T]he current US bankruptcy system *grew directly out of the US unique capitalist system* which *rewards entrepreneurialism* as well as *extensive consumer spending*. It makes sense that a society in which dollars rule would have a forgiving personal bankruptcy system in order to keep consumer spending high … *both systems are part of a larger scheme to keep economic players alive and active in the game of capitalism*. US bankruptcy systems are *among the country's few social programs* and they address many of society's ills. Thus they are broad and form an integral part of the social system from which they sprung.[6] (emphasis added)

Entrepreneurialism, maintenance of consumer spending, and a social safety net are undoubtedly narratives that have justified a liberal bankruptcy discharge.

[2] M Prasad, *The Land of Too Much: American Abundance and the Paradox of Poverty* (Cambridge, Harvard University Press, 2012).

[3] DA Skeel, *Debt's Dominion: A History of Bankruptcy Law in America* (Princeton, Princeton University Press, 2014). See also WC Whitford, 'Changing Definitions of Fresh Start in U.S. Bankruptcy Law' (1997) 20 *Journal of Consumer Policy* 179, 179. (US consumer bankruptcy law is nearly unique in the world in its commitment to the fresh start', but he notes expanding limitations on the fresh start so that it is more of a 'stale start'.) See also T Sullivan, E Warren, and JL Westbrook, *As We Forgive Our Debtors: Bankruptcy and Consumer Credit in America* (New York, Oxford University Press, 1989). '[O]ur bankruptcy law is distinctively American … American [bankruptcy] laws are unique in concept, not merely in detail.'

[4] See Skeel's observation that '[s]ince 1898, bankruptcy professionals have been the single most important influence on the development of bankruptcy law' in Skeel, *Debt's Dominion* (n 3) 47; AK Littwin, 'The Do-It-Yourself Mirage: Complexity in the Bankruptcy System' in KA Porter (ed), *Broke: How Debt Bankrupts the Middle Class* (Palo Alto, Stanford University Press, 2011); AK Littwin, 'The Affordability Paradox: How Consumer Bankruptcy's Greatest Weakness May Account for its Surprising Success' (2011) 52 *William & Mary Law Review* 1933.

[5] See discussion below at section VI and for a useful discussion of the nature of the US system see Littwin, 'The Affordability Paradox' (n 4).

[6] N Martin, 'The Role of History and Culture in Developing Bankruptcy and Insolvency Systems: The Perils of Legal Transplantation' (2005) 28 *Boston College International & Comparative Law Review* 1.

But debtor rehabilitation through counselling and the importance of personal responsibility are also evident in the historical record. Political disagreements about the scope of the fresh start reflect the tensions between these objectives and characterise the history of legislative politics on bankruptcy law.[7] Most histories of US bankruptcy law periodise relatively long intervals of stability punctuated by significant legislative changes, stimulated by critical junctures, and often triggered by supposed 'explosions' in bankruptcy filings.[8] However, even during these stable periods, the low-visibility law in action often altered the law on the books and provided a stimulus for change. Thus, in practice, creditors continually undercut the effectiveness of the fresh start discharge under Chapter 7; referees stretched the application of the Bankruptcy Act in the 1930s providing the basis for Chapter 13 in the 1938 Chandler Act; and local variations and experimentation have continued after the Great Recession as a response to the failure of federal legislative changes to the Act. Politics permeates, therefore, these low-visibility areas of legal change.

US consumer bankruptcy history is also one of unintended consequences and the limits of institutional design. The Bankruptcy Reform Act of 1978 provided an unintended stimulus for bankruptcy law as a consumer rights tool, and created the experimental US Trustee's Office. Originally opposed by creditors, they later promoted this Office as a method of policing debtor abuse in the Bankruptcy Abuse Prevention and Consumer Protection Act of 2005 (BAPCPA), only to find that it mutated into a consumer protection agency in the Great Recession! The state plays a significant role in US consumer bankruptcy law, notwithstanding images of US bankruptcy law as a privatised system. However, this is not the state as a unified, centralised bureaucracy but rather the state as an 'infrastructural power'[9] of public and private actors loosely tied together. Transplanting the US system without this infrastructure may lead to difficulties.

Legal professionals dominated bankruptcy policymaking from the mid-1930s until 1978 when bankruptcy reform changed from 'quiet' to 'loud' politics.[10]

[7] See E Berglöf, H Rosenthal, and EL von Thadden, 'The Formation of Legal Institutions for Bankruptcy: A Comparative Study of the Legislative History' (2001) Background paper for the World Development Report, http://vonthadden.vwl.uni-mannheim.de/fileadmin/user_upload/thadden/research/Berg-Rosen-ThadFeb2001.pdf. David Skeel views US bankruptcy law as compromise between creditor groups and 'prodebtor movements' and populism. He also notes the role of politics where creditor interests have influenced the Republican party and debtor interests the Democrat party, as well as the role of bankruptcy lawyers in expanding the scope of the bankruptcy law. Skeel, *Debt's Dominion* (n 3) 16.

[8] These periods are the conflicts over the original 1898 Act; the 1930s and the development of Chapter 13; the late 1950s until the Bankruptcy Reform Act 1978; the subsequent 'war of ideas' as creditors pressed for changes in the period leading up to BAPCPA 2005, perceived as a partial victory for creditors, and the current era, including the response of bankruptcy law to the Great Recession. See eg Skeel, *Debt's Dominion* (n 3).

[9] See WJ Novak, 'The Myth of the "Weak" American State' (2008) 113 *The American Historical Review* 752.

[10] See P Culpepper, *Quiet Politics and Business Power Corporate Control in Europe and Japan* (Cambridge, Cambridge University Press, 2011). See also E Warren, 'The Changing Politics of American Bankruptcy Reform' (1999) 37 *Osgoode Hall Law Journal* 189, 192: '[M]ost of the perceived genius

A relatively small close-knit group of lawyers, academics, and judges exercised what one writer describes as a policy monopoly[11] from the 1930s until the 1978 Act. This era of quiet politics produced 'mildly pro-debtor'[12] legislation based on a vision of the debtor as an unfortunate or slightly incompetent victim of the credit system. This monopoly was disrupted by policy entrepreneurs for creditor interests after 1978 who changed the policy image of consumer bankruptcy, focusing on the abuser and the 'lifestyle bankrupt', layered incremental changes on to existing legislation in 1984 and 1994, and partially succeeded with the goal of restricting access to bankruptcy through 'means testing' and other provisions in the BAPCPA which raised the costs of bankruptcy filing. The Great Recession of 2008 raised the role of bankruptcy law as a protection for homeowners. Federal legislation did not enact a 'cramdown'—the possibility of writing down the principal of a loan under Chapter 13—but local judicial experiments have developed that promise some relief in bankruptcy for homeowners. The difficulties of achieving 'big bang' legislative change through the federal Congress means that political action continues in other sites, as those defeated in one site move the forum.

II. The Challenge of the Wage Earner Debtor: The 1930s

Consumer bankruptcy was not a carefully planned institution and the 1898 Act viewed bankruptcy as a trader not consumer remedy.[13] The 1898 Act was not viewed at the time as debtor-friendly.[14] Wage earner bankruptcies became a

and warts in the 1978 Bankruptcy Code can be laid at the feet of the bankruptcy professionals [but] in the bankruptcy debates of 1997–98 the special interest groups largely replaced the professionals as influential players.'

[11] See Kevin Ball who argues that for about 30 years from the 1930s, bankruptcy policymaking was dominated by 'a small group of attorneys, bankruptcy judges, and academics [that] used its status to completely rewrite the bankruptcy laws according to its own preferences'. K Ball, 'Bankruptcy and Politics: A Framework for Bankruptcy Policymaking in the United States Congress and Courts' (PhD thesis, Wayne State University 2012) http://digitalcommons.wayne.edu/oa_dissertations/423. Ball draws on the work of FR Baumgartner and PD Jones, *Agendas and Instability in American Politics* (Chicago, University of Chicago Press, 1993) who at p 4 define a policy monopoly as 'structural arrangements supported by powerful ideas'. Baumgartner and Jones refer to several areas of US policy characterised by the attempt by experts to dominate policymaking.

[12] Skeel, *Debt's Dominion* (n 3) 156.

[13] '[C]onsumer bankruptcy has always been a difficult institution to pin down. It was certainly not carefully fashioned by lawmakers. Rather, it crept up through an opening in the 1898 Act and has grown with the expansion of consumer credit ever since.' See DA Moss and GA Johnson, 'The Rise of Consumer Bankruptcy: Evolution, Revolution, or Both' (1999) 73 *American Bankruptcy Law Journal* 311.

[14] Bradley Hansen and Mary Hansen argue that James Olmstead's famous comments about the fresh start representing a 'Hebrew Jubilee' were a warning against regarding bankruptcy as a jubilee and not a statement that it was a jubilee. See BA Hansen and ME Hansen, 'The Role of Path Dependence in the Development of US Bankruptcy Law, 1880–1938' (2007) 3 *Journal of Institutional Economics* 203. See also, JM Olmstead, 'Bankruptcy a Commercial Regulation' (1902) 15 *Harvard Law Review* 829.

political issue in the early 1930s[15] as part of the general critique of the bankruptcy system. Wage earner cases increased by 414 per cent (whereas the population increased 16 per cent) between 1920 and 1930,[16] and an official report in 1931 described them as a 'subject of major importance'.[17]

The system no longer functioned as envisaged in 1898 as a medium of creditor distribution since there were rarely any assets to distribute, and creditor control had failed because of creditor apathy towards potentially small dividends.[18] The straight liquidation bankruptcy of individuals with few assets was perceived as a remedy insufficiently tailored to the distinct situation of the wage earner.[19] A government report, which provided the basis for the Hastings-Michener Bill of 1932, proposed the following typologies of debtor based on cases reported by referees in bankruptcy:

'(1) [T]he strictly fraudulent, whose discharge should be denied.
(2) The honest but unfortunate, overwhelmed with debt who should receive a full discharge on grounds of public policy.
(3) *The honest but temporarily embarrassed harassed (sic) by garnishments or attachments who could pay if given time under the protection of the court.*—The effect of lumping them with the second class and discharging them automatically is to destroy their sense of moral obligation and to promote extravagance and shiftlessness.
(4) *The large borderline class who are neither strictly honest nor strictly fraudulent but whose conduct is not such as to justify a full discharge.*—These are the bankrupts who have recklessly lived beyond their means; gambled away their money or grossly neglected their affairs: incurred judgments for

[15] Wage earner bankruptcies represented the majority of bankruptcies during the late 1920s, when courts, in the face of the failure of creditor control, routinely granted discharge. The level of wage earner bankruptcies seemed to be related to the impact of wage garnishment in certain states. See R Nugent and FM Jones, 'Wage Executions for Debt: Part 1 Frequency of Wage Executions' (1936) 42 *Monthly Labor Review* 285. States with restrictions on wage garnishment have lower bankruptcy filing rates. See eg P Apilado, J Dauten, and D Smith, 'Personal Bankruptcies' (1978) 7 *Journal of Legal Studies* 371; L Lefgren and F McIntyre, 'Explaining the Puzzle of Cross-State Differences in Bankruptcy Rates' (2009) 52 *Journal of Law and Economics* 367.

[16] Note 'Bankruptcy Reform and the Chandler Bill' (1936–37) 46 *Yale Law Journal* 1177 footnote 199, citing Department of Commerce, *Causes of Bankruptcy among Consumers* (Domestic Commerce Series, No 82, 1933).

[17] United States President Herbert Hoover (1929–33), 'Strengthening of Procedure in the Judicial System: Message from the President of the United States Recommending the Strengthening of Procedure in the Judicial System: Together with the Report of the Attorney General on Bankruptcy Law and Practice, S Doc 65, 72d Congress 1st Session' (Washington DC, US Government Printing Office, 1932) S Doc 65, 72d Congress 1st Session. The actual ratio of wage earners to business bankruptcies at this time is difficult to assess because many individuals whose businesses had failed were now employees and classified by officials as wage earners.

[18] See WA Sturges and DE Cooper, 'Credit Administration and Wage Earner Bankruptcies' (1933) 42 *Yale Law Journal* 487, noting that only 116 out of 28,914 bankruptcies in 1931 were involuntary cases.

[19] See Hoover, 'Strengthening of Procedure' (n 17) 8. The bankruptcy courts 'are chiefly engaged in relieving from their debts vast numbers of debtors who obtain their discharges without making any provision for a partial payment of their creditors either out of property or earnings'.

negligence or grossly neglected their affairs ... obtained credit in immediate contemplation of bankruptcy or without the slightest regard as to when or how it might be paid.[20]' (emphasis in original)

The accuracy of these typologies depended on the underlying factual data, and individual bankruptcy law became the focus for pioneering empirical research by realist legal scholars who promoted the ideal of progressive reform through greater knowledge of the law in action.[21] William O Douglas's study of Boston and New Jersey debtors identified unemployment and medical expenses as the primary causes of bankruptcy, with a minority of individuals overextending on consumer credit or home mortgages.[22] In a companion article, Douglas and J Howard Marshall concluded that the vast majority of wage earner cases were 'cases of varying degrees of misfortune precipitated by the increasing demands on and availability of consumptive credit'.[23] Approximately 25 per cent of debtors declared bankruptcy because of deficiency judgements after a home had been foreclosed.[24]

Douglas and Marshall proposed greater availability of optional amortisation plans for debtors that would not require creditor consent and supported greater attempts, following the English approach of the conditional discharge, to separate different types of bankrupt. The inspiration for the amortisation plan was the growth of private organisations, such as the American Amortization Company in Chicago, that negotiated payment plans—of approximately two years—by debtors with their creditors, permitting the debtor to 'avoid bankruptcy, keep his job, and obtain relief from much of his anxiety and fear'.[25]

Reform proposals during this era identified several themes. First, existing bankruptcy law did not adequately provide an opportunity for the wage earner to avoid the stigma of bankruptcy and repay some or all of their obligations

[20] Hoover, 'Strengthening of Procedure' (n 17) 24–25.These categories have a striking similarity to the categories used by the Cork Committee in England. See K Cork, *Insolvency Law and Practice: Report of the Review Committee*, vol 8558 (London, HMSO, 1982).

[21] See DA Skeel, 'Vern Countryman and the Path of Progressive (and Populist) Bankruptcy Scholarship' [2000] *Harvard Law Review* 1075.

[22] WO Douglas, 'Wage Earner Bankruptcies. State vs. Federal Control' (1933) 42 *Yale Law Journal* 591.

[23] WO Douglas and JH Marshall, 'A Factual Study of Bankruptcy Administration and Some Suggestions' (1932) 32 *Columbia Law Review* 25, 53.

[24] Wage garnishment often precipitated bankruptcy either through the hardship it caused to individuals or through loss of a job. Nugent and Jones (n 15) found that bankruptcy rates were extremely high in those states that permitted unrestricted wage garnishments or permitted wage assignments. Individuals would fear loss of employment and might even resort to loan sharks to avoid garnishment. In Texas, a state without a garnishment law, only 9% of bankrupts in 1930 were wage earners. See Hoover, 'Strengthening of Procedures' (n 17) 81. This report noted that '[c]ollectors often use the expression, "Pay Me or I will get your job"'. In England, in comparison, since the Truck Acts of the nineteenth century it was not possible to attach an individual's wages. Wage attachment was only introduced in 1970.

[25] Douglas and Marshall, 'A Factual Study of Bankruptcy Administration' (n 23) 54. They also proposed (at 57) a summary procedure based on the English summary administration for small asset cases. But Douglas had also concluded in his 1932 Yale article (n 22) that few of the Boston debtors would be able to take advantage of this opportunity given their limited repayment capacity.

over time.[26] Second, provisions were necessary for the group of debtors who could repay their debts in full if given extra time and reduced interest charges. The Hastings-Michener Bill of 1932 included section 75,[27] which permitted a debtor to amortise debts over two years with a subsequent discharge of the remaining debt. An individual who chose straight bankruptcy faced the possibility of a suspended discharge with a requirement to make income repayments dependent on their capacity. Individuals with no repayment capacity would obtain an immediate discharge. These provisions were ultimately not enacted but the idea of a *voluntary* wage repayment plan survived in subsequent bills in the 1930s and ultimately became Chapter 13 of the 1938 Chandler Act. Finally, creditors should take some responsibility for over-indebtedness. Several documents refer to the careless extension of credit and over-indebtedness as a consequence of modern salesmanship 'striving to expand sales regardless of credit risk'.[28]

The 1930s US solutions were fashioned for debtors with different payment capacities.[29] The Chandler Act of 1938 reflected the work of the National Bankruptcy Conference, which would also be influential in post-war bankruptcy development.[30] But the major reform of the 1930s for wage earners did not arise from elite lawyers or academics but from a judicial improvisation originating in Alabama,[31] based partly on a failed English model. Valentine Nesbit, a referee in Alabama, developed a repayment system for wage earners, primarily employees of large private and public organisations in Birmingham Alabama,[32] through a very liberal interpretation of section 74 of the 1932 Act.[33] Nesbit administered a

[26] See discussion of development of Chapter 13 in *Perry v Commerce Loan Co* 383 U.S. 392 (1966).

[27] Hoover, 'Strengthening of Procedures' (n 17) 80 argued: '(1) That most wage earners who fall into debt desire to pay their debts in full and wish to avoid the stigma of bankruptcy; (2) that they are driven into bankruptcy chiefly by garnishments and other attachments, even in the midst of an attempt to pay in installments; (3) that at least a third of the wage earners who are now forced into bankruptcy and released from their debts could, if given time and protection, pay their creditors in full; (4) that if the law offered such relief without stigma, a still larger number of wage earners, who now resort to loan companies in an effort to stave off their creditors and gradually get into debt beyond their capacity to pay, would find a means of relief at a comparatively early stage of indebtedness.'

[28] Hoover, 'Strengthening of Procedures' (n 17) 8, 9. 'The creditors are not infrequently to blame for the losses incurred. Credit is often extended carelessly and without adequate inquiry, or with the expectation that profits from the increased volume of sales will exceed probable credit losses. The consequences of modern salesmanship striving to expand sales regardless of credit risk by encouraging persons of moderate means to make purchases on credit which they can ill afford are undoubtedly reflected in the deplorable statistics of bankruptcy.'

[29] In some respects, they resemble the recommendations of the UK Cork Committee in 1982, which proposed a range of alternatives for individual debtors. See ch 3 section III.A.

[30] David Skeel describes the NBC as the 'single most important voice in bankruptcy reform' during this period. Skeel, *Debt's Dominion* (n 3) 90.

[31] See generally, TW Dixon and DG Epstein, 'Where Did Chapter 13 Come from and Where Should It Go' (2002) 10 *American Bankruptcy Institute Law Review* 741.

[32] Dixon and Epstein, 'Where Did Chapter 13 Come From' (n 31) 752. 'Employees of the local industries (principally coal and steel), railroad and public utility employees made up the bulk of the 2,300 debtors, with city, county, state and federal employees also appearing on the list … about one-half of the debtors were African-Americans.'

[33] Dixon and Epstein, 'Where Did Chapter 13 Come From' (n 31) 741.

discretionary equity to balance the interests of debtors and creditors, and introduced an administrative structure of supervisors to collect payments and provide the protection of the court to debtors against further action by creditors. Along with Walter Chandler and the counsel for the National Retail Credit Association, Nesbit drafted the initial Chandler Bill provisions on Chapter 13.[34] According to Nesbit, the programme was popular with creditors, because it 'made collecting their money easier and more certain',[35] and debtors, because it protected their employment and protected them from the stigma of bankruptcy.[36] Nesbit claimed that he was imitating English procedures that allowed for liquidation on a partial payment plan, and in his testimony on the Chandler Bill stated: 'of course there have been similar provisions in the Canadian and British laws … We are just 25 to 30 years behind the Canadians and the British to that extent. They have had a partial payment plan in the British law for several generations.'[37] Nesbit did not identify specific English procedures but may have been thinking of the English administration order.[38] Although Chapter 13 promised benefits to both creditors and debtors, questioning by Congressional House committees demonstrated concern that it could represent a form of federal wage attachment.[39] One commentator thought that the introduction of Chapter 13 would render straight bankruptcy a residual form of relief.[40]

The 1920s and 1930s were, therefore, a period of conversion for the US bankruptcy system. Bradley Hansen and Mary Hansen claim that during this period bankruptcy became identified with consumers rather than traders, and the idea of the fresh start for individuals, as exemplified in the famous dictum of

[34] Dixon and Epstein, 'Where Did Chapter 13 Come From' (n 31) 757. Henry Heiman of the National Association of Credit Men commented that the NBC acting in conjunction with Congress forms an 'ideal model for government-business cooperation and might be adapted for other types of legislation'. Certainly 'creditors … heartily endorsed' Chapter 13. See W Enright, 'Congress Is Ready to Hear Business; Heimann Finds It Receptive to Concrete Proposals Intelligently Made' *The New York Times* (New York, 3 April 1938) 62.

See also, United States Congress House Committee on Judiciary, *Revision of the Bankruptcy Act: Hearing before the Committee, 75th Cong. 1st Sess. on H.R. 6439. Subsequently Amended, Reintroduced and Reported as H.R. 8046.* Serial 9, 1–9 June 1937 (Washington DC, Government Printing Office, 1937). Mr Duffy: 'As I understand this bill which we have before us, it practically sanctions everything that you are doing now. Your practical experience justifies this bill, I think you said?' Mr Nesbit: 'Yes sir; that is true.'

[35] House Committee on Judiciary, *Revision of the Bankruptcy Act* (n 34).

[36] House Committee on Judiciary, *Revision of the Bankruptcy Act* (n 34). According to Nesbit: 'All they want is an opportunity to pay without being adjudged bankrupt. The first question they ask is "Mr Nesbit, is this bankruptcy?"' Testimony of Valentine Nesbit, Committee of Judiciary of House of Representatives on HR 6439 and HR 8046 (1937) 259, 261.

[37] Testimony of Valentine Nesbit (n 36) 259, 261.

[38] An income payment order was also possible under s 51 of the Bankruptcy Act 1914, but was rarely used.

[39] See the valuable contemporary discussion of the Chapter 13 proposals in 'Bankruptcy Reform and the Chandler Bill' (n 16) 1191–97.

[40] J Mulder, 'Ambiguities in the Chandler Act' (1940) 89 *University of Pennsylvania Law Review and American Law Register* 10.

Local Loan Co v Hunt,[41] became dominant, eclipsing that of distribution of assets among creditors. The Democratic Party had by the mid 1920s dropped its original opposition to the institution of bankruptcy, which it had viewed as a vehicle for oppression of small businesses and farmers. Douglas justified the idea of the discharge in terms of encouraging experimentation in business, which we would probably now describe as entrepreneurialism. He thought, however, that the US erred in its rather liberal approach to discharge and that greater controls should be introduced, similar to the English controls on discharge where, for example, an individual who had failed to keep proper books would be penalised.[42]

III. The Wage Earner as Consumer Debtor: 1950s–1978

Lizabeth Cohen describes the post-World War II US as a 'consumers' republic' where democracy became associated with the ability to own a home and a standard package of consumer goods.[43] Consumer credit financed these purchases and the US government provided a variety of subsidies, such as tax deductions, to facilitate the expansion of credit. This era represented a continuation and expansion of the consumer credit economy of the 1930s. Widespread access to credit was supported by both labour and consumer groups. Along with the consumer credit

[41] *Local Loan Co v Hunt* 292 US 234 (1934). Mr Justice Sutherland: 'When a person assigns future wages, he in effect pledges his future earning power. The power of the individual to earn a living for himself and those dependent upon him is in the nature of a personal liberty quite as much, if not more, than it is a property right. To preserve its free exercise is of the utmost importance not only because it is a fundamental private necessity, but because it is a matter of great public concern. From the viewpoint of the wage earner, there is little difference between not earning at all and earning wholly for a creditor. Pauperism may be the necessary result of either. The amount of the indebtedness, or the proportion of wages assigned, may here be small, but the principle, once established, will equally apply where both are very great. The new opportunity in life and the clear field for future effort which it is the purpose of the Bankruptcy Act to afford the emancipated debtor would be of little value to the wage earner if he were obliged to face the necessity of devoting the whole or a considerable portion of his earnings for an indefinite time in the future to the payment of indebtedness incurred prior to his bankruptcy.' This case actually drew on an earlier decision which had primarily justified the fresh start in relation to *business* debtors. See *Williams v US Fidelity & Guaranty Co* 236 US 549, 554–55: '[R]elieve the honest debtor from the weight of oppressive indebtedness and to permit him to start afresh free from the obligations and responsibilities consequent upon business misfortunes.'

[42] See WO Douglas, 'Bankruptcy', *Encyclopedia of the Social Sciences* (London, Macmillan Publishing Co, 1937): 'To quarantine those who have failed because of their own incompetence and to allow those who have failed because of misfortune to make another attempt has been thought to draw the proper distinction between legitimate and illegitimate experimentation. Until a scientific study of the causes of failure is made there will be no factual basis for legislation along the lines of that of other countries."

[43] See L Cohen, *A Consumers' Republic: The Politics of Mass Consumption in Postwar America* (Cambridge, Mass, Harvard University Press, 2003). See also L Hyman, *Debtor Nation: The History of America in Red Ink* (Princeton, Princeton University Press, 2008); G Trumbull, *Consumer Lending in France and the US* (Cambridge, Cambridge University Press, 2013).

boom came a growth in bankruptcy filings.[44] This growth stimulated discussion of consumer bankruptcy in the late 1950s and 1960s as well as an interest in 'consumer' bankrupts who seemed to constitute a new species of bankrupt, with few assets except their future income capacity along with a limited ability to pay for bankruptcy.[45] Similar comments had been made about the new wage earner bankrupt in the 1930s. Historical amnesia is a common disease in bankruptcy policymaking. Bankruptcy regulation was increasingly linked to consumer credit regulation and the darker side of debt collection and creditor enforcement.[46]

Lawyers and legal academics dominated bankruptcy policymaking during this period. The American Bar Association (ABA), through its subcommittee on consumer bankruptcy chaired by the counsel for Beneficial Finance, expressed concern in 1961 about the growth in consumer bankruptcies and the need for further study.[47] The Association also supported[48] several congressional bills during the 1960s to introduce a 'needs-based' bankruptcy with individuals being required to demonstrate that they could not make some repayment over a three-year period.[49]

The National Bankruptcy Conference (NBC) and the National Association of Referees in Bankruptcy were key actors during this period.[50] The Conference annually presented to Congress proposed amendments to the Bankruptcy Act as

[44] The classic article is V Countryman, 'The Bankruptcy Boom' (1963) 77 *Harvard Law Review* 1452. Legal articles on Chapter 13 in the late 1950s and early 1960s often prefaced their analysis with reference to the large rise in 'consumer' bankruptcies. See eg WE McCarty, 'Wage Earners' Plans-Chapter XIII' (1961) 45 *Marquette Law Review* 582 ('serious concern' about the rising number of straight bankruptcy petitions).

[45] See eg BC Hilliard Jr and W Hurt, 'Wage Earner Plans under Chapter XIII of the Bankruptcy Act' (1963) 19 *The Business Lawyer* 271: 'It would appear we have geared ourselves–perhaps inextricably–to a consumer-credit economy. A new and extremely numerous class of debtors has been created, and continues to increase, made up of those whose incomes are derived from wages, salaries, or commissions. The Bankruptcy Act of 1898, intended to cope with business failures, did not envision the problems of wage-earner debtors or afford realistic procedures with respect to them.'

[46] See generally National Commission on Consumer Finance, *Consumer Credit in the United States* (Washington, US Government Printer, 1972).

[47] See 'Bar Study Asked on Bankruptcies: Investigation Urged into Reasons for Growth of Consumer Failures' *New York Times* (New York, 11 February 1961) 29.

[48] Senator Charles Grassley referred to these when introducing HR 2415 1998: 'In the 1960s, Congress considered several such proposals. See HR 12784, 88th Cong, 2d Sess (1964); HR 292, 89th Cong, 1st Sess (1965); S 613, 89th Cong, 1st Sess (1965); HR 1057 & HR 5771, 90th Cong, 1st Sess (1967). United States, Bankruptcy Reform Act of 2000: Conference Report (to Accompany HR 2415) (Washington DC, US GPO, 2000).

[49] These bills either required a debtor to demonstrate that adequate relief could not be provided by a three-year Chapter 13 plan, or permitted a referee to convert a voluntary proceeding in bankruptcy to a Chapter 13 without the debtor's consent. See HR 12784 88th Congress 2d Session (1964) and S 613 HR 292 89th Congress 1st Session (1965), proposing a mandatory Chapter 13 as a condition of discharge. Harvard law professor and member of the National Bankruptcy Conference Vern Countryman critiqued these proposals noting that the 'proposals seemed objectionable to most members of the National Bankruptcy Conference'. V Countryman, 'Proposed New Amendments for Chapter XIII' (1966) 22 *Business Lawyer (ABA)* 1151. See also WK Adam, 'Should Chapter XIII Bankruptcy Be Involuntary?' (1965) 44 *Texas Law Review* 533.

[50] On the legislative role of the National Conference of Referees in Bankruptcy, see BL Zelenko, 'The Role of the Referee in Legislative Reform of the Bankruptcy Act' (1969) 43 *Journal of the National Conference of Referees in Bankruptcy* 101. See generally RW McDufee, 'Wage Earner (Chapter XIII) Proceedings in the Bankruptcy Court' (1962) 17 *The Business Lawyer* 677.

well as commenting on and opposing proposals from other sources.[51] In 1956, Charles Horsky, Chairman of the NBC, described its role as a veritable 'Ministry of Justice'[52] in bankruptcy law—'a body of experts and specialists who will explore new ideas, take into account economic and political changes, and see to it that law keeps abreast of progress in other areas'.[53] One member claimed in 1958 that much bankruptcy legislation had been sponsored and drafted by the Conference.[54] Its discussion of Chapter 13 is, therefore, of interest, revealing the thinking of central actors in the US bankruptcy 'knowledge regime' of this period.

Several annual conferences[55] of the NBC during the 1950s discussed Chapter 13 filings, which then represented only between 10 and 15 per cent of bankruptcies.[56] Most filings were in southern states such as Alabama, and a few northern states such as Maine. Its lack of use was attributed to factors such as the low debt ceiling, the absence of knowledge of its potential by lawyers and consumers, the lack of enthusiasm by referees outside a few states for the process, and the inability to deal effectively with secured debt. Committees of the NBC proposed greater publicity for the benefits of Chapter 13, including a series of law review articles targeted at states with low rates of Chapter 13 participation.[57] The consensus of the

[51] See testimony of Frank Kennedy to House Hearings Before the Subcommittee on Bankruptcy of the Committee on the Judiciary US Senate Second Session on SJ Res 100 A Bill to Create a Commission to Study the Bankruptcy Laws of the US (1969) 84. Kennedy indicated that the conference had 'about 50 members', 'half of whom are practitioners, and the other half divided fairly evenly between referees in bankruptcy and law professors … an effort is made to keep the conference representative of the several interests that are involved in bankruptcy cases, including secured and unsecured creditors, and debtors … The sponsoring organizations include the American Bankers Association, the section of Corporation of Banking and Business Law of the American Bar Association, the Commercial Law League of America, the American Institute of Certified Public Accountants, National Association of Credit Management and four others … the principal activity of the conference is the consideration and drafting of proposals to amend the Bankruptcy Act. As the members of the Judiciary Committee of the Senate know, the conference presents to Congress every session, I should say, a number of drafts of proposed amendments. We also oppose some proposals that emanate from other sources and seek modifications of proposals that come from other sources.'

[52] See Minutes of National Bankruptcy Conference, 1956 at 30 (US bankruptcy archives, University of Pennsylvania). The reference is to BN Cardozo, 'A Ministry of Justice' (1921) 35 *Harvard Law Review* 113.

[53] Minutes of National Bankruptcy Conference, 1956 at 30.

[54] S Krause, 'What's New in Bankruptcy?' (1958) 13 *The Business Lawyer* 468. On the legislative role of the National Conference of Referees, see Zelenko, 'The Role of the Referee' (n 50) 103.

[55] Skeel, *Debt's Dominion* (n 3) 95. The author provides a history of the development of the NBC.

[56] In 1951, Walter Chandler chairman of the subcommittee on wage earners reported that 'Chapter XIII has been successful wherever tried'. National Bankruptcy Conference Summary of Proceedings New York City February 23–25, 1951 (US Bankruptcy Archives, University of Pennsylvania) 42.

[57] The Committee noted that the value of Chapter 13 was not only the benefits of creditor repayment but 'the intangible value measured in terms of satisfaction and moral strength derived by an honest debtor from the payment of his obligations in full'. Appendix G 1957 Summary of Proceedings National Bankruptcy Conference 1957 Annual Meeting, Washington, Nov 1–2 1957, 49 (US Bankruptcy Archives, University of Pennsylvania) For the articles promoting greater use by states that had low usage of Chapter 13, see CE Nadler, 'Rehabilitation of the Insolvent Wage Earner under the Bankruptcy Act: A Challenge to Minnesota' (1957) 42 *Minnesota Law Review* 377; CE Nadler, 'Rehabilitation of the Insolvent Wage Earner under the Bankruptcy Act in Florida' (1957) 10 *University of Florida Law Review* 465; CE Nadler, 'Rehabilitation of the Insolvent Wage Earner in Georgia under the Bankruptcy Act' (1958) 63 *Commercial Law Journal* 67.

Conference was that Chapter 13 served a useful purpose but that debtors should not be actively steered towards it by courts, as suggested by the Judicial Conference (comprised of senior judges).[58]

A quantum leap in interest by the NBC in Chapter 13 occurred in the early 1960s, when Asa Herzog,[59] a leading member of the NBC, expressed strong reservations about the current administration of Chapter 13.[60] In 1963 the NBC noted both substantial growth in popular discussion about the rise of non-business bankruptcies, and that the ABA had established a committee on consumer bankruptcy which favoured a 'needs based' bankruptcy. James Maclachlan, a Harvard Law School bankruptcy law professor and a founding member of the NBC, thought that an 'involuntary Chapter XIII might be the answer—to the problem of the consumer debtor'.[61] MacLachlan was in the minority on this issue, and the Conference disapproved of the Canadian concept of a conditional discharge. The Conference did propose measures to make Chapter 13 more efficient and attractive to debtors, but maintaining debtor choice of chapter.[62]

Conflict existed therefore between the position of expert representatives of creditor groups who, along with the ABA, favoured a needs-based bankruptcy, and the position of the NBC and the National Association of Referees in Bankruptcy who were sympathetic to a more effective use of a voluntary Chapter 13 for wage

[58] See Resolutions 49–51, National Bankruptcy Conference Summary of Proceedings, 1958 Annual Meeting, Washington DC, 25. This vote was a response to a Judicial Conference resolution (Report of the Committee on Bankruptcy Administration of the Judicial Conference) that district judges direct referees in bankruptcy to consider whether a case was appropriate for Chapter 13 and if so to recommend this to the debtor and his lawyer. The NBC concluded that: 'The choice of remedies should be made by the bankrupts with the advice of their attorneys and … it is not the function of the court to influence or interfere with such choice or remedy.' Resolution 51 stated that 'the court may suggest the availability of Chapter XIII in appropriate cases, leaving the final decision to the debtor and his counsel'. See further ER Sloan, 'Wage Earners' Plan' (1958) 7 *University of Kansas Law Review* 175.

[59] Herzog was a bankruptcy court judge from 1958 to 1975. His obituary described him as 'widely regarded as Dean of the nation's bankruptcy system'.

[60] See Annual Conference of the National Association of Referees in Bankruptcy 1962, 72, 85 (Bankruptcy archives, University of Pennsylvania). In his view, Chapter 13 practice in many districts was a violation of the Bankruptcy Act with 'production-line' routines by trustees who exercised excessive power over debtors' lifestyles. He thought that they should simply act as 'distributing agent' and the conference approved a proposal to change the title of the trustee to distributing agent. Herzog was himself criticised later for not encouraging the use of Chapter 13 in New York. RJ Cole, 'Personal Finance: Wage Earner Plan' *New York Times* (New York, 10 October 1968) 73. See also DT Stanley and M Girth, *Bankruptcy: Problem, Process, Reform* (Washington DC, Brookings Institution, 1971) 74. The Brookings study found that Chapter 13 cases represented 17% of bankruptcies in 1964. Substantial state variations existed in its use, ranging from 76% in northern Alabama to 4% in northern Illinois. These differences continue to exist.

[61] He commented that 'it [is] outrageous for people to buy, contemplating paying out of future earnings, and then deciding they do not want to … Bankruptcy is drawn up in a commercial framework. The bankruptcy law was not drawn up with reference to this sort of thing at all: Proceedings of the National Bankruptcy Conference, October 25–26, 1962, 49. See also JA MacLachlan, 'Puritanical Therapy for Wage Earners' (1963) 68 *Commercial Law Journal* 87.

[62] This position may have reflected the influence of Harvard law professor Vern Countryman who became chair of the NBC committee on consumer bankruptcy in the mid 1960s. Countryman was also Reporter on the Chapter 13 Rules in 1973. David Skeel notes at 135 that 'Countryman tirelessly promoted the interests of consumer debtors'. Skeel, *Debt's Dominion* (n 3).

earners as a form of debtor rehabilitation but opposed the idea of an imposed Chapter 13.

Debates on several bills introduced during this period to bring in a needs-based bankruptcy highlighted the competing arguments.[63] These bills were not successful partly because of organised opposition by the NBC and the National Association of Referees in Bankruptcy. The NBC also alerted labour organisations to the potential impact of these bills, spoke against them in congressional hearings,[64] and proposed its own alternative.[65]

The 1967–68[66] hearings on Wage Earners Plans canvassed the opposing views. Those supporting a needs-based approach included the ABA, American Bankers Association, credit unions, industrial bankers (finance companies), the National Federation of Independent Business, and the US Chamber of Commerce. Arguing that bankruptcy proceedings had become a 'near scandal', promoters argued that the Bill would provide greater rehabilitation and self-esteem for a debtor, promote individual responsibility and morality, and would be economically beneficial.[67] A basic premise was that those who 'could pay' should not be able to use straight bankruptcy.[68] To support this claim the ABA cited empirical studies of individual bankruptcy, which concluded that 25–50 per cent of bankrupts could pay their debts from future income.[69]

Opponents of the Bill claimed, first, that it represented discriminatory and punitive 'class legislation' to require only wage earners, generally a lower-income

[63] These Bills included HR 12784, 88th Congress 2d Sess (1964); HR 292, 89th Congress 1st Sess (1965); S. 613, 89th Congress 1st Sess (1965); HR 1057 & HR 5771, 90th Congress. 1st Sess (1967).

[64] Resolution 21 National Bankruptcy Conference, Summary of Proceedings, New York 1964, 14. The Resolution stated: 'that the *attention of labor organizations* be called to the fact that proposals having such effect are under active consideration by interested groups; that the *Conference prepare a brief* on the subject for submission to the Bankruptcy Committee of the Judicial Conference; and that representatives of the Conference for the purpose of opposing the bill, appear at any Congressional hearing with respect to any bill relating to this matter' (emphasis in original).

[65] See Countryman, 'Proposed New Amendments for Chapter XIII' (n 49).

[66] See United States Congress, *Wage Earner Plans under the Bankruptcy Act. Hearings before the Subcommittee No 4 of the Committee of Judiciary, Ninetieth Congress, First Session, on HR 1057 and HR 5771 … May 24 and 25, 1967* (Washington, US Government Printing Office, 1967).

[67] James MacLachlan, Harvard law professor, member of the National Bankruptcy Conference and an author of the Chandler Act, apparently supported the Bill.

[68] See statements of Carrol Wetzel, Chairman, Section of Corporation, Banking and Business Law, and Linn K Twinem, Chairman, Consumer Bankruptcy Committee of the American Bar Association, House Hearings HR 1057 (90th Congress) 1967 *Wage Earner Plans Under the Bankruptcy Act* 38–39. They claimed that bankruptcy proceedings had reached a point of 'near scandal' with debtors needlessly claiming relief.

[69] R Dolphin, *An Analysis of Economic and Personal Factors Leading to Consumer Bankruptcy* (Michigan, Bureau of Business and Economic Research, Graduate School of Business Administration, Michigan State University, 1965). The study claimed that 28% of bankrupts could repay their debts over three years on a Chapter 13 plan living on a 'comfortable' budget. Ibid 98. The study received financial support from an American Bankers Association fellowship. It is not clear how many of the studies cited in legislative hearings by the ABA were sponsored by them. The ABA had indicated in 1961 that it would promote study of the consumer bankruptcy system. See 'Bar Study Asked on Bankruptcies' (n 47) (reporting comments of Linn Twinem, counsel for Beneficial Finance and chairman of the ABA subcommittee on consumer finance).

group, to be subject to this test when corporations or high-income professionals were excluded. Second, many Chapter 13 plans failed (evidence existed that between 30 and 50 per cent of plans were not confirmed) because of debtor moves, default in payments, etc. These issues would be compounded by 'coerced' plans which might simply result individuals in quitting their job. Finally, the AFL-CIO claimed that not only did the proposals discriminate against workers, but they also were an invasion of privacy of the worker who would be treated like a ward of court, losing control of their affairs. Vern Countryman, speaking as Vice Chair of the NBC, viewed the legislation as a thinly disguised involuntary Chapter 13. In a rhetorical flourish, he likened the proposals to a form of involuntary servitude and noted that when similar proposals had been made in the 1930s they had been characterised as 'un-American'.[70]

Chapter 13 was not, however, the only consumer bankruptcy issue discussed during this period. A common theme in congressional hearings was the ineffective nature in practice of the bankruptcy discharge.[71] Repeat player creditors, primarily finance companies, had developed techniques to circumvent the bankruptcy discharge. These included the use of broad security interests in household goods, procuring reaffirmations of individual debts, taking advantage of the limited effect of a bankruptcy discharge in state courts,[72] and aggressive use of the fraud exception to discharge. Finance companies exploited the fraud exception by requiring substantial financial details from consumers, coupled with the debtor's promise that this was an accurate statement of their financial affairs, knowing that any mistake could be used later to found a non-dischargeability claim. The Brookings Institution study of bankruptcies filed in 1964 found that 41 per cent of bankrupts reported post-bankruptcy collection efforts and 12 per cent paid the debt in response. In addition, about one-third of bankrupts had agreed to repay some of the debts discharged in bankruptcy.[73] Bankruptcy relief often proved to

[70] '[T]he involuntary feature is contrary to the genius of our institutions … We have outlawed peonage and other forms of involuntary servitude and have largely outlawed imprisonment for debt … We can hardly be expected now to approve a system whereby the debtor's opportunity for rehabilitation is to be delayed for a period of bondage during which his future earnings are sequestered for the benefit of his existing creditors.' (Countryman, 'Proposed New Amendments for Chapter XIII' (n 49) 74.)

[71] See eg in 1968 the testimony of bankruptcy referees Asa Herzog, Conrad Cyr, Judge Edward Weinfeld. See also Hearings before Subcommittee no 4 of Ctte on the Judiciary HR 91st Congress HR 6665 and HR 12250 and testimony of Vern Countryman. See also Royal Jackson, Office of Bankruptcy Division of Administrative Office of the US Courts: 'For the more than twenty years that I have served in the Bankruptcy division, this matter of discharge of debts has been a source of complaint. These complaints have come largely from bankrupts and members of the bankruptcy bar, who have been plagued by the harassment of creditors who ignore the discharge granted in the Federal court and continue to sue bankrupts on discharged debts in State courts after the bankruptcy proceeding has been closed. In my judgment, this is the worst defect in the Bankruptcy Act', 32.

[72] Reforms to the Bankruptcy Act in 1970 conferred on bankruptcy courts the power to determine whether a debt was dischargeable. For a discussion see V Countryman, 'The New Dischargeability Law' (1971) 45 *American Bankruptcy Law Journal* 1.

[73] Stanley and Girth, *Bankruptcy* (n 60).

be illusory.[74] For a significant number of debtors the fresh start and clear field for future effort embodied in the rhetoric of *Local Loan Co v Hunt* did not match the reality of the law in action.

Notwithstanding the conflicts over Chapter 13, substantial agreement did exist during the 1960s on certain matters. First, the Bankruptcy Act needed to respond to the new mass phenomenon of consumer debt and consumer bankruptcy, dominated by no-asset cases. Second, the general goal should be rehabilitation; budget and debt counselling should be part of bankruptcy, as well as part of a preventive strategy.[75] Daniel Cowans, vice president of the National Association of Bankruptcy Referees commented that: 'many Americans get into difficulty because they do not know how to live in this kind of economy. They did not know how to manage their money.'[76] The major conflict was on the extent to which an individual should be persuaded or coerced into choosing Chapter 13 rather than Chapter 7.

These issues framed the background to the 1970 Bankruptcy Commission, formed in response to the 'rising tide of consumer bankruptcies'.[77] The Commission's report in 1973 espoused the values of an 'open credit society'[78] underpinned by the moral obligation to repay debts. The primary functions of bankruptcy were relief of hardship from individual enforcement, rehabilitation of debtors so that they could be more productive, and a meaningful fresh start. Access should be dependent on counselling, which would assist individuals to make a rational decision between Chapter 13 and straight bankruptcy. Budgetary counselling would also be provided to bankrupts. The Commission was enthusiastic as to the potential of a reformed Chapter 13 providing the solution for debtors with a regular income but no assets.[79] Individuals should be encouraged to file for Chapter 13, but the Commission rejected forced participation by debtors which in the Commission's view had little chance of success.

The Commission's major recommendation was the separation of administrative from judicial functions and the creation of a federal administrative agency

[74] Asa Herzog of the NBC commented that in many cases 'the net effect of … bankruptcy discharge is a tendency to get rid of a few medical bills [with the debtor still owing] virtually the same amount that he did before'. Testimony of Asa Herzog in United States, Bankruptcy: Hearings before Subcommittee No. 4 of Committee on the Judiciary of the House of Representatives 91–1, on SJ Res. 88, HR 6665 and HR 12250, October 1, 1969, Serial No 7 (Washington DC, US Government Printing Office, 1969).

[75] See eg Maine Bankruptcy Referee Conrad Cyr in 1968 Hearings, Hearings before the Subcommittee on Bankruptcy and the Committee on the Judiciary US Senate (2d Sess) SJ Res 100 A Bill to create a Commission to Study the Bankruptcy Laws of the US (1969) '"debtor rehabilitation" rather than asset liquidation is the main objective'. 'While under the jurisdiction of the bankruptcy court the bankrupt receives no budgetary instruction or other social or economic assistance.'

[76] Testimony to Hearings before the Subcommittee on Bankruptcy and the Committee on the Judiciary US Senate (2d Sess) SJ Res 100. A Bill to create a Commission to Study the Bankruptcy Law of the US (1969).

[77] Report of the Commission on the Bankruptcy Laws of the United States (n 45) 1.

[78] See discussion of 'Philosophy' in chapter 3. This model was contrasted with a socialist command economy.

[79] 'No feature of the present Bankruptcy Act has received as much general acclaim as Chapter XIII.' Report of the Commission, ch 6.

which would substitute uniform administration for the existing patchwork quilt of local courts and have the ability to offer budget and counselling services that would give meaningful relief to consumer debtors who were perceived as poor debt managers.[80] The creation of an administrative agency fitted with the wider movement in the US for the rebirth or creation of administrative agencies.[81]

The Commission proposals formed the basis for the Bankruptcy Reform Act of 1978, but the administrative model failed to gain acceptance because of vehement opposition by judges and lawyers and a lack of support by financial interests who believed that a government agency would be debtor friendly and encourage bankruptcy filings.[82]

The Bankruptcy Reform Act of 1978 embraced Chapter 13 as the preferred alternative for debtors, with the intention that straight bankruptcy would become a residual form of relief.[83] The Act provided many incentives for debtors to choose Chapter 13 over Chapter 7, such as the ability to cramdown security interests and receive a 'super discharge' of debts, which would not be dischargeable under Chapter 7. The 1978 Act also abolished the requirement of creditor acceptance of a plan, instead substituting judicial approval. The Act did protect debtors against some of the practices of consumer finance companies, requiring judicial approval for reaffirmations. The Act also introduced a limit on the dischargeability of student loans, notwithstanding general opposition to this by bankruptcy insiders in the congressional debates. Finally, it substituted the term 'debtor' for 'bankrupt' throughout the Act. Most commentators seem to share David Skeel's conclusion that the 1978 Act was mildly 'pro-debtor', but note also the absence of deep ideological divisions between interest groups[84] with all parties agreed on the

[80] The Bankruptcy Commission cited the Brookings Institution study which concluded that the leading reason for bankruptcy (in 31% of cases) was 'poor debt management'. See Stanley and Girth, *Bankruptcy* (n 60) 47: 'too many debts, unwise refinancing, overspending.' Wage garnishment was the most common 'immediate cause' of bankruptcy. The Brookings Commission study had concluded that the existing system was subject to pervasive 'administrative and fiscal error and confusion' (n 60) 4.

[81] See eg the rebirth of the Federal Trade Commission (FTC) in the 1970s after withering criticism. See RA Posner, 'The Federal Trade Commission' (1969) 37 *The University of Chicago Law Review* 47.

[82] Extravagant but not untypical arguments were that a bankruptcy agency would result in a 'huge bureaucracy with tentacles reaching into every area of the country and marked with all the weaknesses of inept officialism, expensive red tape and corruption'. Asa Herzog, Bankruptcy Judge and member of the NBC quoted in E Posner, 'The Political Economy of the Bankruptcy Reform Act of 1978' (1997) *Michigan Law Review* 47, 78.

[83] See HR Rep no 95–995 at 118 (1977): 'the premises of the bill with respect to consumer bankruptcy are that use of the bankruptcy law should be a last resort; that if it is used, debtors should attempt repayment under chapter 13.'

[84] Eric Posner's public choice analysis of the Act (Posner (n 82)) constructs it as primarily the outcome of a variety of creditor, state, and federal interests vying for advantage, with debtors represented only by proxy through lawyers and academics. Bruce Carruthers and Terence Halliday note the 'relative ideological neutrality of the legislation'; indeed that 'political ideology … was absent altogether' in the US. See B Carruthers and T Halliday, *Rescuing Business: The Making of Corporate Bankruptcy Law in England and the United States* (Oxford, Oxford University Press, 1998) 147. Nunez and Rosenthal note the absence of roll-call votes (a sign of a 'salient policy debate') on the 1978 Act. S Nunez and H Rosenthal, 'Bankruptcy "Reform" in Congress: Creditors, Committees, Ideology and Floor Voting in the Legislative Process' (2004) 20(2) *Journal of Law Economics and Organization* 527.

importance of credit in the economy and the role of bankruptcy as a safety net in 'welfare state capitalism'.[85]

Unintended consequences of the Act were the construction of individual bankruptcy as a consumer law issue and the growth of a consumer bankruptcy bar.[86] The many new provisions in the 1978 Act attracted the interest of consumer public interest lawyers. The more powerful bankruptcy stay on individual actions in the 1978 Act and liberal discharge rules might be used to protect their clients against evictions, mortgage foreclosures, problems with welfare overpayments, or state authorities withholding licences because of unpaid debts. Consumer bankruptcy law[87] overtook other areas of public interest litigation, such as truth in lending and warranty law. It became a substitute for the limits of existing consumer protection, and by the mid 1990s a flourishing consumer bankruptcy bar existed.[88] This emphasised a consumer rights narrative of bankruptcy law, and consumer bankruptcy became an integral aspect of bankruptcy law courses, which experienced a significant growth in US law schools after the 1978 Act.

IV. Layering and Changing the Narrative: 1978–97

The period from 1978 until the passage of the BAPCPA in 2005 was characterised by a large growth in household credit, facilitated by deregulation of interest rates, increased liquidity in financial markets, and computer technology which enabled more targeted pricing of credit.[89] This is also the period of 'high globalisation' when the lower-middle classes of the rich world found their incomes under pressure.[90] Credit provided a method of compensating for stagnating wages, at least in the short run, but which might result in longer-term costs such as bankruptcy.[91] Between 1929 and 1985, increases in consumer bankruptcies had tracked the

85 Posner, 'The Political Economy' (n 82) 60.

86 See Skeel, *Debt's Dominion* (n 3) 192–93. Although the NBC had taken an interest in consumer bankruptcy, and were sympathetic to consumer bankrupts, no practising consumer bankruptcy lawyers were on the Board until Henry Sommer became a member in the 1980s.

87 See H Sommer, 'The New Law of Bankruptcy: A Fresh Start for Legal Services Lawyers' (1979) 13 *Clearinghouse Review* 1.

88 See J Braucher, 'Lawyers and Consumer Bankruptcy: One Code, Many Cultures' (1993) 67 *American Bankruptcy Law Journal* 501. And see W Whitford, 'The Ideal of Individualised Justice Consumer Bankruptcy as Consumer Protection, and Consumer Protection in Consumer Bankruptcy' (1994) 68 *American Bankruptcy Law Journal* 397, 401: 'It is time for consumer advocates to think of consumer bankruptcy as a primary vehicle for delivering the elusive goal of consumer justice.' The ability of lawyers to market to potential bankrupts was increased by the reduced restrictions on advertising following the decision of the US Supreme Court in *Bates v State Bar of Arizona* 433 US 350 (1977).

89 See eg R Brown and S Burhouse 'Implications of the Supply-Side Revolution in Consumer Lending (2005) 24 *St Louis University Public Law Review* 363.

90 See B Milanovic, *Global Inequality: A New Approach for the Age of Globalization* (Cambridge Mass, Harvard, 2016) 20.

91 See the discussion of the effects of short-term rises in consumer credit on bankruptcy rates in R Lawless, 'The Paradox of Consumer Credit' (2007) *Illinois Law Review* 347.

rise in outstanding debt, but after 1985, consumer filings outpaced the increase in consumer credit.[92] This was also the period of the unravelling of US welfare capitalism, which had relied on industrial relations policies of private firms to provide substantial benefits to employees.

The large increase in bankruptcies from 1979 to 1980 (from 196,976 to 314,886) immediately after the passage of the Act provided the opportunity for creditor lobbying for greater restrictions on bankruptcy access. Technical amendments were necessary in the immediate wake of the 1978 Act, but the 1981 hearings also provided an opportunity for groups to promote substantive change. A 'consumer credit coalition'—'a loose confederation of consumer credit issuers such as credit unions, finance companies, and consumer loan oriented banks'[93]—argued (once again) that future income should be taken into account in determining access to bankruptcy and that those with the means to pay a portion of their debts should be channelled to Chapter 13. They sponsored congressional bills to this effect during this period, and supported a business school study that, similar to the earlier sponsored studies of the 1960s, claimed that a substantial percentage of bankrupts interviewed could have repaid a significant portion of their debts.[94] These creditor amendments were unlikely to pass in a Congress that was split on the need for bankruptcy reform. Congress, however, had to act when the Supreme Court in 1982 declared unconstitutional the powers of the newly created bankruptcy judges under the 1978 Act.[95] Creditor groups tacked their amendments to this issue.[96] Ultimately, a compromise was reached in the Bankruptcy and Federal Judgeship Act of 1984. Political gridlock often results in the enactment of broad legislative standards, passing on the hard choices to the judiciary, and this Act introduced an open-textured 'substantial abuse' test that could only be raised by a bankruptcy judge.[97] The 1986 amendments conferred power on the Federal US Trustee Service to review for abuse.

[92] See Moss and Johnson, 'The Rise of Consumer Bankruptcy' (n 13) 327. See also D Ellis, 'The Effect of Consumer Interest Rate Deregulation on Credit Card Volumes, Charge-Offs, and the Personal Bankruptcy Rate' (1998) (Federal Deposit Insurance Corporation—FDIC) www.fdic.gov/bank/analytical/bank/bt_9805.html.

[93] Unsigned memorandum, 'Legislative History of the Bankruptcy and Federal Judgeship Act 1984', (US National Bankruptcy Archives, University of Pennsylvania, Kenneth Klee papers, Box 3). This loose coalition became the National Coalition for Bankruptcy Reform. See Skeel, *Debt's Dominion* (n 3) 189–91.

[94] See Purdue University, Credit Research Centre, and Krannert Graduate School of Management, *Consumer Bankruptcy Study* (2 vols, 1982). The study was critiqued systematically in T Sullivan, E Warren, and J Westbrook, 'Limiting Access to Bankruptcy Discharge: An Analysis of the Creditors' Data' (1983) *Wisconsin Law Review* 1091.

[95] See *Northern Pipeline Construction Co v Marathon Pipe Line Co* 458 US 50 (1982). See 'Bankruptcy Courts Are Going Bust' *The New York Times* (New York, 28 September 1982) A22.

[96] Labour groups also supported reform, concerned about the effects of the Supreme Court decision in *National Labour Relations Board v Bildisco* 465 US 513 (1986). Congress was split on whether to address only the judicial status issue, with those wishing to restrict access to bankruptcy holding to ransom the judicial reforms. See V Countryman, 'Credit Extenders Who Want to Hold Debtors in Bondage' *The New York Times* (New York, 25 October 1982) A18.

[97] Section 707(b).

The substantial abuse provision legitimated the idea that abuse existed in the bankruptcy system, and the provision was an ideological victory for creditors.[98] In 1990, a new Bankruptcy Coalition was formed, comprising the American Bankers Association, Credit Union National Association, Mastercard, the National Association of Federal Credit Unions, and the National Retail Federation.[99] During this period, the coalition of creditor interests unsuccessfully sponsored a series of 'technical amendments'.[100] It also supported the creation of the National Bankruptcy Review Commission in 1994, a measure generally opposed by Democrats. However, it was Republican control of Congress in 1997 that provided the opportunity for the introduction of what would ultimately become, eight years later, the BAPCPA of 2005.

A. Changing Narratives and 'The War of Ideas'

Bankruptcy policymaking changed during this period from being dominated by legal technical experts, such as the NBC, to one driven by an increasingly powerful creditors lobby, reflecting the growth and consolidation of the consumer credit industry which was pushing to restrict access to bankruptcy.[101] These changes in bankruptcy policymaking reflected broader changes in US politics during this period. Although US policymaking has always been subject to lobbying by private interest groups, and this was reflected in its knowledge regime (for example, Brookings, American Enterprise Institute, Urban Institute), John Campbell and Ove Pedersen argue that this structure seemed unable to provide clear policy solutions to the economic problems of the late 1970s, such as stagflation. One consequence was the proliferation of new 'competitive and contentious' organisations. Post-1978 US politics reflected a 'continuing escalation in ideological rancor, polarisation and divisiveness in Washington', resulting in 'a war of ideas that grew increasingly vicious'.[102] David Skeel entitles his chapter on post-1978

[98] See Skeel, *Debt's Dominion* (n 3) 147. The author refers to it as a symbolic victory.

[99] See A Wiese, 'Are You Participating in the Bankruptcy Process? Only if the Credit Industry Becomes More Involved in Helping Americans Avoid the Need to File Will the Bankruptcy Problems be Solved' (1991) (March) *Credit Magazine* 26.

[100] These proposed amendments included a requirement to gather more statistical information on the assets and liabilities of debtors, to require a debtor to be counselled on bankruptcy choices, to limit the number of filings under Chapter 13, to extend plans from three to five years, and to loosen restrictions on reaffirmations.

[101] Elizabeth Warren argues that bankruptcy reform in the US before the 1980s reflected the influence of bankruptcy professionals such as the NBC but that since that period the 'special interest groups largely replaced the professionals as the influential players'. Warren, *The Changing Politics* (n 10).

[102] See JL Campbell and OK Pedersen, *The National Origins of Policy Ideas: Knowledge Regimes in the United States, France, Germany, and Denmark* (Princeton, Princeton University Press, 2014) 3. JL Campbell and O Pedersen, 'Policy Ideas, Knowledge Regimes and Comparative Political Economy (2015) 13 *Socio-Economic Review* 679, 685.

bankruptcy developments 'Credit Cards and the Return of Ideology in Consumer Bankruptcy'.[103]

A dominant narrative of bankruptcy in the 1960s was that of a technical subject best delegated to professional experts. The image of a bankrupt in the professional community seemed to be that of an unfortunate, perhaps mildly incompetent individual, who needed assistance.[104] After 1978, a contest for authority emerged as to the policy image of bankruptcy, the characteristics and motives of debtors, and the appropriate policy response.[105] This was both a scholarly and political battle, where the outcome depended not on the strength of technical arguments but on politicians, policy entrepreneurs, and the media.[106]

Substantial increases in consumer bankruptcy filings had been defining aspects of the discussions of bankruptcy reforms in the 1930s and 1960s. It was not surprising, therefore, that the supposed explosion in filings in the 1990s, during a period of apparent economic prosperity, framed political and policy discussion. Was the increase simply a reflection of increased household debt,[107] greater and more aggressive extension of credit to more risky consumers,[108] or an erosion of personal responsibility? Debtor irresponsibility dominated many media stories. Alan Greenspan, Chair of the Federal Reserve, was quoted as stating that 'personal bankruptcies are soaring because Americans have lost their sense of shame in filing for bankruptcy court protection'.[109]

Important theoretical and empirical work on consumer bankruptcy examined these questions. Progressive legal scholarship in the US provided scientific support, through a series of path-breaking empirical studies, for the idea of bankruptcy as a safety net for a middle-class (defined in terms of home ownership,

[103] Skeel, *Debt's Dominion* (n 3) ch 7.

[104] See generally Ball, 'Bankruptcy and Politics' (n 11).Whether these views were widely shared by the public is difficult to assess. Efrat's study of the portrayal of bankrupts in the elite media concluded that bankrupts were portrayed as disreputable and possibly fraudsters even in the early 1960s. See R Efrat, 'Bankruptcy Stigma: Plausible Causes for Shifting Norms' (2005) 22 *Emory Bankruptcy Developments Journal* 481; R Efrat, 'The Evolution of Bankruptcy Stigma' (2006) 7 *Theoretical Inquiries in Law* 365; R Efrat, 'The Moral Appeal of Personal Bankruptcy' (1998) 20 *Whittier Law Review* 141.

[105] See Warren, *The Changing Politics* (n 10). See also JF Witt, 'Narrating Bankruptcy/Narrating Risk' (2003) 98 Northwestern University Law Review 303. John Pottow develops this theme in his analysis of the lobbying landscape surrounding the enactment of BAPCPA. He argues that consumer bankruptcy policymaking was transformed by policy entrepreneurs for creditors from a technical question to the political issue of addressing personal responsibility. See JAE Pottow, 'A U.S. Perspective on the Contextual Terrain of Political Economy in Insolvency Reform' in S Ben-Ishai and A Duggan (eds), *Canadian Bankruptcy and Insolvency Law : Bill C-55, Statute c. 47 and Beyond* (London, LexisNexis, 2007). See generally Ball, 'Bankruptcy and Politics' (n 11) ch 6.

[106] PA Hall, 'Policy Paradigms, Social Learning, and the State: The Case of Economic Policymaking in Britain' (1993) 25 *Comparative Politics* 275. See also Warren, *The Changing Politics* (n 10).

[107] See Lawless, 'The Paradox' (n 91).

[108] See Moss and Johnson, 'The Rise of Consumer Bankruptcy' (n 13) 347–48.

[109] Quoted in M Jacoby, 'Negotiating Bankruptcy Legislation through the News Media' (2004) 41(4) *Houston Law Review* 1091, 1097.

education, and occupational status) subject to increased pressures.[110] This narrative differed from earlier studies that associated bankruptcy with lower-income blue-collar workers.[111] Exogenous factors, such as unemployment, family breakdown, and healthcare problems, drove financial failure and bankruptcy.[112] In the US, middle-class two-income families with high levels of debt were particularly vulnerable to changes in life events, for example, loss of employment, illness, and family breakdown.

Studies indicated few 'can pays' existed among those who used straight bankruptcy—Chapter 7. This challenged the assertion that too many individuals were exploiting bankruptcy, and supported consumer choice concerning the Chapter 13 option.[113] Sullivan, Warren, and Westbrook concluded that bankruptcy was not an ideal solution to the problems of the middle class, but given the changes in the US social security and health care system, played a crucial safety net role. The US health and welfare system was closely linked to secure long-term employment, and as that was eroded, a great risk shift[114] occurred, shifting risk from employers and the government to individuals, with a consequent increase in middle-class insecurity and bankruptcy.

The political significance of Sullivan, Warren, and Westbrook's middle-class analysis—the title of their book published in 2000 was *The Fragile Middle Class*—was to defend the existing system of bankruptcy by universalising its potential benefits. Since the great majority of the US population define themselves as middle class, bankruptcy was a phenomenon that might affect a broad range of the population. Universalising benefits is a strategy for maintaining political support for welfare state institutions and creating political resistance to their erosion. Sweden is an example of this technique, where the middle-class benefits significantly from a system of universal entitlement to benefits.[115]

A competing model of bankruptcy emerged from the new law and economics approach within the legal academy. This approach hardly existed in the

[110] See Sullivan, Warren, and Westbrook, *As We Forgive Our Debtors* (n 3); TA Sullivan, E Warren, and JL Westbrook, *The Fragile Middle Class: Americans in Debt* (New Haven, Yale University Press, 2000).

[111] See eg P Schuchman, 'The Average Bankrupt: A Description and Analysis of 753 Personal Bankruptcy Filings in Nine States' (1983) 88 *Commercial Law Journal* 288.

[112] In 2007, 'more than three in five consumer bankruptcy filings … were related to medical costs and lost income due to illness and injury'. See JS Hacker, 'The Middle Class at Risk' in K Porter (ed), *Broke: How Debt Bankrupts the Middle Class* (Stanford, Stanford University Press, 2012) 220.

[113] See T Sullivan, E Warren, and J Westbrook, 'Who Uses Chapter 13?' in J Niemi, I Ramsay and W Whitford (eds), *Consumer Bankruptcy in Global Perspective* (Oxford, Hart Publishing, 2003) ch 13.

[114] See JS Hacker, *The Great Risk Shift: the Assault on American Jobs, Families, Health Care and Retirement* (Oxford, Oxford University Press, 2006). Hacker points out that once the complex public/private nature of the US health and welfare system is taken into account, the US did not before the risk shift allocate substantially less resources than European states to these areas.

[115] The Scandinavian model of welfare provided 'benefits tailored to the tastes and expectations of the middle classes but nonetheless retained universalism of rights'. G Esping-Andersen, *The Three Worlds of Welfare Capitalism* (Princeton, Princeton University Press, 1990) 31.

period before the 1978 Act. This modelled bankruptcy as a rational cost-benefit choice and investigated the potential impact of ex post protections such as state exemptions in bankruptcy on the cost and availability of credit.[116] Conceptualising bankruptcy as a form of mandatory insurance, it highlighted the trade-off between insurance protection in bankruptcy and its impact on risk-taking behaviour (moral hazard) and opportunism.[117] Econometric studies studied the correlation between generous wealth exemptions (such as a homestead) and the cost and availability of credit for entrepreneurs and consumers and the distributional effects of exemptions on different groups.[118] The law and economics approach challenged Sullivan and others' adverse events theory of bankruptcy, arguing that debtor calculation of financial benefits affects the bankruptcy decision.

Economists attempted also to measure the supposed decline in the stigma of bankruptcy during the late 1990s, but with mixed success given the limits of econometric studies.[119] Economic public choice analyses also claimed that the existing US bankruptcy system reflected the interests of judges, legal academics, and bankruptcy lawyers—the bankruptcy establishment.[120]

Academic debate continues as to the impact of adverse events and the effects of moral hazard in bankruptcy law.[121] Although the economic conception of the rational actor calculating costs and benefits is not intended to be a picture of reality,[122] the law and economic studies could be used by groups to provide a scientific support for a common-sense discourse of bankruptcy abuse by opportunists and rational calculators. The economic argument that the costs of these actions would be passed on to other consumers, primarily more poor

[116] See eg the overview by MJ White, 'Bankruptcy and Consumer Behavior: Theory and US Evidence' in G Bertola, R Disney, and CB Grant (eds), *The Economics of Consumer Credit* (Cambridge, MIT Press, 2006). MJ White, 'Corporate and Personal Bankruptcy Law' (2011) 7 *Annual Review of Law and Social Science* 139.

[117] B Adler, L Polak, and A Schwartz, 'Regulating Consumer Bankruptcy: A Theoretical Inquiry' (2000) 29 *The Journal of Legal Studies* 585.

[118] See White, 'Bankruptcy and Consumer Behavior' (n 116) and 'Corporate and Personal Bankruptcy Law' (n 116).

[119] One study, for example, concluded that higher defaults on credit cards must be explained by declining stigma because it was not explained by other variables! See DB Gross and NS Souleles, 'An Empirical Analysis of Personal Bankruptcy and Delinquency' (2002) 15 *Review of Financial Studies* 319. An economic study of the period between 1980 and 2000 attributes the rise in bankruptcies to increases in credit availability and a reduction in the costs of bankruptcy, which might include the ability to access credit after bankruptcy and 'stigma'. I Livshits, J MacGee, and M Tertilt, 'Accounting for the Rise in Consumer Bankruptcies' (2010) 2 *American Economic Journal* 165.

[120] 'The current business and consumer bankruptcy systems thus substantially benefit the bankruptcy bar, the bankruptcy judges, and the academics whose consulting income increases with the cost, complexity and court centeredness of the system. These groups have dominated the current reform debates and past debates as well. Informal speculation plausibly suggests that we have the consumer bankruptcy system that the lawyers want.' Adler, Polak, and Schwartz, 'Regulating Consumer Bankruptcy' (n 117) 611.

[121] See the studies on the impact of illness and uninsured medical bills on bankruptcy cited in MJ White, 'Economics of Corporate and Personal Bankruptcy Law' (2014) unpublished paper on file with author.

[122] An early intervention had adopted a behavioural rather than rational economic approach. See TH Jackson, 'The Fresh Start Policy in Bankruptcy Law (1985) 98 *Harvard Law Review* 1393.

individuals, could feed a 'rhetoric of reaction'.[123] Creditor groups sponsored further studies during the 1990s, and 2000s, which claimed that significant numbers of bankrupts could repay a portion of their debts,[124] and promoted a famous sound bite that bankruptcies represented an annual '$400 tax' on every American, a claim that was read into the Congressional Record, even though it lacked empirical support.[125]

V. BAPCPA 2005—the Great Recession and the Future

The BAPCPA 2005, enacted after a tortuous eight-year passage through Congress,[126] reflected earlier drafts by industry lobbyists in the 1980s. Senator Howard Grassley introduced the initial Bill in Congress as a 'progressive culmination' of efforts begun in the 1960s to deny relief under Chapter 7 if a court concluded that a debtor could pay substantial amounts of debt under Chapter 13.[127] The Bill would restore 'personal responsibility and integrity in the bankruptcy system and ensure that the system is fair for both debtors and creditors'.[128] The primary mischiefs identified were the perceptions that bankruptcy was increasingly used as a first rather than last resort, that responsible Americans were subsidising abusers through an implicit bankruptcy tax, and that loopholes and incentives in the existing system encouraged opportunistic behaviour.[129]

The main instrument to achieve responsibility was a statutory means test as a condition of access to straight bankruptcy for individuals with primarily consumer debts.[130] Other changes included required pre- and post-bankruptcy

[123] See AO Hirschman, *The Rhetoric of Reaction: Perversity, Futility, Jeopardy* (Cambridge, Harvard University Press, 1991).

[124] These are referred to in footnote 18 in United States Congress, 'Bankruptcy Abuse Prevention and Consumer Protection Act of 2005 : Report of the Committee on the Judiciary to Accompany S. 256 Together with Dissenting, Additional Dissenting, and Additional Minority Views' (Washington DC, US Government Printing Office, 2005) Report 109–31. See eg United States Congress, *Bankruptcy Reform Act of 1999: Hearing before the Subcommittee on Commercial and Administrative Law of the Committee on the Judiciary, House of Representatives, One Hundred Sixth Congress, Second Session, on HR 833.* (Washington DC, US Government Printing Office 2000).

[125] See E Warren, 'The Phantom $400' (2004) 13 *Journal of Bankruptcy Law & Practice* 77.

[126] Bankruptcy Abuse Prevention and Consumer Protection Act of 2005 (BAPCPA), Pub L No 109–8, 119 Stat 23 (codified in scattered sections of 11, 12, 18, 28 USC). For a comprehensive account of the legislative process see S Jensen, 'A Legislative History of the Bankruptcy Abuse Prevention and Consumer Protection Act of 2005' (2005) 79 *American Bankruptcy Law Journal* 485.

[127] See 146 Cong. Rec. 26462–26464 (2000) (statement of Sen. Chuck Grassley) (introducing H.R. 2415 in 1998 (an early version of the BAPCPA).

[128] Bankruptcy Abuse Prevention and Consumer Protection Act of 2005, Report of the Committee on the Judiciary House of Representatives to Accompany s 256, 109 Congress First Session 3 (2005).

[129] Report of the Committee on the Judiciary House of Representatives to Accompany s 256 (ibid) 3–5.

[130] 'The heart of the bill's consumer bankruptcy reforms consists of the implementation of an income/expense screening mechanism ("needs-based bankruptcy relief" or "means testing"), which is intended to ensure that debtors repay creditors the maximum they can afford.' Report of the Committee on the Judiciary House of Representatives to Accompany s 256 (ibid).

counselling; random audits of debtor filings; greater obligations on bankruptcy lawyers to certify the correctness of debtors filings; a five-year (rather than three-year) requirement for a Chapter 13 repayment; limits on refilings,[131] and repeat filings as a mechanism to stay enforcement action;[132] and limits on cramdowns on security over automobiles. Finally, increased responsibilities were conferred on the regulator, the US Trustee, to police the means test and regulate the bankruptcy system.

The interest group story of the passage and enactment of BAPCPA often dominates. BAPCPA was 'written by, bought, and paid for by the consumer credit industry, especially the credit card industry'.[133] Howard Nunez and Stephen Rosenthal's study confirms the significance of campaign contributions by the credit card industry in creating the bipartisan support for BAPCPA.[134] However, even the interest group story is not reducible to that of the unalloyed political power of creditor interests to write their views into law.[135] The automatic exemption from the means test for debtors with income lower than the state median protected lower-income debtors. Increased exemption protections were inserted for pension plans, special provisions included for applying the means test to veterans,[136] and social security payments excluded from the definition of 'income 'in the means test.[137] Some creditors benefited at the expense of other creditors. Secured creditors (for example, automobile lenders) were able to secure specific benefits at the expense of unsecured (for example, credit card companies) as a price for their support.[138] Although the opponents of the Bill could not match the resources of the creditors' coalition, they did succeed in framing bankruptcy as a feminist issue, thus expanding the debate and resulting in several amendments intended to protect women.[139]

The narrative of personal responsibility dominated congressional debates on BAPCPA. Only those who 'were rendered unable to pay their debts through no fault

[131] Section 1328(f) now prohibits discharge under Chapter 13 where discharge under Chapters 7, 11 or 12 in the preceding four years; 727(a)(8) increases from seven to eight years for refiling of Chapter 7.

[132] Section 362(c)(3) and (4).

[133] AM Dickerson, 'Regulating Bankruptcy: Public Choice, Ideology, & Beyond' (2006) 84 *Washington University Law Review* 1861. See also the discussion in Ball, 'Bankruptcy and Politics' (n 11) 138: '[R]eformers defined their efforts in terms of promoting personal responsibility'.

[134] Nunez and Rosenthal (n 84).

[135] See S Soederberg, 'The US Debtfare State and the Credit Card Industry: Forging Spaces of Dispossession' (2013) 45 *Antipode* 493.

[136] See revised section 707(b)(2)(b).

[137] See section 101(10A)(B). John Pottow queries whether the credit lobby might have been concerned about the lobbying power of the American Association of Retired Persons.

[138] See WC Whitford, 'A History of the Automobile Lender Provisions of BAPCPA' [2007] *University of Illinois Law Review* 143. And see interesting discussion by Melissa Jacoby of the use of the media by debtors' groups to 'reframe' the bankruptcy debate: 'Negotiating Bankruptcy Legislation Through the News Media' (2004), 41 *Houston Law Review* 1091.

[139] These included: excluding child support payments from disposable income under Chapter 13, creating a super-priority for repayment of spousal and child support payments under Chapter 7, and permitting expenses incurred to maintain the family of the debtor from family violence to be included as expenses in determining a debtor's means.

of their own' should access bankruptcy.[140] This 'is a nation of personal responsibility where people are expected to meet their obligations', stated President Bush when signing the Bill into law. Protection should be for the 'innocent, "vulnerable" victim'.[141] The ABA's call for greater personal responsibility in the 1960s debate had not been successful, but in the 2005 world of neo-liberalism it chimed with an ideology of individualisation of responsibility. 'Can pay/should pay' became a central trope. 'The heart of [BAPCPA's] consumer bankruptcy reforms [are] to help ensure that debtors who *can* pay creditors *do* pay them'.[142] Dickerson's analysis of the congressional debates concluded that legislators *did* agree on certain principles: that some debtors 'tried to game the system' and should not be given relief; that many consumers had taken on too much debt; and that a significant tranche of deserving debtors did exist.[143] These typologies of debtors resemble those identified in the early 1930s.

Debate continues as to the impact of BAPCPA,[144] for example, whether its provisions have reduced or delayed filings that would otherwise have been made under the previous legislation. The long-term impact of BAPCPA on bankruptcy filings is difficult to separate from other causes such as the decline in household debt.[145] Studies suggest that the increase in filing costs[146] caused by greater paperwork, rather than the means test,[147] has reduced or delayed access to

[140] Dickerson, 'Regulating Bankruptcy' (n 133) 1856.She notes, at 1894, that 'personal responsibility' was used almost seventy times during debates concerning the proposed bill'.

[141] Dickerson, 'Regulating Bankruptcy' (n 133) 1895.

[142] *Ransom v FIA Card Services* 562 US 1, 2. (Supreme Court of the United States).

[143] Dickerson, 'Regulating Bankruptcy' (n 133) 1873–75.

[144] For some studies on the impact of BAPCPA on particular groups of consumers see eg AP MacArthur, 'Pay to Play: The Poor's Problems in the BAPCPA' (2008) 25 *Emory Bankruptcy Developments Journal* 407 (looking at impact on poor consumers); K Porter, 'Going Broke the Hard Way: The Economics of Rural Failure' (2005) 2005 *Wisconsin Law Review* 969. See RM Lawless and others, 'Did Bankruptcy Reform Fail?' (2008) 82 *American Bankruptcy Law Journal* 349. Its provisions on serial filing appear to have failed to achieve their objective partly through judicial dislike of the provisions. S Greene, 'The Failed Reform: Congressional Crackdown on Repeat Chapter 13 Bankruptcy Filers' (2015) 89 *American Bankruptcy Law Journal* 241.

[145] See CE Weller, BJ Morzuch, and A Logan, 'Estimating the Effect of the Bankruptcy Abuse Prevention and Consumer Protection Act of 2005 on the Bankruptcy Rate' (2010) 84 *American Bankruptcy Law Journal* 327; SJ Spurr and KM Ball, 'The Effects of a Statute (BAPCPA) Designed to Make It More Difficult for People to File for Bankruptcy' (2013) 87 *American Bankruptcy Law Journal* 27. See R Lawless, 'Annual U.S. Bankruptcy Filings on Track for 6.7% Decline' *Credit Slips*, http://www.creditslips.org/creditslips/2016/07/annual-us-bankruptcy-filings-on-track-for-67-decline.html#more.

[146] See LR Lupica, 'The Consumer Bankruptcy Fee Study: Final Report' (Social Science Research Network 2011) SSRN Scholarly Paper ID 2132913 http://papers.ssrn.com/abstract=2132913; LR Lupica, 'The Costs of BAPCPA: Report of the Pilot Study of Consumer Bankruptcy Cases' (2010) 18 *American Bankruptcy Institute Law Review*. The study indicated almost 25% increases in costs and legal fees with substantial variations between states.

[147] The Federal US Trustee's office indicates that approximately 12% of Chapter 7 debtors had income above their state median in 2013 but that in only a small percentage of these cases did the US trustee attempt to seek dismissal after consideration of the debtor's circumstances: *Annual Report of Significant Accomplishments* (Washington, US Trustee Program, 2013). These data do not capture those individuals who might have filed but were deterred by the means test.

bankruptcy[148] for individuals earning below the median state income, the individuals who were intended to have continuing access to straight bankruptcy. As to its effects on credit one study conducted immediately after the passage of the Act concluded that although the Act had reduced losses accruing to credit card companies, the savings were not passed on to 'responsible Americans'.[149] Progressive scholars writing in 2014 conclude that although BAPCPA represents 'far reaching changes' in the law, 'most of the fundamental components of the prior system remain unchanged'.[150]

The introduction of mandatory counselling illustrates the legislation in practice.[151] Counselling had long been proposed for debtors in the US—certainly since the 1960s. Under the BAPCPA, bankrupts must obtain pre-bankruptcy counselling, 'in order to make an informed choice about bankruptcy, its alternatives, and consequences'.[152] Counselling in financial management is also a condition of discharge so that debtors can 'hopefully avoid future financial distress'.[153]

[148] See S Albanesi and Jaromir Nosal, 'Insolvency after the 2005 Bankruptcy Reform' (New York, Federal Reserve Bank of New York, 2015) Staff Report No 725, https://papers.ssrn.com/sol3/papers.cfm?abstract_id=2594037.

[149] See M Simkovic, 'The Effect of BAPCPA on Credit Card Industry Profits and Prices' (2009) 83 *American Bankruptcy Law Journal* 1.

[150] E Warren, JL Westbrook, K Porter, and J Pottow, *The Law of Debtors and Creditors: Text, Cases and Problems* (Denver, Aspen, 2014).

[151] Counselling was proposed by the Bankruptcy Commission in 1973, and the 1994 Commission endorsed the concept of voluntary debtor education.

[152] See United States Congress, 'Bankruptcy Abuse Prevention and Consumer Protection Act of 2005', Part 1, 3.

[153] This counselling must include instruction on: budget development; money management; wise use of credit; consumer information; coping with unexpected financial crisis. Bankruptcy becomes, therefore, a site of discipline and learning where individuals can become financially literate, See regulations on credit counselling at 28 C.F.R. §§ 58. The US Trustee Service approves qualified credit counselling agencies. The instruction must include the following topics (58.33): (1) budget development, which consists of the following: (i) setting short-term and long-term financial goals, as well as developing skills to assist in achieving these goals; (ii) calculating gross monthly income and net monthly income; and (iii) identifying and classifying monthly expenses as fixed, variable or periodic; (2) money management, which consists of the following: (i) keeping adequate financial records; (ii) developing decision-making skills required to distinguish between wants and needs, and to comparison shop for goods and services; (iii) maintaining appropriate levels of insurance coverage, taking into account the types and costs of insurance; and (iv) savings for emergencies, for periodic payments and for financial goals; (3) wise use of credit, which consists of the following: (i) identifying the types, sources and costs of credit and loans; (ii) identifying debt warning signs; (iii) discussing appropriate use of credit and alternatives to credit use; and (iv) checking a credit rating; (4) consumer information, which consists of the following: (i) identifying public and non-profit resources for consumer assistance; and (ii) identifying applicable consumer protection laws and regulations, such as those governing correction of a credit record and protection against consumer fraud; and (5) coping with unexpected financial crisis, which consists of the following: (i) identifying alternatives to additional borrowing in times of unanticipated events; and (ii) seeking advice from public and private service agencies for assistance. An earlier study of counselling in Chapter 13 cases had concluded that counselling did not seem to result in more plan completions than cases where no counselling was provided. See J Braucher, 'Debtor Education in Bankruptcy: The Perspective of Interest Analysis' in WC Whitford, J Niemi-Kiesilainen, and I Ramsay (eds), *Consumer Bankruptcy in Global Perspective* (Oxford, Hart Publishing, 2003).

Michael Sousa conducted a study of debtors' experiences of counselling.[154] Sousa concludes that pre-filing counselling did not achieve a legislative objective of leading debtors to rethink their decision about filing for bankruptcy. Counselling either confirmed the correctness of an individual's decision to file for bankruptcy or helped to allay any fears about declaring bankruptcy. Most debtors thought that the two-hour financial education course was insufficient to provide long-term effects and was often inappropriate since many individuals filed for bankruptcy because of external economic changes unrelated to financial capability.[155] Sousa further concludes that the existing mandated course is 'by and large misguided'.[156] This failure of institutional design could be explained by the argument that the proponents of counselling did not care about its success but inserted the provisions primarily as another hurdle for potential bankrupts which might deter or delay bankruptcy filing. However, since counselling is monitored by the Federal Trustee Office one might expect that the process could be reformed so that it may be difficult to predict the long term role of counselling.

A. The Great Recession as a Critical Juncture?

The Great Recession was a critical juncture in relation to consumer credit regulation in the US and provided the opportunity for the creation of the new Consumer Financial Protection Bureau inspired by the agenda-setting work of Elizabeth Warren, who constructed credit as a potentially dangerous product, and the consequent need for the equivalent of a Consumer Product Safety Commission in the area of credit.[157]

An important question raised during the crisis was the role of bankruptcy law in addressing the problems of individuals unable to maintain repayments on their mortgage or who experienced negative equity. Widespread mortgage foreclosures have a devastating effect not only on individuals, but also on communities. The existence of non-recourse mortgages in several states, a legacy of the Great Depression, did permit some homeowners to walk away from their home without any further liability, but the use of this option was seen as potentially detrimental to communities.[158]

Over-indebted homeowners have some protection in US bankruptcy law. Homestead exemptions provide protection against unsecured creditors. In some cases,

[154] MD Sousa, 'Just Punch My Bankruptcy Ticket: A Qualitative Study of Mandatory Debtor Financial Education' (2013) 97 *Marquette Law Review* 391.

[155] See Sousa, ibid 443. This study also reviews other studies of counseling pre and post BAPCPA.

[156] Sousa, ibid 466.

[157] See E Warren, 'Unsafe at Any Rate' (2007) Summer *Democracy Journal*. See A Levitin, 'The Consumer Financial Protection Bureau: An Introduction' (2012–13) 32 *Review of Banking and Financial* Law 321. See also discussion in D Skeel, *The New Financial Deal: Understanding the Dodd-Frank Act and Its (Unintended) Consequences* (New Jersey, John Wiley & Sons, 2010).

[158] But see the discussion in R Harris and A Meir, 'Non-Recourse Mortgages—A Fresh Start' (2013) 21 *American Bankruptcy Institute Law Review* 119.

debtors might be able to retain a home by getting rid of unsecured debt in Chapter 7 and continuing to pay a mortgage. Chapter 13 can be used strategically to prevent foreclosure through the use of the stay. However, Chapter 13 requires individuals to have a plan for curing arrears and for many individuals this proves an insurmountable problem. Proposals were, therefore, made at the outset of the crisis to permit an individual to write down the principal value of the loan. Chapter 13, without this cramdown of principal, usually resulted in a delay in foreclosure rather than saving the home.[159] Academics such as Adam Levitin argued that the Chapter 13 bankruptcy procedure administered by the US bankruptcy courts was the most effective and fair method of addressing housing debt overhang at no cost to the taxpayer.[160] The bankruptcy system could distinguish those genuinely in need of a write-down from opportunists. Moral hazard would be unlikely since lenders would be sanctioned for bad borrowing decisions and debtors required to live on a three- to five-year Chapter 13 programme before being discharged.[161]

When he was a presidential candidate, Barack Obama promised cramdown legislation, but subsequently gave tepid support to proposed legislation introduced on this topic when he became president, preferring the creation of individualised negotiation possibilities through the Home Affordable Modification Program (HAMP).[162] The International Monetary Fund subsequently assessed these measures as only partially successful.[163] Concentrated political opposition by finance capital to mortgage principal write-down played a significant role in the failure of the bankruptcy cramdown provisions.[164] The discourses of personal responsibility and moral hazard were also influential. Obama wished to help 'responsible

[159] See AM White and C Reid, 'Saving Homes—Bankruptcies and Loan Modifications in the Foreclosure Crisis' (2013) 65 *Florida Law Review* 1713.

[160] AJ Levitin, 'Resolving the Foreclosure Crisis: Modification of Mortgages in Bankruptcy' [2009] *Wisconsin Law Review* 565; MJ White and N Zhu, 'Saving Your Home in Chapter 13 Bankruptcy' (2010) 39 *Journal of Legal Studies* 33.

[161] Variations on this cramdown approach were proposed with the objective of creating incentives for borrowers to stay in their home (eg by relating the cramdown to declines in property prices in the relevant ZIP code) and conferring on lenders a right to receive a percentage of any appreciation in value. See EA Posner and L Zingales, 'A Loan Modification Approach to the Housing Crisis' (2009) *American Law and Economics Review* 19.

[162] See eg the Helping Families Save their Homes in Bankruptcy Acts 2008, 2009, and the account in K Roberts and S Kaper, 'Out of Their Depth' (2012) *National Journal*, www.nationaljournal.com/magazine/the-white-house-s-housing-fumbles-20120322. This article provides a blow-by-blow insider account of the administration of the Obama debt-relief program.

[163] See IMF (2012), *World Economic Outlook*, ch 2 'Household Debt'. See B Applebaum, 'Cautious Moves on Foreclosures Haunting Obama' *New York Times* (20 August 2012) A1.

[164] See S Labaton, 'Ailing, Banks Still Field Strong Lobby at Capitol' *New York Times* (5 June 2009) A1. 'The defeat of the bankruptcy proposal is a testament to the enduring influence of banks, even as the industry struggles financially and suffers from its role in the economic crisis … [I]t poured millions of dollars into lobbying: four of the industry's top trade groups spent nearly as much on lobbying in the first three months of this year as they did in all of 2001 … Throughout it all the banks took advantage of the Obama administration's seeming ambivalence. Despite its occasional populist rhetoric, the White House was conspicuously absent from weeks of pivotal negotiations this Spring.' See also Applebaum, 'Cautious Moves on Foreclosures Haunting Obama' (n 163).

borrowers' and the administration was convinced that most Americans, even in a deep recession, would not support their 'neighbours being bailed out at public expense'.[165] The televised rant in 2009 by Rick Santelli, a media pundit, against cramdown, which sparked the creation of the Tea Party, confirmed the administration's view.[166] According to one account, the Obama administration was driven by two ideological concerns: 'contract sanctity and moral hazard'.[167] The administration believed that the most important task for government after a bank crisis is to get the banks lending again by ensuring their stability by recapitalisation. Reducing an overhang of consumer debt is a secondary objective. Aggressive deleveraging of household debt might threaten the banks' stability. Mian and Sufi argue that this approach was misconceived since the threat to the banking system had passed by 2009 and aggressive deleveraging would have stimulated consumption by middle- and lower-income groups.[168] Ideas as much as the lobbying of narrow interest groups contributed to the failure to enact provisions on mortgage principal write-down.

The failure to adopt federal legislation is not, however, the end of the story. Bankruptcy judges in many districts introduced mediation programmes to assist homeowners in negotiating with lenders. In some cases this might result in principal write-down. Judges adapt the law to perceived local needs through practices that may result in long-term changes in bankruptcy practice.

VI. The Role of the State in US Bankruptcy Law

The idea of an administrative agency to oversee and administer consumer bankruptcies has a long history in the US.[169] Lawyers and judges have consistently opposed the creation of such an agency. The Bankruptcy Reform Act 1978 did not implement the Bankruptcy Review Commission's proposals for an administrative agency because of the strong opposition by bankruptcy judges. Creditors also opposed the creation of an agency because they thought that it would be debtor-oriented.[170] An experimental trustee service within the Department of Justice was established in a number of states as a political compromise. It had a precarious

[165] Labaton, 'Ailing, Banks Still Field Strong Lobby at Capitol' (n 164).

[166] See discussion of this in A Mian and A Sufi, *House of Debt: How They (and You) Caused the Great Recession, and How We Can Prevent It from Happening Again* (Chicago, University of Chicago Press, 2015) 135.

[167] K Roberts and S Karper, 'Out of their Depth' *National Journal* (22 March 2012). Applebaum, 'Cautious Moves on Foreclosures Haunting Obama' (n 163).

[168] See Mian and Sufi, *House of Debt* (n 166) 135–46.

[169] See discussion in Littwin, 'The Affordability Paradox' (n 4) 1981–86.

[170] See discussion in Carruthers and Halliday (n 84) 406–16, and Skeel, *Debt's Dominion* (n 3) 142–47. Skeel notes at 145 the opposition of Linn Twinem of Beneficial Finance, who feared that a state agency would encourage an 'explosion' of bankruptcies.

pilot role until 1986, when it was confirmed after several positive assessments of its operation.[171] It was also given power to intervene where there was the possibility of substantial abuse by a debtor.

The US Trustee Service now has general oversight of the bankruptcy process, including appointing and supervising the work of the panel trustees[172] in Chapter 7, supervising the administration of Chapter 13 cases, enforcing provisions regulating debt advice agencies[173] (including lawyers), licensing credit counselling agencies, and developing the credit counselling requirements under the BAPCPA. It may apply for a denial of discharge under section 727 and polices the means test under section 707. The BAPCPA also conferred power on it to conduct random audits of bankruptcy filings. The US Trustee Service can appear and be heard in any case or proceeding under the bankruptcy code.[174] Bankruptcy fees provide funding for the agency but the actual appropriation is determined by Congress.

Described as a 'watchdog' on its creation in 1978,[175] its mission is 'to promote the integrity and efficiency of the bankruptcy system for the benefit of all stakeholders—debtors, creditors and the public'.[176] In the early 2000s, its dominant mission was that of reducing bankruptcy abuse by debtors. It commenced a national enforcement initiative in response to apparent public concern about abuse of the bankruptcy system.[177] The annual reports of this period highlight its enforcement action against debtors under section 707(b) and actions against debtors' attorneys and petition preparers.[178] The agency claimed in 2002 that 'abuse of the system is more widespread than many would have estimated'.[179] The consumer bankruptcy

[171] A useful survey of its development until the mid-1990s is in National Bankruptcy Review Commission (US), *Bankruptcy: The Next Twenty Years: National Bankruptcy Review Commission Final Report, October 20, 1997* (Washington, US Government Printer) 844–57.

[172] Generally, lawyers from the private bar.

[173] See 28 USC ¶ 586; ¶¶ 526–528 Bankruptcy Code and ¶ 101 (12A), which defines 'debt advice agency'.

[174] 11 USC ¶ 307.

[175] House Report No 989, 95th Congress, 2nd Session at 88 (reprinted in 1978 US Code Congressional & Administrative News at 5787, 5963, 6049).

[176] See the United States Department of Justice website:www.justice.gov/ust/eo/ust_org/index.htm.

[177] See United States Trustee Program, *Annual Report of Significant Accomplishments, Fiscal Year* (Washington DC, US Government Printing Office, 2002). It provides the example of: 'A Chapter 7 debtor in Dallas agreed to dismiss her case, preventing discharge of $122,527 in consumer credit card debt, after the U.S. Trustee filed a motion to dismiss for substantial abuse and completed discovery. The debtor, a commercial airline pilot, earned $11,500 per month and paid $3,100 per month on the mortgage for her $385,000 home. Just before filing, she bought a $50,000 Mercedes to replace her repossessed $90,000 Mercedes.'

[178] In 2004, the following comment was highlighted in the report: 'Manhattan and the New York City area provide special challenges for civil enforcement because certain living expenses that appear to be on the high side are reasonable for the area. Nevertheless, in New York City we have identified debtors who have lived lavishly off credit card debt, and who have the ability to repay debts with some old-fashioned belt tightening under a Chapter 13 or Chapter 11 plan. My office aggressively investigates and pursues actions against these abusive debtors.' Greg Zipes, trial attorney, New York City.

[179] JC Marshall, 'Civil Enforcement: An Early Report' (2002) 18 *Journal of the National Association of Bankruptcy Trustees* 39.

bar probably viewed the agency as a police officer rather than a watchdog.[180] The increased powers for the agency in BAPCPA—perceived as a statute written by creditors—further fuelled a suspicion of the agency as creditor-oriented, and during the late 2000s the progressive Credit Slips blog had several posts questioning the interpretative guidelines of the agency.[181] The 2007 Annual Report, however, signals a change in tack at the agency and identifies potentially abusive conduct by sub-prime lenders as a priority. And in 2008, mortgage servicer abuse and improper attempts by a credit card servicer to recover discharged debts, rather than debtor abuse, were lead stories in the annual report. The agency identifies in its 2009 report a series of abuses by mortgage servicers, such as excessive and unwarranted charges, and by 2010 consumer protection had become one of the agency's top priorities.[182]

Both creditor and debtor groups have feared that a government bankruptcy agency would be a partisan for creditors or debtors. However, a brief examination of the experience of the agency does not indicate that it fits the popular theory of agency capture—where an agency becomes captured by interest groups. This flawed theory does recognise that agencies are rarely politically neutral administrators and are subject to political influence. The greater attention to consumer protection reflects the changing economic and political context in the wake of the Great Recession. Like all agencies, the Trustee Service operates within constraints. The US Trustee Service has limited resources to pursue its goals in an age of austerity[183] and is dependent on Congress for funding.[184] Changes in bankruptcy filings affect its funding. Establishing priorities is a continuing challenge for the agency and as a decentralised agency with 21 regional offices it must balance uniformity and the recognition of local differences which may be embedded in

[180] See J Birnbaum, 'Law Makes Debt Relief Harder for Homeowners' The New York Times (New York, 12 January 2008) http://www.nytimes.com/2008/01/12/business/yourmoney/12money.html accessed 21 July 2015 It quotes a bankruptcy lawyer stating that the US Trustee Office 'is conducting audits … and aggressively working to push them (debtors) into Chapter 13'. Reference is also made to the 'long arm of the Trustee programme'.

[181] See eg Bob Lawless on the guidelines on secured credit payments or K Porter, 'Big (Bad?) US Trustee', *Credit Slips: A Discussion on Credit, Finance and Bankruptcy* (25 September 2006) www.creditslips.org/creditslips/2006/09/big_bad_us_trus.html.

[182] Eg pursuing 'mortgage servicers that engage in misconduct against homeowners in bankruptcy by inflating claims, imposing impermissible fees and charging fees for services they do not perform or do not document'. United States US Department of Justice, 'United States Trustee Programme; Annual Report: Fiscal Year 2010' (Washington, Government Printer, 2010), www.justice.gov/ust/annual-reports-significant-accomplishments; US Department of Justice, 'United States Trustee Programme; Annual Report: Fiscal Year 2011' (Washington, Government Printer, 2011). See also United States US Department of Justice, 'United States Trustee Programme; Annual Report: Fiscal Year 2013' (Washington, Government Printer, 2013) 3, www.justice.gov/ust/annual-reports-significant-accomplishments. 'Protecting consumer debtors from being victims of unscrupulous creditors, bankruptcy petition preparers … and those who use the bankruptcy system to perpetrate fraud.'

[183] See, for example, United States US Department of Justice, 'United States Trustee Programme; Annual Report: Fiscal Year 2012' (Washington, Government Printer, 2012) 7, www.justice.gov/ust/annual-reports-significant-accomplishments: 'In face of budgetary challenges, the Program continued to pursue activities critical to its mission, while prudently undertaking cost cutting measures.'

[184] Congress determines the proportion of fees to be allocated to the agency.

local legal culture. It must maintain legitimacy and a reputation for effectiveness with a variety of political constituencies, speaking to multiple audiences—of lawyers, standing trustees, panel trustees, and creditors—about its work.[185] Its ability to act may depend on working with other agencies, as occurred in the US$25 billion mortgage settlement in 2012 concerning abusive practices in mortgage servicing, foreclosure and bankruptcy by the five largest mortgage servicers in the US.

The role of the state in the US bankruptcy system is sometimes viewed as limited, compared with the significant role of public administrators in France or the 'officialism' of the Insolvency Service in the United Kingdom. This is a potentially misleading contrast based on a Weberian view of the state as a unified and centralised bureaucracy. If one thinks of the state in terms of 'infrastructural power', defined as the ability to 'penetrate civil society and implement policy',[186] then the US has a substantial infrastructure devoted to regulating and processing bankruptcy. This includes not merely the Federal Trustee Service, but also bankruptcy judges, standing trustees in Chapter 13 (effectively publicly appointed administrators), private trustees (private lawyers carrying out public functions under Chapter 7), and bankruptcy clerks who process the great majority of Chapter 7 cases.[187] These groups (judges, lawyers) all have representative associations that play a role in both policymaking and implementation. This mixture of public and private actors represents a further US characteristic of harnessing private power to achieve public objectives.[188] William Novak argues that 'the American

[185] See the discussion of the importance and complexity of reputation to agencies in D Carpenter, *Reputation and Power: Organizational Image and Pharmaceutical Regulation at the FDA: Organizational Image and Pharmaceutical Regulation at the FDA* (Princeton, Princeton University Press, 2014) 43.

[186] Novak comments that 'while the despotic power of the American state (until recent times) might have been limited, the scale and scope of its infrastructural power is and always has been extensive. From the founding of the first national governing institutions to the conquest of western lands; from the creation of a vast public infrastructure for the promotion of commerce to the construction of a powerful defense and military establishment; from the expansion of governmental powers of police, regulation, administration, and redistribution to the invention of new ways of policing citizens, aliens, races, morals, and gender relations in the production of national culture, the infrastructural power of the American state seems at times boundless, even borderless, as American legal, corporate, economic, and cultural forms spread across the globe. It is this power-infrastructural power that renders commentary about American state weakness or statelessness unintelligible.' Novak, 'The Myth of the "Weak" American State' (n 9) 763.

[187] For a study of the role of private trustees see Serena Laws, 'What is Owed: Debt: Bankruptcy and American Citizenship' (PhD thesis, University of Minnesota 2011). Laws conducted a nationwide survey of Chapter 7 panel trustees. The 2005 amendments in the BAPCPA harness the role of lawyers as gatekeepers, imposing penalties on them if they do not adequately monitor information provided by their clients.

[188] Angela Littwin argues that the contemporary bankruptcy infrastructure in the US performs well because it is headed by federal judges (providing prestige) who provide a backstop, with lawyers managing most of the administrative work, including diagnosis, and identifying problems (ombudsman role), and acting as lobbyists for the system. The private nature of lawyer financing means that the infrastructure expands and contracts with changes in the economy. The disadvantage of this system is that policies are mediated through the cost calculations and values of the intermediaries, possibly undermining the objectives of the policy. The importance of the US bankruptcy infrastructure in managing the system is a factor that may limit the exportation of the US model to countries without such an infrastructure. Littwin, 'The Affordability Paradox' (n 4).

state is and always has been more powerful, capacious, tenacious, interventionist, and redistributive than was recognised in earlier accounts of US history'.[189] This understanding of the US helps us to reframe the idea that US bankruptcy administration reflects deep cultural values of distrust of state bureaucracies as 'despotic' institutions. This rhetoric of despotism surfaced in the 1930s and 1970s when the US attempted to introduce a federal agency to oversee and process bankruptcy cases. But the rhetoric emanated primarily from the existing administrators, namely judges and lawyers.

VII. Discussion

Several themes emerge. First, there is the long historical conflict going back to the 1930s between those groups desiring greater steering of individuals to Chapter 13 types of plans and those defending consumer choice and the maintenance of a liberal access to bankruptcy. Substantial continuity exists in creditors' demands for a needs-based bankruptcy. It is not a post-1979 idea. Proponents appealed to personal responsibility and morality in the 1930s. The rise of neo-liberalism and the trope of increasing individualisation of responsibility undoubtedly provided a more favourable backdrop for creditors' demands. The changes in the composition of Congress, a substantial and well-organised lobbying campaign, and the ability to tap into ideas of personal responsibility provided the opportunity for bringing together a broad coalition to support the passage of the BAPCPA.

The trajectory of individual bankruptcy law in the US evokes Duncan Kennedy's characterisation of the continuing conflicts in US law between a private law of liberal and strict excuses, representative of a conflict between liberal and conservative structures of thought in private law.[190] Both sides of the conflict appeal to cultural norms as support for their interpretation of bankruptcy law. The interweaving of the scholastic and political in the battle of competing paradigms of individual bankruptcy characterises US bankruptcy law history, with neither side scoring a definitive victory. This conflict between different visions of bankruptcy is a continuing process, occurring within many sites, legislatures, courts, and the law in action, rather than a cycle that achieves any long-term equilibrium or settlement. The conflict has resulted in a complex law that often takes away with one hand what it gives with the other. Yes, an individual gets a fresh start, but not for student loans and several other debts.

Progressive sociolegal bankruptcy scholarship in the US is now less optimistic about the ability of bankruptcy to provide an adequate safety net or even a 'fresh start'.[191] Some argue that reforms should focus on simplification of existing

[189] Novak, 'The Myth of the "Weak" American State' (n 9).

[190] See D Kennedy, *A Critique of Adjudication [Fin de Siècle]* (Cambridge, Harvard, 1997).

[191] See generally, KA Porter (ed), *Broke: How Debt Bankrupts the Middle Class* (Stanford, Stanford University Press, 2011). The system is increasingly costly, discriminates on the basis of race (J Braucher,

procedures,[192] drawing inspiration from the English debt relief order[193] and the French *rétablissement personnel*,[194] and that a more effective social safety net should be developed. Jacob Hacker concludes that 'bankruptcy relief for approximately 1.5 million middle-class families each year is ultimately an enormously wasteful, inefficient and incapable means of providing economic security to those who most need it'.[195] Yet a recent economic study is more optimistic suggesting that the pre-BAPCPA Chapter 13 may have provided significant financial benefits and economic stability to debtors.[196] The debate continues.

The development of US bankruptcy law illustrates repeated failure of institutional design, the gap between the law in books and the law in action, and a certain contingency. The early choice of lawyers and courts as bankruptcy administrators created a status quo bias against the introduction of an administrative agency. US bankruptcy law resembles an adaptive evolutionary process. Thus, consumer bankruptcy was not widely perceived as a solution for consumer debt problems in the 1970s.[197] David Caplovitz, who conducted important studies on US consumer debt in the 1960s and 1970s, commented in 1977 that he could not understand why so few consumers filed for bankruptcy, attributing the reluctance to social stigma. Caplovitz's comments seem strange if bankruptcy was a deeply rooted historical form of social safety net or method of maintaining consumer demand. US corporate bankruptcy law in Chapter 11 has provided the source for the development of a transnational legal order in corporate bankruptcy. The idea of the US fresh start has undoubted appeal but a closer inspection indicates the complexities of the scope and meaning of the fresh start which are at the heart of political conflicts over individual bankruptcy in the US. It would be surprising if simply transplanting the fresh start would avoid such conflicts in other countries.

D Cohen, and RM Lawless, 'Race, Attorney Influence, and Bankruptcy Chapter Choice' (2012) 9 *Journal of Empirical Legal Studies* 393); filers report similar or worse financial situations over a year after their discharge (K Porter and D Thorne, 'The Failure of Bankruptcy's Fresh Start (2006) 92 *Cornell L Rev* 67); 'bankruptcy households are more likely to experience renewed financial difficulties, accumulate much less wealth, and use expensive credit sources, such as payday loans. Moreover financial hardship persists even more than ten years after the filings' (S Han and G Li, 'Household Borrowing after Personal Bankruptcy' (2011) 43 *Journal of Money, Credit and Banking* 491). Homeowners who constituted over 50% of filers in the 2007 Consumer Bankruptcy project rarely managed to save their homes in Chapter 13: MB Culhane, 'No Forwarding Address: Losing Homes in Bankruptcy' in K Porter (ed), *Broke: How Debt Bankrupts the Middle Class* (Stanford, Stanford University Press, 2012).

[192] See RJ Mann, 'Making Sense of Nation-Level Bankruptcy Filing Rates' in J Niemi, I Ramsay, and WC Whitford (eds), *Consumer Credit, Debt and Bankruptcy: Comparative and International Perspectives* (Oxford, Hart Publishing, 2009).

[193] See discussion below, ch 3.

[194] See discussion below, ch 4.

[195] Hacker, 'The Middle Class at Risk' (n 112) 234.

[196] See W Dobbie and J Song, 'Debt Relief and Debtor Outcomes: Measuring the Effects of Consumer Bankruptcy Protection' (2014) 105 *American Economic Review* 1272.

[197] D Caplovitz, 'The Social Benefits and Costs of Consumer Credit' in RM Goode (ed) *Consumer Credit* (Leiden, Sijthoff, 1978) 135–36.

3

Drift, Conversion, and Layering: England and Wales

The truth is that nobody knew what was happening and nobody cared … the liberty of the subject was not well protected if he was a civil debtor.

OR McGregor, *Social History and Law Reform* (Hamlyn Lecture, 1981) 64.

I. Introduction

Lord McGregor's comments in 1981 echo Paul Rock's characterisation of debt collection in 1972 as a topic of 'low visibility'.[1] But the Cork Committee was about to propose a new framework for English insolvency law in 1982, noting that the problem of the 'consumer debtor' was the most pressing issue.[2] The primary solution proposed, based on no empirical research and a cursory review of foreign approaches, was an update of the administration order procedure of 1883, responding to criticisms that had existed from the introduction of the procedure.

This chapter analyses how England and Wales adjusted its personal insolvency law to the growth of the consumer debtor. The period includes a severe recession in the early 1990s and the Great Recession of 2008. Contemporary solutions for the over-indebted in England and Wales now represent a complex number of alternatives: bankruptcy with a discharge after one year, but also the possibility of payments over three years if an individual has surplus income; a debt relief order (DRO) for those with 'no-income and no assets', also promising a discharge after one year; an individual voluntary arrangement (IVA) where an individual pays a percentage of their debt over a period of usually five years and may be able to retain their home; the administration order in the county court which permits repayment and composition of debts, and private debt management plans which in theory promise full repayment over an average of eight years, but which do not often go to term.

[1] P Rock, *Making People Pay* (London, Routledge, 1973) 4.

[2] *Insolvency Law and Practice: Report of the Review Committee*, cmd 8558 (HMSO 1982) ('Cork report') para 272.

This complex system may on an optimistic reading represent the success of a relatively pragmatic and experimental system responding to private actors' needs. However, it is best understood as a process of drifting, layering, and conversion with unintended consequences for consumers flowing from measures such as the Enterprise Act 2002. Drifting reflected political and bureaucratic choices for inaction, and judicial neglect in the case of the county court administration order. McGregor's diagnosis was correct in this case. Substantial change in England and Wales came through conversion of a commercial statutory solution by entrepreneurial private actors developing the IVA as a consumer remedy, now the primary consumer remedy as indicated in Figure 3.1. However, the opportunity for this development followed both governmental inaction in failing to implement legislation in 1990 and the example of publicly subsidised initiatives by the Birmingham Debt Advice Centre and Citizens Advice Bureaux (CABs). CABs demonstrated the role of, and market for, money advice and debt management plans. Social entrepreneur Malcolm Hurlston imported the US model of creditor financed debt advice in the mid 1990s[3] and accounting entrepreneurs subsequently saw opportunities for filling a niche not met by existing programmes and developed the consumer IVA in the late 1990s. From these beginnings in the mid 1990s has grown the UK 'over-indebtedness industry'.[4] This industry is now a significant political actor[5] that also serves government objectives of providing a convenient alternative to state provision of advice and debt-settlement mechanisms.[6] This alternative comes at the cost of required government oversight of unfair and misleading practices associated with some sectors of the industry.[7]

[3] Through the creation of the Consumer Credit Counselling Service (now known as Step Change Debt Advice).

[4] See below at section II.

[5] See eg the Debt Resolution Forum whose members include many of the large debt management companies and 'promotes professional standards for resolving debtors' financial problems, focused on the quality of advice provided to consumer debtors by all DRF members'. It is represented on stakeholder groups and makes submissions to regulators. See Debt Resolution Forum, www.debtresolutionforum.org.uk/director-profiles.php. Another organisation is the Debt Managers Standards Association (DEMSA), founded in 2000, which promotes 'good practice in the debt management industry'. It is a member of the IVA Standing Committee (see below).

[6] See eg Great Britain: National Audit Office, *Helping Consumers to Manage Their Money: Money Advice Service* (London, The Stationery Office, 2013) para 16.

[7] See eg The Financial Conduct Authority, 'Debt Management Firms Must Raise Their Game, Says FCA' (Financial Conduct Authority, 22 September 2014) www.fca.org.uk/news/debt-management-firms-must-raise-their-game. The FCA has a series of rules and guidance on debt collection in its rulebook on consumer credit. See eg FCA CONC 8.2 (debt advice rules), 8.7 (charging for debt counselling and advice). See also the very critical Office of Fair Trading 2010 report on debt management companies 'Debt Management Guidance Compliance Review' (London, OFT 1274, 2010). A summary of its findings can be found at a House of Commons note L Conway, 'Debt management businesses' 27 March 2012, 4–5. Following this review a large number of firms (87) exited the market. In addition the FCAs treatment of this sector as high risk has led to licences being revoked. See eg 'FCA contacting 16,000 customers of debt management firm, PDHL' https://www.fca.org.uk/news/press-releases/fca-contacting-16000-customers-debt-management-firm-pdhl.

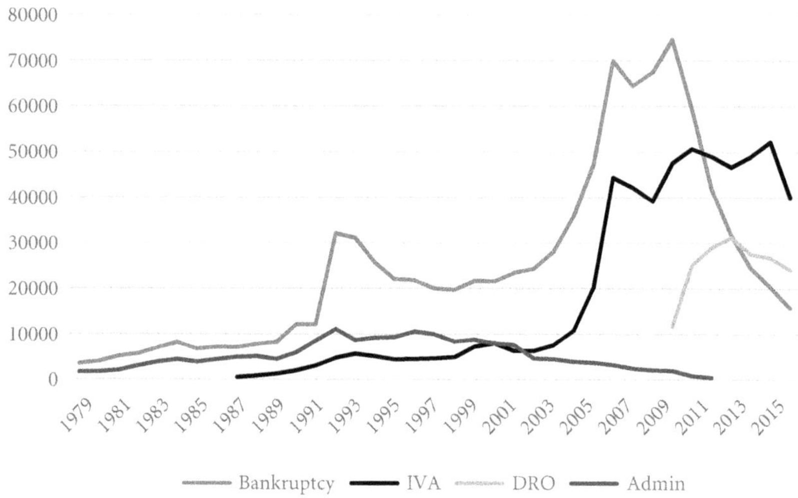

Figure 3.1: Bankruptcies, IVAs, administration orders, and DROs, England and Wales 1979–2015 (IVAs 1987–2015, administration orders 1979–2011, DROS 2009–2015)

Source: Insolvency Service, Annual Insolvency Statistics.

A narrative of 'can pay should pay' now dominates public policymaking with the primacy of repayment plans and residual relief available for the deserving poor under the debt relief order that came into force in 2009. The idea of 'straight bankruptcy' with a swift discharge as a primary consumer remedy is increasingly a suppressed political alternative in the UK.

The deregulation of the credit market in the early 1980s with measures such as the abolition of terms controls on hire purchase and the end of the monopoly of building societies on housing finance, fuelled a credit boom with the household debt/income ratio growing from 25 per cent to 68 per cent between 1981 and 1988.[8] This period of liberalisation was followed by the severe recession in 1990–91 which tested the mechanisms in the UK for protecting consumers caught in an economic recession. Figure 3.1 indicates the general increase in insolvencies over this period and Figure 3.2 shows the large increase in the percentage of non-trader bankruptcies, particularly in the period leading up to the Great Recession. Figure 3.3 places these data in the context of other Anglo-Saxon countries, showing that England and Wales consistently has a significantly lower level of insolvency per 1,000 capita than both Canada and the United States. These data do not however take into account the large number of debt management plans with approximately 150,000 plans commenced each year in England and Wales.

[8] National Consumer Council, *Credit and Debt: The Consumer Interest* (London, HMSO, 1990) Table III.7.

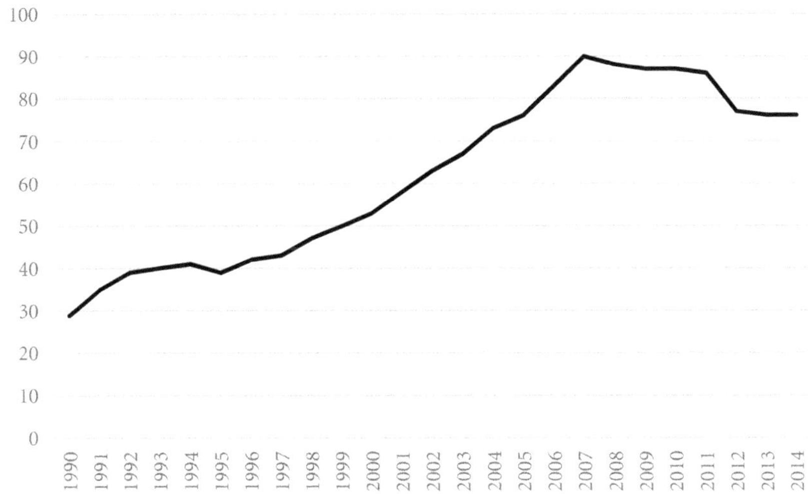

Figure 3.2: Non-trader insolvencies, England and Wales 1990–2014 (thousands)

Source: Insolvency Service, Annual Insolvency Statistics.

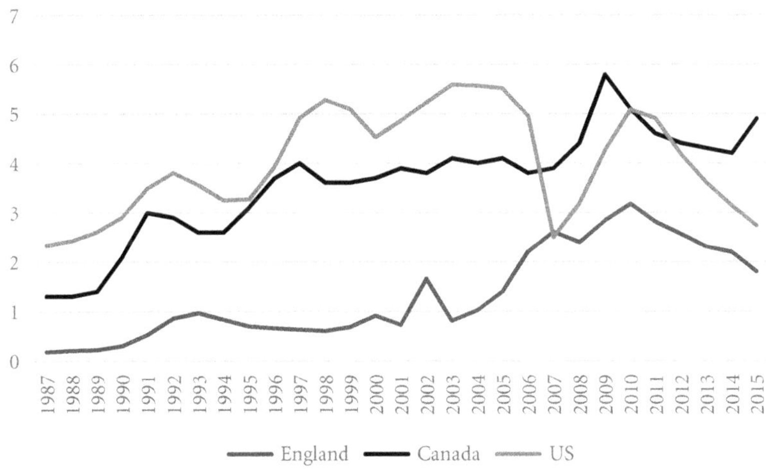

Figure 3.3: England and Wales, Canada, and US insolvency rates per 1,000 population, 1987–2011

Source: Canada, Office of Superintendent of Bankruptcy; England and Wales, Insolvency Service; US, R Lawless, Credit Slips http://www.creditslips.org/creditslips/2016/07/annual-us-bankruptcy-filings-on-track-for-67-decline.html#more. Note that US rates are based on individuals 25+ whereas the other countries are individuals 18+.

II. The Players in English Personal Insolvency Reform

Government departments play a significant role in personal insolvency law administration and policymaking in England and Wales. The Insolvency Service, a specialist executive agency of the Department for Business, Energy and Industrial Strategy, originates from Joseph Chamberlain's introduction of 'officialism' in 1883 as a response to the failure of creditor control in bankruptcy.[9] The Insolvency Service acts as regulator, policy developer, and enforcer of 'commercial morality'.[10] It also administers individual insolvencies that are not profitable for the private sector.[11] In its own words, it 'ensure[s] that the insolvency framework remains world-class and fit for purpose'.[12] It provides a forum for bringing together the actors and views of the insolvency policy community. As part of the international network of insolvency regulators it also acts on behalf of the government and the insolvency community in negotiating on issues such as European harmonisation, ensuring, for example, that London remains an important site for corporate restructuring. Much of its work is financed by fee for service on a user-pay basis. It therefore has an interest in reducing its involvement in administering insolvencies with no assets or income. It survived the Thatcher government's attempt to privatise it in the late 1970s as part of an ideologically driven programme of government deregulation. Unlike in the US, professional groups opposed a reduction in this state role of monitoring and investigating commercial bankruptcies.[13] Professionals viewed the existence of the state agency as a method of ensuring that professional standards would be maintained, enhancing the prestige of the profession.

The Ministry of Justice (formerly the Lord Chancellor's Office) has an interest in bankruptcy as it oversees court resources. The overlapping nature of the two ministries creates potential for jurisdictional conflict. Personal insolvency proposals by the Ministry of Justice have generally been tacked on to wider measures addressing the court service.[14] A general objective of the Ministry has been to

[9] See V Markham Lester, *Victorian Insolvency: Bankruptcy Imprisonment for Debt, and Company Winding Up in Nineteenth Century England* (Oxford, Oxford University Press, 1995) 208–09.

[10] Eg by disqualifying directors and imposing Bankruptcy Restriction Orders.

[11] The Insolvency Service acts under a variety of statutory powers contained in the Insolvency Acts 1986 and 2000, the Company Directors Disqualifications Act 1986, the Employment Rights Act 1996, and the Companies Acts 1985 and 2006.

[12] Written evidence Insolvency Service to the House of Commons Business and Enterprise Committee. See House of Commons Business and Enterprise Committee, *The Insolvency Service* Sixth Report of Session 2008–09 HC 198 ev 19.

[13] See B Carruthers and T Halliday, *Rescuing Business: The Making of Corporate Bankruptcy Law in England and the United States* (Oxford, Oxford University Press, 1998) 114–15.

[14] Examples include s 13 of the Courts and Legal Services Act 1990 and the Administration Order, Enforcement Restriction Order, and Debt Management Provisions in the Tribunals, Courts and Enforcement Act 2007.

divert 'petty' debt cases from the courts in order to reduce costs so that courts can concentrate on dispute resolution and high-value cases.[15] The Ministry successfully opposed the Cork Committee's proposals for a specialised insolvency court.[16] This opposition by the Ministry represented both concerns about costs and the views of the judiciary. The Ministry also failed to bring into force modernisation of the county court administration order in 1990 and 2007, although these provisions had been enacted by Parliament.[17] The Ministry's promotion of the DRO in the late 2000s removed low-value insolvency cases from the court system.

Several professional groups have an interest in insolvency. No widespread consumer insolvency bar exists as in the US, although bankrupts have sometimes benefited from the public interest activity of cause lawyers.[18] Private insolvency professionals dealing with consumers in the UK are primarily accountants. They have not generally acted as spokespersons for consumer debtors' easy access to bankruptcy relief. Indeed, the most recent proposals by the main professional body, The Association of Business Recovery Professionals (R3) propose an extension of the discharge period from one to three years.[19] US studies indicate that some US bankruptcy lawyers view their role as protecting the 'little guy', part of crusading consumer protection.[20] A 'crusading accountant' may be an oxymoron and certainly less common in the UK.

Insolvency practitioners are part of the 'over-indebtedness industry', a significant part of the personal insolvency landscape of the twenty-first century, but almost unknown before the 1990s.[21] A major study of debt advice in 1995 hardly

[15] Eg in its consultation document *A Choice of Paths* (2004) the Department of Constitutional Affairs (predecessor of the Ministry of Justice) stated at page 9 that the management of long-term debt was not a 'proper role for the court … as it is not a part of the court's core functions of dispute resolution and enforcement regulation'.

[16] See Carruthers and Halliday, *Rescuing Business* (n 13) 143.

[17] See discussion below of s 13 of the Courts and Legal Services Act 1990 and the provisions in the Tribunals, Courts and Enforcement Act 2007 addressing administration orders, enforcement restriction orders and debt management plans.

[18] See eg *R v Lord Chancellor ex parte Lightfoot* [2000] 2 WLR 318 (although in this case the court rejected the argument that the bankruptcy deposit contravened an individual's human rights to access to the courts).

[19] R3, Association of Business Recovery Professionals, 'The Personal Insolvency Landscape—A Way Forward for Formal Debt Relief' (Association of Business Recovery Professionals, 2014) www.r3.org.uk/media/documents/policy/policy_papers/personal_insolvency/R3_Personal_Insolvency_Landscape_Jan_2014.pdf?utm_medium=email&utm_source=Association+of+Business+Recovery+Profes sionals&utm_campaign=3561079_Personal+Insolvency+Landscape&utm_content=PesonalInsolvenc yLandscape&dm_t=0,0,0,0,0.

[20] See J Braucher, 'Debtor Education in Bankruptcy: The Perspective of Interest Analysis' in W Whitford, J Niemi-Kiesilainen and I Ramsay (eds), *Consumer Bankruptcy in Global Perspective* (Oxford, Hart Publishing, 2003).

[21] By the mid 1980s, pioneers such as the Birmingham Money Advice Centre had developed informal alternatives that outstripped the number of administration orders. See J Davies, 'Delegalisation of Debt Recovery Proceedings: A Socio-Legal Study of Money Advice Centres and Administration Orders' in I Ramsay (ed), *Debtors and Creditors—A Socio-Legal Perspective* (Abingdon, Butterworths Law, 1986) 194. For an outline of this development see I Ramsay, 'Bankruptcy in Transition: The Case of England and Wales—The Neo-Liberal Cuckoo in the European Bankruptcy Nest?' in Whitford, Niemi-Kiesilainen, and Ramsay (eds), *Consumer Bankruptcy* (n 20)) 214–17.

discusses private debt management services, although it recognised an unmet need for advice.[22] By 2009, approximately 150 fee-charging debt management companies existed, although the market is dominated by one-stop shops that offer a range of services, from consolidation loans to insolvency.[23]

The industry can be divided into three groups: the for-profit private sector; charities financed primarily by creditors; and publicly financed debt advice agencies. The first category includes the one-stop shops. The large debt buying companies, such as Max Recovery (a subsidiary of JP Morgan) which claims to be one of the largest single unsecured creditors in bankruptcies and IVAs, are a second group within this category.[24] Finally, there are intermediaries such as TDX (a subsidiary of Equifax), which acts as the nominee (representative) for large numbers of creditors with IVA debts, establishing repayment levels to maximise recovery. TDX acts on behalf of many financial institutions in determining whether to accept or reject IVA offers. The concept of the 'apathetic creditor' uninterested in bankruptcy because of the small returns no longer reflects reality. Computerisation and algorithms, along with economies of scale, have rendered debt collection and management a highly profitable industry.

The second category of creditor financed advisers include the Step Change Debt Charity (formerly Consumer Credit Counselling Service (CCCS)) which provides free debt advice and has the largest share of free-to-client debt management programmes. It also acts as an advocacy organisation. Lastly is the publicly subsidised sector dominated by Citizens Advice, most of whose funding comes from central and local government, which relies on volunteers, but has specialist money advice units and also lobbies for change through a research and campaigns agenda.

These groups play several public roles. First, as advisers to consumers they may not only respond to consumer needs but shape individual debtors' expectations and preferences between different debt solutions. Private debt management companies have little interest in promoting bankruptcy for consumers, and issues of steering consumers to repayment plans rather than bankruptcy has been a continuing issue.[25] Charities funded by creditors may be less likely to promote solutions that write off debt. The promotion of alternatives to bankruptcy may create a general atmosphere where bankruptcy and debt write-off becomes a suppressed alternative Second, these groups actively lobby on legislation and regulations addressing debt relief. In addition, representatives of these groups contribute to low-visibility but influential policy committees.[26] They can, therefore, play a key

[22] See E Kempson, *Money Advice and Debt Counselling*, vol 797 (London, Policy Studies Institute, 1995).

[23] For an overview see London Economics, *Debt Advice in the UK: Final Report for The Money Advice Service* (London, London Economics, 2012). See also S Collard, 'An Independent Review of the Fee-Charging Debt Management Industry' (Personal Finance Research Centre, University of Bristol, 2009) 2, http://oro.open.ac.uk/40183/.

[24] See description in letter by Max Recovery to Insolvency Service Policy Directorate, 8 February 2010 (on file with author).

[25] See the FCA Report (n 7).

[26] Eg on the development of the IVA, see below section IV.

role in implementing or frustrating public policy objectives underlying insolvency remedies.

The financial industry also plays an influential role through its lobby group the British Bankers Association. It is a long-term repeat player. It unsuccessfully opposed the Labour government's liberalisation of discharge for consumers in 2002, but successfully altered subsequent public policy through concerted action in the marketplace in the mid 2000s to reduce access to insolvency relief and prevent the introduction of a more liberal IVA procedure for writing down debts.

Consumer groups in the UK have differed in their interest in insolvency. The middle-class consumers' association (now Which?) showed little interest in over-indebtedness during the 1980s and 1990s. Its main concern was the consumer as creditor, and it lobbied hard for deposit protection during the passage of the Insolvency Act 1986. The National Consumer Council, established with public support in the 1970s to represent the disadvantaged consumer, did take an interest,[27] but it was the publicly funded Citizens Advice that campaigned to highlight over-indebtedness during the late 1990s, lobbied to reduce financial barriers to access to bankruptcy and briefed MPs on this issue during the passage of the Enterprise Act 2002.

Party politics are also relevant. Reforms during the 1980s reflected the values and priorities of the Conservative government, which demonstrated little concern for the plight of consumer debtors. In contrast, the New Labour government, while embracing entrepreneurialism, also promoted the interests of consumers and was concerned with issues of financial and social inclusion, and established a task force on over-indebtedness in 2000 and proposed significant reforms in the 2007 Tribunals, Courts and Enforcement Act (though several proposals have not been implemented). The limits of parliamentary time mean that major legislative changes are unlikely to occur in this technical area of law unless they coincide with a government priority or electoral pledge.[28] Thus, in 2002, bankruptcy reform to achieve a more entrepreneurial economy was fast-tracked through Parliament as part of a flagship Enterprise Act. Recent reforms to remove debtor-initiated insolvency cases from the courts chime with government policy to reduce public service costs. Since comprehensive reform in this area is rare, insolvency reforms are often layered onto existing legislation. Even the 2002 amendments were layered onto an older quasi-criminal bankruptcy law. However, significant changes can be made by being tagged to deregulation initiatives and through the exceptional procedure

[27] See National Consumer Council, *Consumers and Debt* (1982); National Consumer Council, *Credit and Debt: The Consumer Interest* (n 8). Two single issue groups have lobbied on bankruptcy reform: The Association of Bankrupts founded in 1983 by Joha McQueen and the Bankruptcy Advisory Service founded in 1997 by Gill Hankey.

[28] Thus Carruthers and Halliday note that the development of the 1986 reforms cannot be understood without a broader understanding of the 'current of Mrs Thatcher's policies to downsize government, to privatize industry, to stimulate entrepreneurship, and to clean up markets so they would be safe for ordinary investors ... the particular cast of the insolvency reforms, and the very fact of their Parliamentary passage, testified to the affinity between professional agendas and wider party ideology'. See Carruthers and Halliday, *Rescuing Business* (n 13) 148.

of a Legislative Reform Order[29] (discussed below in relation to the IVA) which can modify primary legislation. In addition, the executive can act swiftly in the UK if it wishes: in 2013 it immediately reversed the effect of a significant victory for debtors discharging debt owing to the public social fund by making such debts non-dischargeable.[30] This must be set within the context after the Great Recession of a policy preference in this area for soft law, and achieving results through codes of practice and voluntary measures, albeit under the threat of regulation.[31]

The groups and ministries outlined in the preceding paragraphs constitute the knowledge regime on personal insolvency in England and Wales and they generally agree on a master narrative of 'can pay should pay'. Some of these groups conduct policy-oriented research, but empirical research on personal insolvency is modest. While some demographic information on bankrupts is now available in England and Wales, no detailed studies of bankrupts similar to the US consumer bankruptcy project exist. Empirical research has not been characteristic of English policymaking in this area, so little is known about central policy questions such as the success of the central consumer remedy, the IVA. The most extensive review of the system in the early 1980s, undertaken by the Cork Committee, conducted no empirical research, instead constructing a consumer debtor image based on a professional view of debtors as 'mildly incompetent'. The Enterprise Act (2002) provisions on individual insolvency were based on a narrative of a distinction between the 'responsible risk-taker' and the 'culpable bankrupt'.[32] The absence of systematic research confers an advantage on insiders to the system who claim to 'know' the social reality of debtors and creditors.

A characteristic of US bankruptcy policymaking has been the role of the legal academy in conducting empirical research since the early studies by Douglas and other realist scholars in the 1930s. Academic lawyers in England and Wales have,

[29] See Legislative and Regulatory Reform Act 2006. There are strict preconditions for the use of this procedure. These are: '(a) the policy objective intended to be secured by the provision could not be satisfactorily secured by non-legislative means; (b) the effect of the provision is proportionate to the policy objective; (c) the provision, taken as a whole, strikes a fair balance between the public interest and the interests of any person adversely affected by it; (d) the provision does not remove any necessary protection; (e) the provision does not prevent any person from continuing to exercise any right or freedom which that person might reasonably expect to continue to exercise; (f) the provision is not of constitutional significance.'

[30] See the case of *Secretary of State v Payne and Cooper* [2011] UKSC 60. Reversed prospectively by Insolvency (Amendment) Rules 2012 (SI 2012/469).

[31] See eg Department for Business, Innovation and Skills, 'Consumer Credit and Personal Insolvency Review: Summary of Responses on Consumer Credit and Formal Response on Personal Insolvency' (London, Department for Business, Innovation and Skills, 2011) URN 11/1063, www.gov.uk/government/uploads/system/uploads/attachment_data/file/31840/11-1063-consumer-credit-and-personal-insolvency-responses.pdf. 'The evidence suggests that while regulation can sometimes be necessary, much can be achieved through other means. A voluntary approach can have clear benefits not just for business but for consumers as well. Businesses are not burdened with the cost of implementing new regulations and consumers do not have to wait for regulations to come into force before increased protections are introduced.'

[32] See discussion of the background to the Enterprise Bill in HC Research Paper 02/21 Enterprise Bill 2002, April 2002, 98–102.

until recently, contributed modestly to policy analysis of consumer insolvency and have not engaged in empirical research.[33] Basic questions about the role of bankruptcy as a creditor's or debtor's remedy were hardly examined.[34] Privacy laws have been interpreted to screen bankruptcy court records from research access, so evidence-based policy is hard to develop.

III. Drifting—the Sad Life of the English Administration Order

In 1861, England and Wales abolished the trader restriction on insolvency, which had over the preceding 300 years become 'mired in … legal technicalities' of determining whether a particular occupation constituted a 'trade'.[35] The extension of a discharge to non-traders in 1861 was not intended to expand access for debtors but to enhance creditor power to bring a bankruptcy action against a wider group in society. It was opposed by Members of Parliament who thought that it might be used by 'unscrupulous moneylenders' against gentlemen and landowners.[36]

Bankruptcy law, which envisaged a liquidation of assets, was unsuited to working-class debtors with few or no assets and limited earnings. The working-class debtor faced the possibility of imprisonment for debt throughout the nineteenth and twentieth centuries (a possibility that was not effectively abolished for ordinary debts in England and Wales until 1970).[37] Commentators during this

[33] See the exploratory study by J Tribe, 'Bankruptcy Courts Survey 2005—A Pilot Study: Final Report—January 2006' (Social Science Research Network, 2006) SSRN Scholarly Paper ID 1329109, http://papers.ssrn.com/abstract=1329109: D Milman, *Personal Insolvency Law, Regulation And Policy* (Aldershot, Ashgate, 2005).

[34] But see J Kilborn and A Walters, 'Involuntary Bankruptcy as Debt Collection: Multi-Jurisdictional Lessons in Choosing the Right Tool for the Job' (2013) 87 *American Bankruptcy Law Journal* 123.

[35] V Markham Lester, *Victorian Insolvency* (n 9) 16.

[36] ibid 136.

[37] It is true that the Debtors Act 1869 abolished imprisonment for debt but it retained the possibility of imprisonment if the court thought that the debtor had the means to pay. Evidence was often provided by the plaintiff and imprisonment often depended on the discretionary decision of the county court judge with wide variations between circuits. See discussion in GR Rubin, 'Law, Poverty and Imprisonment for Debt, 1869–1914' in GR Rubin and D Sugarman (eds), *Law, Economy and Society, 1750–1914, Essays in the History of English Law* (Abingdon, Professional Books Ltd, 1984). In 1969 the Lord Chancellor introduced the Administration of Justice Bill 1969 with the following comments: 'The judges have, of course, done their best, in difficult circumstances, to exercise this jurisdiction humanely. However, as the Committee showed, conditions in the courts really do not give them a chance to distinguish between the persistent, dishonest debtors and those who are merely inadequate. The persistent, dishonest debtors may often be clever enough to avoid actually going to prison, while those who are inadequate suffer from their inability to manage their affairs. The sanction of imprisonment serves little purpose and it contributes to the overcrowding of our already overcrowded prisons. This is, I believe, the only country in Western Europe where imprisonment for ordinary civil debt has been retained.' See HL Deb 4 December 1969, vol 306, cols 196–262. The government retained in the 1970 amendments the power to imprison for contempt debtors for non-payment of central and local government taxes. This was contrary to the recommendations of the Payne Committee. Sir Jack Jacob was very critical of this in his 1987 Hamlyn lectures. See J Jacob, *The Fabric of English Justice* (London, Sweet and Maxwell, 1987) 201–02.

period noted the discrimination in judicial approaches to working-class debtors (regarded as feckless) and those small businessmen ('who may have missed success by the merest chance'[38]) who could afford to access the bankruptcy laws. At the same time, wage garnishment was not possible in England and Wales, given the strictures of the nineteenth-century Truck Acts and the Wages Attachment Abolition Act 1870.[39] Wage attachment would not be introduced in England until 1971. The absence of wage garnishment in England and Wales marks a potentially important institutional difference from the US where liberal state garnishment laws were associated with high bankruptcy filing rates in the 1920s.[40]

Joseph Chamberlain's 1883 Bankruptcy and Insolvency Act established the framework for twentieth-century bankruptcy law in England and Wales. Chamberlain, then a radical liberal, introduced the administration order as a response to claims of unequal treatment of working-class insolvents. He described the role of the administration order in the following words:

> But the more important provision which he had made for dealing with this subject was that under which a County Court Judge might, in future, make an order for the payment by a debtor who owed less than £50, by instalments or otherwise, of all or any part of his debts. A debtor, who was brought up on a judgment summons or a County Court plaint, might state that he was indebted to other persons, might give in a schedule of his debts, and propose an arrangement for discharging them, and if the Court thought it reasonable it might at once confirm it, so that a small debtor would then be in exactly the same position as a large debtor, who had succeeded in making a composition with his creditors, or in arranging for a scheme of liquidation. Although he had not abolished in all cases imprisonment for debt, yet, if these provisions became law, it could be no longer said that any inequality existed in the law as between rich and poor. The resort to imprisonment to secure payment would be much rarer, and a large discretion would be vested in the Judges to arrange for the relief of the small debtor by a reasonable composition.[41]

The administration order provided a wage earner with the possibility of a repayment or composition order in the county court, administered by the court and with the possibility of an ultimate discharge and immunity from further collection action during the period of the order.[42] It responded to the criticisms of the

[38] See P Johnson, 'Creditors, Debtors and the Law in Victorian and Edwardian England' in W Steinmetz (ed), *Private Law and Social Inequality in the Industrial Age: Comparing Legal Cultures in Britain, France, Germany, and the United States* (Oxford, Oxford University Press/German Historical Institute London, 2000) 503. Gerry Rubin cites a comment in *The Times* in 1873 highlighting the class nature of bankruptcy law which was out of reach of the poor debtor. See Rubin, 'Law, Poverty and Imprisonment' (n 37) 275.

[39] The history of the protection of the worker's wage packet from deductions can be found in Great Britain, *Report of the Committee on the Enforcement of Judgment Debts* (Cmnd 3909) (London, HM Stationery Office, 1969) 149–52.

[40] See R Nugent and FM Jones, 'Wage Executions for Debt: Part 1 Frequency of Wage Executions' (1936) 42 *Monthly Labor Review* 285.

[41] 277 Part Deb HC (3rd series) (1883) 834.

[42] The original s 122 stated: '122. (1.) Where a judgment has been obtained in County Court and the debtor is unable to pay the amount forthwith, and alleges that his whole indebtedness amounts to a sum not exceeding fifty pounds, inclusive of the debt for which the judgment is obtained, the

inaccessibility of bankruptcy for the working class and provided an alternative collection remedy to imprisonment for debt.

The administration order was, therefore, an early attempt to adjust bankruptcy law to the situation of wage earners. But it had a limited success in England and Wales (see Figures 3.4 and 3.5), although it did provide a model for Valentine Nesbit's practice in Birmingham, Alabama, in the 1930s,[43] which was later codified in Chapter 13 of the US Bankruptcy Code in 1938. It also influenced European reformers in the late 1980s[44] who wished to introduce a discharge after an attempt at partial repayment by a debtor.

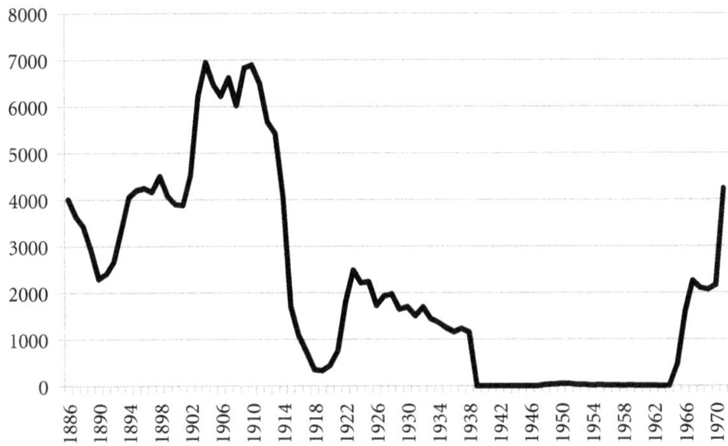

Figure 3.4: Administration orders 1886–1971, England and Wales

Source: Civil Judicial Statistics and data in P Polden, Appendix 3, *A History of the County Court, 1846–1971* (Cambridge, Cambridge Univ Press, 1999).

County Court may make an order providing for the administration of his estate, and for the payment of his debts by instalments or otherwise, and either in full or to such extent as to the County Court under the circumstances of the case appears practicable and subject to any conditions as to his future earnings or income which the Court may think just'. Chamberlain was advised on section 122 by Judge Motteram, a Birmingham County Court judge who may have adopted a similar practice in his court. See (1883–84) *Solicitors Journal* 789.

[43] See Testimony of Valentine Nesbit, Committee of Judiciary of House of Representatives on HR 6439 and HR 8046 (1937) in United States Congress House Committee on Judiciary, *Revision of the Bankruptcy Act: Hearing before the Committee, 75th Cong. 1st Sess. on H.R. 6439 … Subsequently Amend, Reintroduced and Reported as H.R. 8046 Serial 9, June 1–9, 1937* (Washington, Government Printing Office, 1937). Nesbit in discussing his repayment system for wage earners stated: '[O]f course there have been similar provisions in the Canadian and British laws … We are just 25 to 30 years behind the Canadians and the British to that extent. They have had a partial payment plan in the British law for several generations.' Nesbit did not identify the specific English procedure but it is possible that he was thinking of the Administration Order.

[44] See N Huls, 'American Influences on European Consumer Bankruptcy Law' (1992) 15 *Journal of Consumer Policy* 125.

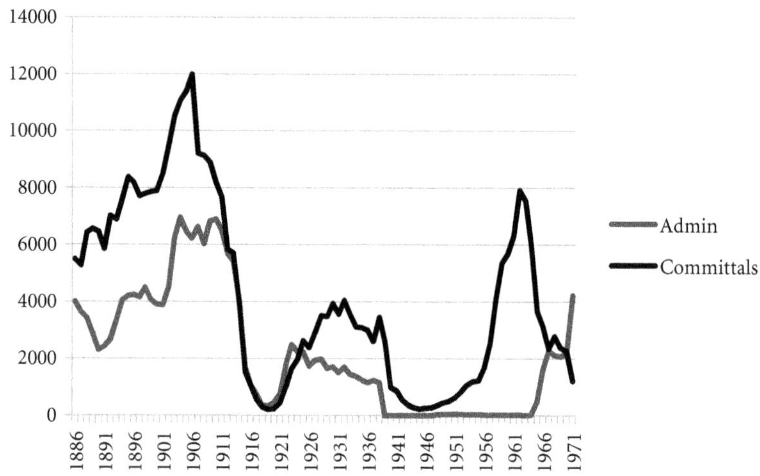

Figure 3.5: Administration orders and committals enforced, 1886–1971

Source: Civil Judicial Statistics and data in P Polden, Appendix 3, *A History of the County Court 1846–1971)* (Cambridge, Cambridge University Press, 1999).

The administration order drifted for most of the twentieth century with no attempt either to address known defects in the procedure, identified as early as 1887[45] and 1908,[46] or raise the ceiling on debts from the original £50. During the interwar period 'few people seemed interested in the administration order'.[47] Judges rarely made composition orders,[48] court administrators disliked the significant work involved in effective management of administration orders, and by 1964 only four administration orders had been made. However, from the mid 1960s, successive government committees identified the order as the central mechanism for addressing the new phenomenon of the 'multiple consumer

[45] See Bankruptcy (Administration Orders) Committee, 'Report of a Committee Appointed by the Lord Chancellor and the Board of Trade to Inquire into the Working of s 122 of the Bankruptcy Act 1883' (Great Britain) C (2nd series) 1887, 5139, 2.

[46] See *Report of the Departmental Committee on Bankruptcy Law* (Cmd 4068, 1908) paras 170–80. For example, that a debtor could only apply for an order if a judgment existed against them. Judge Edward Abbott Parry in his book *Law and the Poor* (Dutton & Co, New York, 1914) argued at p 121 that the order had failed partly because the fifty-pound limit was too small but primarily because the Treasury levied 'harsh and unreasonable fees'.

[47] See P Polden, *A History of the County Court, 1846–1971* (Cambridge, Cambridge University Press, 1999) 142. The primary political action in the 1930s concerned abuses of repossession of goods let on hire purchase where a coalition of industry representatives and poverty activists negotiated a consensus reform implemented in the Hire-Purchase Act 1938. See P Scott, 'The Twilight World of Interwar British Hire Purchase' (2002) 177 *Past & Present* 195, 223.

[48] Eg in 1966, approximately 5% of orders represented orders for less than full repayment. See *Judicial Statistics England* (Lord Chancellor's Department, Cmd 3344, 1966–67) Table 23.

debtor' and providing an alternative to bankruptcy.[49] The Payne Committee in 1969, referring to the 'huge expansion of consumer credit that has taken place during the last quarter of a century' conceptualised the administration order as the response to the problem of 'the multiple debtor'.[50] A revised administration order would be 'one of the important and essential modes of enforcement'. The ceiling on debts was raised several times during the period from the 1960s to the 1980s (£50 to £300 in 1965; £500 in 1970; £1,000 in 1972; £2,000 in 1977; and £5,000 in 1981) and several reforms introduced.[51] Empirical studies of the orders found that 'the typical person who received an administration order was male, under 50 in employment earning lower than average income with two or more dependents and approximately six consumer debts'.[52] An official study in the 1980s found that almost 50 per cent of the orders lasted for up to 10 years.[53]

A. Adjusting the Administration Order to the Consumer Debtor? The Cork Committee

The Cork Committee report identifies the consumer debtor as a novel phenomenon, noting that the 'wage earner with little or no capital assets of any value, can today incur credit to an extent undreamed of a hundred years ago'.[54] The Committee identified reform of insolvency law to address this phenomenon as its top priority.[55] However, no empirical analysis was undertaken of the debt recovery system, the demographics and situation of the 'consumer debtor', or existing bankrupts as a prelude to reform. The Cork Committee adopted this approach generally throughout the report so that, as Carruthers and Halliday note, the final report was 'experiential and pragmatic'.[56]

The Committee's proposals on consumer debtors drew on a subcommittee chaired by Ritchie Penny,[57] a county court registrar. Penny proposed a 'mini

[49] See Great Britain, Report of the Committee on the Enforcement of Judgment Debts (n 39) 69, 762. See also Cork Report (n 2) para 272.

[50] ibid paras 49, 69.

[51] Permitting an order to be made for more than 10 years (!) (1977) and finally a reform, originally proposed in 1908, that orders could be made on a court's own motion was introduced in 1984.

[52] Davies, 'Delegalisation of Debt Recovery Proceedings' (n 21) 193.

[53] See Lord Chancellor's Department, *Civil Justice Review* (London, HMSO, 1987) para 609.

[54] Cork report (n 2) para 272.

[55] ibid para 272. '[T]he most urgent need of all is for the introduction of a simple, accessible, and inexpensive procedure for dealing with the ordinary consumer debtor…'

[56] Carruthers and Halliday, *Rescuing Business* (n 13) 130. Notwithstanding the importance attached by the report to the 'consumer debtor', Bruce Carruthers and Terence Halliday in their extensive analysis of the Cork report do not discuss consumer bankruptcy or consumer debtors. Consumers only appear in the narrative as creditors, represented by consumer organisations lobbying for better protection against fly-by-night contractors and companies taking deposits but subsequently failing.

[57] The other members were David Graham, John Hunter, Chris Taylor, Gerry Weiss, and Trevor Taylor.

bankruptcy', which would be a modified administration order with powers for the administration of any assets to be handled by the court or passed on to the Official Receiver. This combination of a repayment alternative with the possibility of administration and liquidation of assets would subsequently be used by the government to justify the non-implementation of legislation.

The subcommittee submitted a questionnaire to county court registrars and undertook modest reviews of Australian and Canadian proposals.[58]

Registrars responded that administration orders were unpopular with court staff because they took up significantly more time than was recognised in the existing staffing formula;[59] debtors were generally not aware of the possibility of an administration order, could only apply if they already had a judgment debt; and the ceiling on debts was too low.[60]

The responses also provide insight into judges' perception of debtors. Penny viewed most consumer debtors as 'incompetent or mildly dishonest' a view shared by another registrar,[61] while one thought that orders were used by 'unscrupulous debtors to avoid payment of their debts'.[62] Several registrars lamented the loss of the power to imprison debtors under the judgment summons procedure,[63] but concluded that it would be politically unpopular to reintroduce it and such a proposal would affect the image of the report.[64] Bankruptcy was often conceptualised as a creditors' rather than debtors' remedy.

Penny's views are evident in the final report which commented that debt counselling might 'assist in sorting out debtors' muddles at an early stage',[65] that the 'majority of debtors are incompetent rather than dishonest'[66] and that 'the great majority' of bankruptcies result from 'imprudence or extravagance'.[67] However,

[58] See generally National Archives BT 260/25.

[59] The South Eastern registrars commented that: '[I]n the County court, each function is given a rating by points to indicate how much staff time is expected to be spent on it. The staffing complement of a given court is then calculated with reference to these points ratings. AOs [administration orders] attract very few points but absorb a great deal of staff time and effort; they are both complicated and tedious to record and chase.' See similar comments from Registrar Lowis, of the Exeter County Court.

[60] One judge seemed uncertain as to whether they could order repayments of less than 100% notwithstanding the possibility to do so in the legislation, and uncertainty existed on how to deal with secured debts such as hire purchase. None of the judges favoured a specialist insolvency court.

[61] Registrar Hebbert in Halifax, who thought that the 'cunning debtor' was rare; debtors were 'usually bad managers at their wits end'.

[62] Registrar Swangren.

[63] See response of South Eastern Circuit Registrars. 'One belief is common to nearly all our members, the abolition of the judgment summons procedure for most cases of debt has proved to be regrettable. The advantage of the judgment summons was that it was backed up by the threat of imprisonment for contempt.' BT 260/25.

[64] ibid. See South Eastern Circuit registrars. 'One belief is common to nearly all our members: the abolition of the judgment summons for most cases of debt has proved to be regrettable.'

[65] Cork report (n 2) para 349.

[66] ibid para 241.

[67] ibid para 549.

later in the report the Committee rejected the proposition that fraud and serious misconduct are seldom found in cases of personal insolvency.[68]

The Committee proposed an administration order lasting no more than three years and an 'enforcement restriction order' for individuals with no assets and no repayment capacity. The objectives of the administration procedure were to facilitate the regular payment of debts by insolvent consumers or small traders, provide for financial rehabilitation, provide an alternative to bankruptcy and provide a simple procedure for recovering debts. Where an individual with no prospect of making any payments was concerned, the enforcement restriction order would be made 'on such terms as the court may deem just and expedient'.[69]

The Department of Trade and Industry proceeded with the business aspects of the Cork Committee's proposals in the Insolvency Act 1986 which reduced the discharge period in straight bankruptcy from five to three years. The focus here was not on consumer debtors, for whom bankruptcy was assumed to be too costly. Consumer constituencies lobbied for greater remedies for consumer creditors who had paid deposits to failed businesses,[70] but no consumer groups lobbied for more effective and simple consumer insolvency.[71] Indeed, an influential report by insolvency lawyers in the early 1990s concluded that the use of the bankruptcy system by consumers to discharge debts was 'an abuse of the system' because bankruptcy was not designed for 'the small consumer debtor'.[72]

The government transferred responsibility for reform of the administration order to the Lord Chancellor's Office (now the Ministry of Justice), the government department responsible for the courts and legal administration. This department conducted the Civil Justice Review[73] in the mid 1980s as part of a modernisation of the court system. This review portrayed a failing picture of the administration order and recommended reforms to the administration order similar to those outlined by the Cork Committee. Section 13 of the Courts and Legal Services Act 1990 enacted these reforms,[74] permitting a court to make a composition order with repayments over no more than three years and a discharge at the end of this period. Deductions from repayments would be made for the court service for administering the order, but the debtor would not pay a fee. However, section 13, although enacted by Parliament, has never entered into force. Under British

[68] ibid para 719. 'The view expressed in the Consultative Document that fraud and serious misconduct are seldom found in cases of personal insolvency not associated with corporate failure is one which, in the light of our own experience and the substantial evidence submitted to us, we cannot share.'

[69] ibid para 81.

[70] See discussion in Carruthers and Halliday, *Rescuing Business* (n 13) 139.

[71] The Association of Bankrupts did lobby the Insolvancy Service and MPs for a more humans bankrupty system. Bryan Gould MP who had received a letter from the Association noted during passage of the Insolvency Bill that the Bill 'is remiss in not providing a simpler and less expensive alternative proceeding for insolvencies at the lower end of the scale … [it] does not adequately address that problem.' Parliamentary Debates (HC) Official Report, Standing Committee E, 18 June 1985, col 381.

[72] Justice, *Insolvency Law: An Agenda for Reform* (London, Justice, 1994).

[73] See *Civil Justice Review* (London, Cmnd 394 HMSO, 1988).

[74] Section 13 of the Courts and Legal Services Act 1990.

parliamentary procedure, discretion is often conferred on the executive as to the timing of implementation of legislation. Annual reports of the Lord Chancellor's Office in the early 1990s discussed preparations for the implementation of section 13 and the media reported its imminent implementation,[75] but over 25 years later the section is still not in force!

This executive veto has never been satisfactorily justified.[76] It seemed to be based primarily on a fear in the early 1990s of the increased court costs of processing large numbers of debtors and on opposition by the judiciary. A newspaper article in 1992 suggested that there was 'considerable dragging of judicial heels as courts are reluctant to be inundated with cases during a recession'.[77] Figure 3.6 indicates the general decline of the administration order from the early 1990s and its steep decline from the late 1990s may indicate that consumers turned to other alternatives.

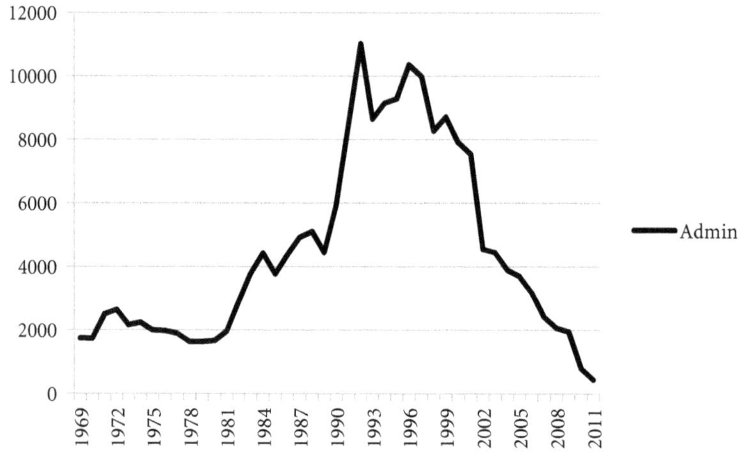

Figure 3.6: Administration orders 1969–2011
Source: Civil Judicial Statistics.

In other European countries, the recession of the late 1980s and early 1990s provided a critical juncture, setting the stage for the introduction of debt

[75] See D Boliver, 'Taking Voluntary Steps to Avoid the Bankruptcy Court' *The Guardian* (4 September 1993) 30. 'Next year administration orders should become more widely available.'

[76] The initial argument highlighted the increased costs for courts with an anticipated rise in administration orders in the recession of the early 1990s. Arguments later developed that section 13 might be interpreted to include secured debt, permitting a mortgage to be written down over three years, and by 2005 the Ministry of Justice claimed that the administration order was unworkable for insolvents because it did not include assets of a debtor and provided no method for investigating an individual's affairs. The Insolvency Service, 'Relief for the Indebted—An Alternative to Bankruptcy', www.detini.gov.uk/consultation12b.pdf.

[77] I Gregory, 'Debtors Have Alternative Choices to Bankruptcy' *The Independent* (4 April 1992).

adjustment laws in France, Germany, and Scandinavian countries. Although the UK government did enact some measures to protect homeowners threatened with repossession (measures which were resurrected in the Great Recession), and mortgage foreclosures reached record levels during this period, it did not bring section 13 into force, thereby preventing access to relief for many consumers. Individual bankruptcies almost tripled between 1990 and 1992, with a substantial percentage representing consumer rather than business debt (29 per cent to 39 per cent) (Figure 3.2).

The use of bankruptcy by consumers was frowned upon by bankruptcy insiders and the Insolvency Service, which was stretched to deal with the increased numbers of low-value bankruptcies that it claimed it did not have the resources to properly investigate. Both viewed section 13 as the more appropriate alternative for many debtors.[78] But nothing transpired. Many individuals were informally insolvent[79] but, unable to pay the costs of bankruptcy, had no opportunity for relief.

In 1998, the New Labour government included in its review of the enforcement of civil judgments the task of considering 'what amendment is needed for the successful implementation of section 13 of the Courts and Legal Services Act 1990'[80] During the late 1990s, over-indebtedness became a significant public issue and in 2000, the New Labour government convened a 'debt summit', established a task force on over-indebtedness and developed an 'Overindebtedness Action Plan' in 2004.[81]

An empirical study of administration orders in the early 2000s painted an almost scandalous picture of their management by county courts with high levels of default and little consistency in application between courts. Users of the orders were primarily female lone parents, 70 per cent of whom were unemployed; almost two-thirds had serious health problems or carer responsibilities.[82] Composition orders were made in 22 per cent of cases even though over 80 per cent of the orders for full payment would not be cleared in three years,[83] and (unpublished) court

[78] D Flynn, 'Are the Institutions of Insolvency Achieving their Purpose? Bankruptcy and Individual Voluntary Arrangements (IVAs) in England and Wales' in H Rajak (ed) *Insolvency Law: Theory and Practice* (London, Sweet & Maxwell, 1993) 115. '[T]he Insolvency Service looks to the introduction of Section 13 of the Courts and Legal Services Act 1990 as potentially providing a useful and, in many cases far more "appropriate" remedy both for debtors with few if any assets and for creditors. The reformed Administration Order procedure holds out the promise of relief for the debtor at far less cost in administrative resources than bankruptcy.'

[79] See J Ford and M Wilson, 'Personal Debt and Insolvency' in H Rajak (ed), *Insolvency Law Theory and Practice* (London, Sweet & Maxwell, 1993).

[80] Geoff Hoon outlining the terms of reference in answer to a Parliamentary question by Melanie Johnson, HC Deb 25 March 1998 vol 309 cc 141-2W 141W.

[81] See DTI and DWP, *Tackling Overindebtedness* (London, HMSO, 2004).

[82] See E Kempson and S Collard, *Managing Multiple Debts: Experiences of County Court Administration Orders among Debtors, Creditors and Advisors* (London, Department for Constitutional Affairs, 2004).

[83] ibid 33.

guidelines stated that a composition order could be made in these situations. Local legal culture seemed to determine the making of composition orders.

In 2004, the government recognised the failure of the existing administration order,[84] and although reform provisions were included in 2007 legislation, once again the relevant sections have never been brought into force.[85] As a consequence, the administration order withered to almost complete extinction by 2013. Successive governments, acting through the Lord Chancellor's Office and the Ministry of Justice, failed to implement these reforms to the administration order and provide adequate resources to the court service, which in any event disliked its role in processing orders. Technical arguments were made against its implementation but the relevant departments were content to see it fail since it was a subsidised service in an era of privatisation. Its functions could be carried out by the private and voluntary sectors with minimal court involvement, leaving 'the court free to focus on its core roles of dispute resolution and enforcement regulation'.[86] In response to a freedom of information request, the Ministry of Justice stated in 2015:

> [T]he Government does not currently plan to implement all the outstanding powers in the Act. Any such powers would only be implemented if the Government were satisfied that there was a compelling case for doing so. The Government suspended work on the introduction of the reformed Administration Order scheme and the Enforcement Restriction Order in 2009 due to cost and there are no current plans to revisit this.[87]

IV. Conversion: The Individual Voluntary Arrangement

The failure to implement section 13 in 1990 left a significant lacuna in insolvency alternatives for consumers. The IVA procedure, enacted in the Insolvency Act 1986, permits an individual to make a composition, through a licensed insolvency practitioner (generally an accountant), with their unsecured creditors, provided 75 per cent of creditors in value accept the proposal.[88] Unlike bankruptcy, an individual might retain control of their property, including a home, in an IVA. The Cork Committee assumed that the normal repayment period would be three years and envisaged its applicability to three classes of debtor: directors of companies who had given personal guarantees, members of professions not

[84] Department for Constitutional Affairs, 'A Choice of Paths: Better Options to Manage Over-Indebtedness and Multiple Debt, Consultation Paper CP 23/04', 6, www.dca.gov.uk/consult/debt/debt.pdf.

[85] See Part 6 Administration Orders of the Tribunals, Courts and Enforcement Act 2007 C. 15.

[86] Above n 84 at para 29.

[87] Ministry of Justice response to FOI request 9 October 2015.

[88] See generally on IVAs, Part VIII Insolvency Act 1986.

permitted to take advantage of limited liability, and traders.[89] Consumers were not identified as possible beneficiaries of this remedy.

During the late 1980s and early 1990s only a modest number of IVAs were registered. The high costs and relatively cumbersome procedure, requiring the debtor to obtain a 'nominee' (licensed insolvency practitioner) to report to the court on the proposal, convene a meeting of creditors and then have the nominee act as supervisor, were cited as reasons for this modest uptake.[90] The courts reduced these costs by a practice direction permitting a 'concertina order',[91] a documents-only process without court attendance.[92] By the mid 1990s, IVA were the domain of small insolvency practitioners. Almost half the cases exceeded three years, with employee and consumer cases representing only 27 per cent of cases.[93] The large banks in the UK developed centralised recovery units to monitor the relative performance of IVAs from different insolvency practitioners and actively participated through standardised voting proxies exercised by large accounting firms.[94]

By the early 2000s, the New Labour government concluded that the IVA was a policy failure.[95] The introduction of the one-year (reduced from three years) discharge in the Enterprise Act 2002 was a response and contemporary commentators predicted the demise of the IVA.[96] Figure 3.1 indicates, however, the significant rise of IVAs after the Enterprise Act 2002 so that it is now the dominant insolvency alternative.

The IVA market was transformed in the early 2000s with the entry of a new model of insolvency practitioner.[97] High-volume processors with a business model that cut costs and advertised extensively, these firms offered IVAs as an alternative to existing public and private debt management plans. Debt Free Direct was the pioneer of this model. This business model transformed the market so that large

[89] Cork report (n 2) ch 7.

[90] See K Pond, 'The Individual Voluntary Arrangement Experience' [1995] *Journal of Business Law* 118.

[91] Practice Note (Ch D: Bankruptcy: Voluntary Arrangements) (No. 1 of 1991) Chancery Division 13 December 1991 [1992] 1 WLR 120; [1992] 1.

[92] David Milman argues that 'the courts have played a key role in promoting the successful operation of the IVA', D Milman, *Personal Insolvency Law, Regulation And Policy*, new edition (Aldershot, Ashgate Publishing, 2005) 132. See also the changes introduced by the Insolvency Act 2000 (s 3 and Sch 3), which make it no longer obligatory for a debtor to seek an interim order.

[93] K Pond, 'A Decade of Change for Individual Voluntary Arrangements' (1998) 14 *Tolleys Insolvency Law and Practice* 324.

[94] See K Pond, 'Administration of Recoveries in Individual Insolvency: Case Studies of Two UK Banks' (2002) 8 *The European Journal of Finance* 206. Pond notes that modifications demanded by creditors related primarily to increased income contributions, increased duration, property revaluation and a windfall clause, limiting the supervisor's fee. He concluded that 'IVAs are far more creditor friendly than in the past and … they reflect less and less the wishes of debtors'. During this period, a 31% failure rate existed with the average dividend of 30p in the £.

[95] 'At the same time it is the Government's view that Individual Voluntary Arrangements (IVAs) have been an ineffective alternative to bankruptcy.' This was attributed to high fees and low returns. See Parliamentary Research Paper 02/21 Bill 115 2001–02 Enterprise Bill, 98.

[96] See M Green, 'New Labour: More Debt—The Political Response' in J Niemi, I Ramsay, and WC Whitford (eds), *Consumer Credit, Debt and Bankruptcy: Comparative and International Perspectives* (Oxford, Hart Publishing, 2009) 405.

[97] Eg Debt Free Direct established in 1997 and now part of the Fairpoint Group.

high-volume providers now have a significant share of the market (see Table 3.1). The terms of debt relief were shaped by negotiations between these firms and creditors. Repayment norms on IVAs were extended from three to five years and homeowners expected to contribute a portion of equity at the end of five years to the repayment of unsecured debts. Fees are deducted from the monthly payments.

Table 3.1: IVA Registration by firms regularly processing over 3,000 cases per annum during period 2009–14

	2009–10	2010–11	2011–12	2012–13	2013–14
Debt Free Direct	7,945	5,284	3,646	4,423	2,950
Freeman Jones	4,439	5,396	5,466	4,642	3,208
Grant Thornton	9,540	7,206	6,346	4,015	2,900
Payplan	5,259	4,986	5,806	6,386	5,263
One Advice	2,169	3,304	5,655	7,587	9,261
Other	24,721	24,104	24,172	20,486	38,140
Total	**53,673**	**50,820**	**51,091**	**47,539**	**61,722**

Source: Freedom of Information request, Insolvency Service England and Wales.

Meanwhile, the Enterprise Act 2002 reduced the discharge period to one year and removed many bankruptcy disabilities. This liberalisation was not aimed at the protection of consumers, but rather represented New Labour's entrepreneurial agenda to reduce the downside risks for small businesses. The White Paper preceding the Act had recognised the growing role of consumer insolvencies and the fact that the UK seemed to be moving to a situation similar to the US and Australia where consumer bankruptcies dominated. It saw this area as a work in progress to be developed by the Insolvency Service and the Ministry of Justice.[98]

The narratives framing the background to the insolvency provisions of the Act included a distinction between the 'responsible risk-taking' and 'culpable bankrupt' with a further subtext of can pay should pay. The price for making bankruptcy more available for the majority was to 'come down hard' on 'the estimated 7–12% of bankrupts who are culpable'[99] through a new bankruptcy restriction order.[100] Peter Mandelson, Secretary of State at the Department of Trade and Industry, promoted the entrepreneurial aspects of the Bill by reference to US

98 See para 1.46–1.48 The Insolvency Service, *Insolvency—A Second Chance* (CM 5234) (London, DTI, The Stationery Office, 2001).

99 DTI press notice, *Byers Outlines Details of Bankruptcy Study*, 2 July 1999.

100 See s 281A of, and Sch 4A to, the Insolvency Act 1986. The objectives of the order are '[t]o protect the public and commercial community, by enabling the court to make a BRO so that a culpable bankrupt will continue to be subject to the restrictions of bankruptcy for a period of 2 to 15 years. To allow lenders and public to differentiate between culpable and non-culpable and make better informed decisions in their dealings with bankrupts. To deter fraud and misconduct.' Insolvency Service, Evaluation of the Bankruptcy Restriction Order Appendix A2: Evaluation Planning Paper for Bankruptcy Restrictions Order provisions (London, Insolvency Service, 2007). The provisions appear to have had limited impact since lenders use their own criteria for lending based on credit reference

experience with a liberal discharge.[101] Melanie Johnson, the minister responsible for the Bill in Parliament, stated in debates that in the US 'if people do not have one or two failures under their belt … they are hardly regarded as serious entrepreneurs'.[102] Bankruptcy reform was appended to a flagship Enterprise Bill that had a swift passage through Parliament, given executive control of Parliament. Credit card companies attempted to undermine the discharge proposals by commissioning a research report that claimed that the proposals would result in a 50 per cent increase in bankruptcies.[103] The government responded by commissioning research to undermine the credibility of the report, concluding that 'its econometric work is so seriously flawed that it should not in any way be relied upon'.[104] Conservative MPs also opposed the inclusion of consumers within the more liberal discharge procedures. They argued that the relaxation of the discharge would reduce personal responsibility, result in an explosion in consumer bankruptcies and a reduction of credit to marginal risks.[105] The liberal US bankruptcy law was

data. See Insolvency Service, *Enterprise Act 2002—the Personal Insolvency Provisions: Final Evaluation Report* (London, Insolvency Service, 2007).

[101] 'In the US some of the most successful entrepreneurs are those who have failed once or twice. Banks and society as a whole don't write people off as failures. They see them as people who have learned', *The Guardian*, 24 June 2000, 29, quoting Peter Mandelson.

[102] Melanie Johnson, MP Parliamentary Under Secretary of State for Competition Consumers and Markets quoted in the *Independent*, 11 June 2000. She quoted statistics that 31.5% of English people say that fear of failure would prevent them from starting a business. In the US, the rate is only 21%. I Ramsay, 'Functionalism and Political Economy in the Comparative Study of Consumer Insolvency: An Unfinished Story from England and Wales' (2006) 7 *Theoretical Inquiries in Law* 625, 646.

[103] The report had been commissioned by the credit card company MBNA which also lobbied MPs. The research is discussed at HL Deb 21 October 2002 vol 639 cc 1133–1140.

[104] 'Last week, we commissioned independent research into the significant part; that is, section 6 of the CEBR research. We commissioned it from Professor John Van Reenen of the department of economics at University College, London. The professor concluded that, the econometric work contained in Section 6 is so seriously flawed that it should not in any way be relied upon to judge the impact of the Enterprise Bill on personal bankruptcies.' Lord McIntosh, HL Deb 28 October 2002 vol 640 c 79.

[105] See eg M Waterson:

> 'Consumer credit might become more restrictive in terms of both its availability and the conditions that are applied. The Consumer Credit Association says: "wholly unsecured credit could become a thing of the past. In other words, lenders will increasingly ask for security or for a guarantor." So the sort of people whom the Government are trying to benefit might be worse off under the Bill, because they are less likely to have assets or know people who are in a position to guarantee their borrowings.
>
> I am reliably informed that another feature of the US market is that, as a result of the US approach to bankruptcy, a whole new sector of predatory lenders has sprung up to service the marginalised group who cannot get credit anywhere else. Most commentators would agree that notions of responsibility in the USA have been eroded simply by the ease with which bankruptcy can occur. It has also been estimated that the average American family pays $400 a year for the cost of bankruptcy across the US economy.
>
> There is another practical issue. As the Under-Secretary of State will know, credit reference agencies tend to keep their records on consumers and their credit ratings for six years. If, as part of the Bill, the Government aim to make it easier for consumers and businesspeople to go in and out of bankruptcy, does the hon. Lady accept that a consumer with a bankruptcy record is unlikely to be able to get credit even if they come out of bankruptcy within 12 months or 2 months or whatever period?'

M Waterson, UK Enterprise Bill HC Debates Standing Committee 14 May Session 2001–02, cols 645–646.

cited as having eroded 'notions of responsibility in the USA' and reference was made to the famous, but misleading, sound bite that bankruptcy in the US costs the average American family $400 a year.[106]

The relevant Minister, Melanie Johnson, responded to these criticisms by pointing to the new bankruptcy restriction order and noted the difficulties of distinguishing business from consumer debts. The government did not, however, believe that bankruptcy should become an easily accessible consumer remedy and rejected a Conservative amendment, promoted by Citizens Advice, that individuals on income support should have free access to bankruptcy. In the words of the relevant minister, 'A person's entry into bankruptcy is not a right and should be considered very much a last resort ... bankruptcy is not the only method of dealing with debts.'[107] The ongoing review of the administration order by the Lord Chancellor would in Melanie Johnson's view provide one solution to the problems of lower-income debtors.[108]

The entrepreneurialism agenda of 'responsible risk-taking' was layered on to existing insolvency legislation. Although the Enterprise Act reduced the disabilities associated with being an undischarged bankrupt, it retained the basic technique of the criminal law for enforcing the remaining disabilities, continuing the historical quasi-penal status of bankruptcy.[109] An influential narrative of the Cork Committee had highlighted the role of bankruptcy in contributing to commercial morality and the Committee had promoted stricter standards for the disqualification of directors of failed firms and the radical idea of 'wrongful trading', which permitted the courts to pierce the corporate veil and hold directors liable to contribute to creditors. The new bankruptcy restriction orders which could be sought by the Insolvency Service, were modelled on the directors' disqualification provisions and were intended to protect the public

[106] See UK Enterprise Bill HC Deb 14 May 2002, col 645.

[107] 'As the House will be aware, bankruptcy is not the only method of dealing with debts; nor, depending on the circumstances of the case, does bankruptcy necessarily provide the best outcomes for both the debtor and the creditor ... Bankruptcy should be considered as a last resort ... There are several other routes available to individuals with financial problems, many of which do not require a deposit. Many individuals can, and do, apply to the county court for administration orders and discharge their liabilities through monthly payments, which are set at a level that the individual can afford ... Additionally, growing numbers of individuals with debt problems seek advice and assistance from organisations in the voluntary sector such as the Consumer Credit Counselling Service and Paylink. Those organisations will administer debt repayment plans on behalf of debtors at no cost to the debtor, the administration cost being met by creditors who agree to forgo a proportion of new debt. Several of them offer repayment plans of as little as £1 per week.' HC Deb 17 June 2002 vol 387 col 59.

[108] Melanie Johnson: 'Such matters are for my right hon. and learned Friend the Lord Chancellor to decide. His review of the enforcement of civil court judgments includes reform of county court administration orders. The Government are considering a range of options, both court based and non-court based. We do not intend to take any interim measures such as increasing the scope of the existing county court administration orders scheme, including increasing the limit, before we have considered the options for reform in that wider context. I hope that the hon. Gentleman appreciates that that is the sensible setting for further consideration of the issues.' HC Deb17 June 2002, vol 387,col 61.

[109] See K Möser, 'Restrictions after Personal Insolvency' (2013) *Journal of Business Law* 679. These provisions are rarely enforced.

and commercial community and aid creditors in making credit decisions. The order would continue to apply the restrictions of an undischarged debtor to an individual for a period of 2 to 15 years, and individuals would appear on a register. The most significant factor relating to consumers, which can be taken into account in determining whether a bankruptcy restriction order (BRO) should be made, is whether the consumer 'incurr[ed] before commencement of the bankruptcy, a debt which the bankrupt had no reasonable expectation of being able to pay'.[110] While subject to an order a consumer debtor is prohibited from obtaining credit of more than £500 without disclosing the existence of the order. Failure to disclose is a criminal offence.

Evaluation of the impact of the Enterprise Act in 2007 indicates that the fresh start objectives of the Act were limited by credit reference policies of maintaining the bankruptcy on record for six years.[111] Credit reference agencies did not distinguish in their files between bankrupts with BROs and other bankrupts, undermining the practical significance of BROs. Bankrupts continue to have problems with bank accounts and many institutions such as landlords and insurance companies use bankruptcy as a criterion for rejecting an applicant. Bankrupts continue to experience stigma, although the public at large believes there is now less stigma to bankruptcy.[112] The jury is out on whether the Enterprise Act provisions have encouraged entrepreneurialism. The 2007 evaluation concluded that it had neither affected the level of business start-ups nor the fear of failure.[113] The primary beneficiaries were consumers who already constituted over 60 per cent of bankrupts in 2002. But even the changes for consumers should not be overestimated. For many years before 2002 a summary procedure had operated for small bankruptcies under £20000 with light-touch investigation by the insolvency service and a discharge period of two years.

The Enterprise Bill did not, therefore, represent a 'decisive departure from the Victorian vision of social stigma attaching to debt'.[114] It was a legislative compromise layered onto a statute with much historical scaffolding and supported by competing narratives of responsible risk-taking and commercial morality.

[110] Schedule 4A (2(2)(h)). The Insolvency Service could also accept an undertaking by an individual instead of going to court. Undertakings represent the vast majority of orders and for consumers the most common ground was incurring debts with no reasonable expectation of repayment until the decision of Register Baister in *Official Receiver v Southey* [2009] BPIR 89 where a higher burden of proof was required for bringing such an action.

[111] See The Insolvency Service, 'Enterprise Act 2002—The Personal Insolvency Provisions: Final Evaluation Report 2007' (London, The Insolvency Service, 2007) webarchive.nationalarchives.gov.uk/+/http:/www.insolvency.gov.uk/insolvencyprofessionandlegislation/legislation/evaluation/final-report/report.pdf.

[112] ibid 51. Individuals identified stigma before the Act as the 'possible loss of home, the effect on credit rating and not being able to repay creditors'. After the Act, it was identified with 'having the bankruptcy order advertised and the possible loss of home'.

[113] ibid 16.

[114] John Willcock, 'Enterprise Bill May Stoke Up Consumer Debt' *The Times* (9 May 2002).

V. Framing the Policy Response After the Enterprise Act: Borrowing Binges

The early 2000s was a period of sharply increasing household debt and pressure on wages. As bankruptcies continued to increase after the Act came into force, the media wrote of the 'sharp', 'soaring', and 'alarming' increases in personal insolvency and attributed it to high personal debt[115] and the Enterprise Act 2002. The tabloid *Daily Mail* claimed that individuals were 'living beyond their means', a sign of 'the save not spend culture', and argued that young single women were loading up on credit card debt for 'clothing socializing and holidays'.[116] A bankruptcy registrar reported that bankruptcies were not caused by unemployment but by debts 'out of control … from endless credit cards that have hit the limit'.[117] The *Guardian* ran several stories between 2001 and 2005 on the 'unsustainable borrowing binge' a theme reiterated by insolvency practitioners. A journalist for the paper who had declared bankruptcy was consoled by the fact that 'she was not alone … domestic bankruptcies had multiplied because of a growing debt culture'.[118] Economists Michael Kitson and Frank Wilkinson argued that economic growth during this period had been driven by a 'consumption binge … which has led to high levels of debt and insolvency'.[119]

The image of the debtor in England during this period was increasingly that of an individual 'living beyond one's means' and individuals who 'simply didn't budget properly'.[120] Unlike in France,[121] the image of the debtor in the English media was not one of the passive debtor affected by unemployment and other life changes, but rather an increasingly middle-class actively over-indebted individual. Individual misjudgement, naivety, and myopic borrowing were cited and more financial education proposed. These reports and commentary framed policymaking so that the idea of more accessible bankruptcies for ordinary consumers to write off debt was unlikely to be popular. In retrospect, a different interpretation is that individuals were attempting to maintain consumption levels in a period

[115] See my discussion of this media response in I Ramsay, '"Wannabe WAGS" and "Credit Binges": The Constructions of Overindebtedness in the UK' in Niemi, Ramsay, and Whitford (eds), *Consumer Credit, Debt and Bankruptcy* (n 96)76.

[116] See eg B Barrow, 'Going Bust, the Wannabe WAGs' *Daily Mail* (21 August 2006) http://www.dailymail.co.uk/news/article-401520/Going-bust-wannabe-WAGs.html. My comments on the media are based on an analysis of UK newspaper coverage of debt and bankruptcy during the period 2001–05.

[117] See Stephen Lawson, Association of Business Recovery Professionals, Enterprise and Culture Committee Official Report, Col 2713, Scottish Parliament, Tuesday, 7 March 2006.

[118] A Hardy, 'Finding Life after Debt' *The Guardian* (10 January 2004).

[119] M Kitson and F Wilkinson, 'The Economics of New Labour: policy and performance' (2007) 31 *Cambridge Journal of Economics* 805, 811.

[120] See PricewaterhouseCoopers, *Living on Tick: The 21st Century Debtor* (London, PwC, 2006). This was based on debtors ticking a box 'Expenditure in Excess of Income' on the IVA form. This is an ambiguous category as it does not explain the reasons behind the expenditure being in excess of income.

[121] See below, ch 4.

of relatively stagnant wages.[122] Research in 2007 concluded that the increase in bankruptcies during this period was primarily driven by increases in secured and unsecured debt,[123] rather than the changes enacted by the Enterprise Act.

The Insolvency Service, responding to concerns about increases in bankruptcy, initiated a meeting of stakeholders and established a working group composed primarily of insolvency practitioners and creditors to review the IVA, with a view to making it more accessible as a consumer remedy.[124] The master narrative of can pay should pay was now influential—'the basic position is that if bankrupts can pay they should pay'—in policymaking for consumer debtors. The Insolvency Service viewed the IVA as the best product for consumers, providing benefits to both creditors and debtors.[125] It proposed a streamlined IVA in low-value cases (under £75,000), reducing the majority required for acceptance to 50 per cent, and preventing creditors proposing modifications. These reforms would be implemented through the Legislative Reform Order procedure, which permits modification of primary legislation by a secondary regulation in limited circumstances.[126]

122 The same *Guardian* journalist (n 116) explained that she was not a spendthrift and that 'the money went on supermarket shopping when my wages had run out, on petrol, car repairs and basic furniture for the small rented home I shared with my husband. We did not live a life of excess, but we did live in excess of our income.'

123 See Department of Work and Pensions/Department of Constitutional Affairs, *Tackling Over-indebtedness* (Annual Report, Overindebtedness Task Force, 2006). 'The Bank of England principally attributes the increasing number of personal insolvencies to the rise in household indebtedness and goes on to say that it is unlikely that the recent rise in bankruptcies are due to changes introduced by the Enterprise Act 2002, given that the upward trend in insolvencies was established before the change to legislation.'

124 'On 19 July 2004, the Insolvency Service hosted a forum to discuss Individual Voluntary Arrangements (IVAs) attended by a wide range of stakeholders. From the opinions expressed at the forum, there appears to be a consensus that a re-examination of the individual voluntary arrangement process is overdue, particularly in the case of so called "'consumer" debtors.' The Working Group represented, according to the Insolvency Service, 'a wide range of stakeholders' but it was dominated by insolvency practitioners and other intermediaries. The members were: John Fairhurst of Payplan, Andrew Redmond of Debt Free Direct, Peter Hughes Holland of Numerica, Charles Howson of Accuma, Beverley Budsworth of Budsworth & Co, Pat Boyden of PwC, Steve Treharne of KPMG, Charles Rusbasan of Max Recovery Ltd, Euan McPherson of HBOS, Nick Pearson of Advice UK, Jan Smith of CCCS. See 'Dear ip ch 24 voluntary arrangements).

125 See Insolvency Service, *Improving Individual Voluntary Arrangements* (London, Insolvency Service, 2005).

126 Under the Legislative and Regulatory Reform Act 2006. This places restrictions on the ability to reform primary legislation. In particular, under s 3(1):

> 'A Minister may not make provision under section 1(1) or 2(1), other than provision which merely restates an enactment, unless he considers that the conditions in subsection (2), where relevant, are satisfied in relation to that provision.
>
> (2) Those conditions are that—
> (a) the policy objective intended to be secured by the provision could not be satisfactorily secured by non-legislative means;
> (b) the effect of the provision is proportionate to the policy objective;
> (c) the provision, taken as a whole, strikes a fair balance between the public interest and the interests of any person adversely affected by it;
> (d) the provision does not remove any necessary protection;
> (e) the provision does not prevent any person from continuing to exercise any right or freedom which that person might reasonably expect to continue to exercise;
> (f) the provision is not of constitutional significance.'

A. The Bankers' Campaign on the IVA

The seemingly high profits available in the IVA market demonstrated by early entrants such as Debt Free Direct attracted new entrants. The highly competitive and relatively unregulated market undoubtedly engendered aggressive and misleading marketing practices with cold-calling and some companies promising large write-offs of debts to consumers in a 'government-provided' plan. The major banks, whose bad debt ratios were increasing during this period, partly as a consequence of earlier aggressive marketing of credit and associated payment protection insurance to increasingly risky customers, claimed that IVA fees were too high. Media coverage of IVAs increased substantially during this period (Figure 3.7) with the banks claiming that IVAs were marketed aggressively and misleadingly to consumers with promises of writing off 75 per cent of the debts when these consumers had little chance of sustaining a plan, but could finance the initial plan fees.[127] They also argued that the increases in bankruptcies and IVAs could lead to a reduction in lending, particularly to poorer consumers. The British Bankers Association lobbied the government to take action against misleading advertising,[128] while Eric Daniels, chief executive of Lloyds Bank criticised consumers with a 'cavalier' attitude to debt and claimed that there were increasing numbers of 'lifestyle insolvencies'.[129] Insolvency practitioners from established firms noted the growth of 'IVA factories' as a response to the borrowing binge and hypothesised that a cultural change was occurring where people 'think it's OK

[127] See eg E Lunn and P Collison, 'IVAs Blamed as Debt Crisis Mounts: Are People Being Encouraged to Just Ditch Their Debts?' *The Guardian* (5 August 2006) 3.

> 'It's sending the big banks hopping mad. Tens of thousands of Britons are, they allege, walking away from their debts, encouraged by companies exploiting "individual voluntary arrangements" (IVAs)—and bagging bumper profits for themselves.
>
> The number of IVAs has exploded in recent years. In 1998 there were under 5,000, but last year that number topped 20,000 and experts predict it could be 100,000 within a few years.
>
> The cost to the banks is reaching critical levels. All the major banks this week reported soaring bad debt levels, with Lloyds TSB boss, Eric Daniels, blaming IVAs for much of the problem. Now the banks are hitting back, warning that people are being fooled by misleading press articles and daytime TV adverts from money-grabbing IVA providers.'

[128] See J Treanor, 'Financial: Banks Call for Changes to Debt Advisory Services: Concerns Rise Over Advice on "Bankruptcy Alternative": DTI and OFT Told Adverts May Mislead Consumers' *The Guardian* (29 September 2006) 26; 'Financial: Banks Call for Action Over Debt Advisers' *The Guardian* (29 September 2006) 1: 'Britain's leading banks are urging authorities to change the way debt advisory firms are able to advertise'.

[129] R Clark and K Miller, 'Going for Broke: Every Minute of Every Working Day, Someone in England and Wales is Made Insolvent. Most Are Not Thrusting Entrepreneurs Down on Their Luck, but Feckless Consumers Eager to Walk Away from Credit Card Debts' *Sunday Telegraph* (6 August 2006) 19. Daniels is quoted as stating: 'Twenty years ago a debt was something that people would naturally repay. Today, advice is being given to students that the minute they graduate they should default. It is a huge societal change.' See 'Alarm at "Quickie" Bankruptcy Plan. Debts of Up to £15,000 Could Be Written Off After a Year With No Need for Court' *Mail on Sunday* (26 November 2006) 5. This article noted that the HSBC chief executive 'criticised debt advice companies that urged people to declare bankruptcy'.

not to pay off their debts'.[130] The banking industry trade association, the British Bankers Association (BBA), lobbied the government, initially unsuccessfully through the Department of Trade and Industry, to regulate the industry. Some IVA firms attempted to develop self-regulation to address bad practices, which resulted ultimately in the formation of the trade association the Debt Resolution Forum.[131]

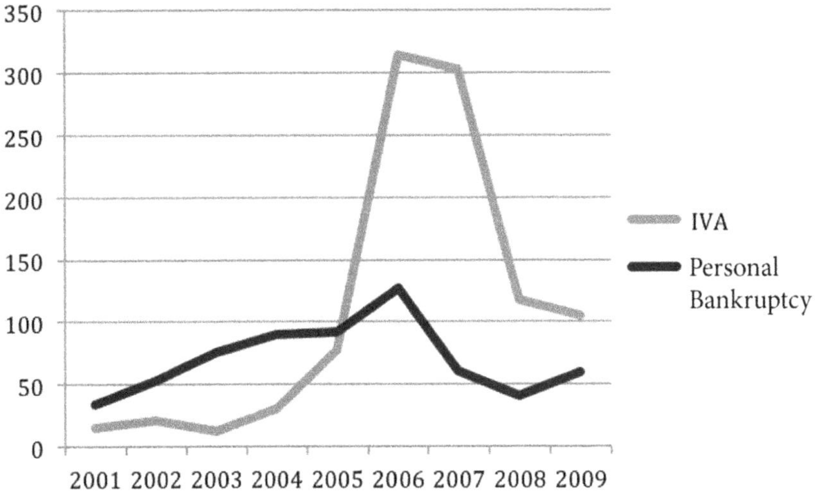

Figure 3.7: Newspaper articles mentioning IVAs and personal bankruptcy 2001–09
Source: Nexis.

The most significant political action by the banks in 2006 was the imposition by major banks, such as HBOS and HSBC, of high 'hurdle rates' for acceptance

[130] See eg 'Alarm at "Shocking Increase" in Walk-Away Debt Pacts: How Debtors Set Up an IVA' *The Times* (4 November 2006) 65. 'Louise Brittain head of the personal insolvency division at Baker Tilly said: 'These figures are quite shocking. The alarming growth in IVAs reflects British consumers' determination to spend beyond their means.' Patrick Boyden, a partner at Price Waterhouse commented on a number of occasions that the rise in IVAs followed a 'borrowing binge' over the last six years and that the increase in bankruptcies reflected a 'cultural shift'. See P Collinson, 'Household Debt Leads to Record Bankruptcies' *The Guardian* (6 November 2004) 32. S Watkins and D Atkinson, 'Banks Will Write Off 4 Billion Pounds as Debt Soars'. Boyden said: 'There is much more acceptance, particularly among the young. They just do not see becoming insolvent as having the same stigma as the older generation.' *Mail on Sunday* (30 July 2006) 1. Boyden conducted a review of IVA clients at PwC, which indicated that a primary reason for turning to an IVA was 'living beyond means'. The study did not probe the reasons for living beyond means. See PricewaterhouseCoopers, *Living on Tick: The 21st Century Debtor* (London, PwC, 2006).

[131] The industry was split on how to reform. See I Dey and R Northedge, 'Debt Firms in Spat Over Regulation' *The Sunday Telegraph* (5 November 2006) City 2. 'A consortium of debt companies … will reveal plans to form the Debt Resolution Forum, a trade body supported by the Insolvency Practitioners Association. But Debt Free Direct, the largest UK debt firm, will unveil proposals for an industry-wide standards system with an independent audit of IVA approval processes and random spot checks.'

of plans.[132] Since the banks would normally have a blocking vote of 25 per cent, they could reject any plan that did not meet the required rate of return. HSBC, for example, would not approve plans that promised a return of less than 40p in the pound, significantly higher than a typical yield of 35p.[133] This had a substantial impact on the numbers of IVAs between 2005 and 2007 (see Figure 3.1) and resulted in profit warnings on the shares of leading IVA companies.

The insolvency intermediary trade association R3 and others criticised this approach as 'frustrating public policy'.[134] Critics argued that the banks' strategy was intended to mask impaired loans and divert debtors to their own high-cost consolidation loans[135] or debt management plans. The Insolvency Service attempted to bring the parties together at a 'debt summit', and a standard form protocol for straightforward IVAs was hammered out by the intermediaries and banks, with the BBA writing an open letter of support to the Insolvency Service in 2007, indicating that their members 'are expected to abide by the terms of the protocol'.[136] The current protocol[137] runs to 47 pages and addresses topics such as the definition of a straightforward IVA marketing and advertising, methods of determining household expenditure for the plan, dealing with home equity, varying a plan and reporting to creditors. It is primarily a statement of existing industry practice: it does not attempt to reduce the majority needed for acceptance of the plan. An IVA standing committee dominated by lenders and insolvency practitioners monitors the application of the protocol.[138] The Insolvency Service did not proceed with the regulation on simplified IVAs. It argued that the non-legislative protocol obviated the need for legislation and that a consensus did not exist on all issues, a prerequisite for a legislative reform order.[139]

[132] See D Atkinson, 'Banks to Seal Escape Route from Debts' *Mail on Sunday* (London, 12 November 2006) 5. E Conway, 'Britons Go Bust at Rate of One per Minute' *Daily Telegraph* (5 August 2006) 1.

[133] See Green, 'New Labour' (n 96) 412.

[134] R3 commented to the review of the Insolvency Service that '[d]uring 2006, banks began to tighten their criteria for approving IVAs … and many imposed so-called hurdle rates, the most well known is HSBC's "40p in the £" requirement. A number of informed commentators, including R3, believe IVAs in 2007 could have reached 65,000, but for bank intervention. The underlying demand and need for IVAs has not reduced. R3believes that excessive blocking of IVA approvals is a frustration of public policy.' Evidence of Association of Business Recovery Professionals in Business and Enterprise Committee, *The Insolvency Service (Sixth Report)* (HC 2008–09, 198) para 4.2.

[135] See D Atkinson, 'Lenders in IVA "Rogue" Loan Abuse; Warning over Debt Consolidation Deals' *Mail on Sunday* (3 June 2007) 5.

[136] 'I am pleased to be able to confirm the continuing support of our members as we move towards full implementation of the new standards. In practice that means that our members are expected to abide by the terms of the protocol in relation to proposals drawn up on the basis of the protocol.' Eric Leenders, Executive Director, BBA Open Letter to the Insolvency Service (18 December 2007).

[137] For the current protocol, see The Insolvency Service, 'Individual Voluntary Arrangement (IVA) Protocol' (10 July 2014) www.gov.uk/government/publications/individual-voluntary-arrangement-iva-protocol.

[138] Of the membership of 20, 17 are either practitioners or lenders.

[139] The Service noted on its website in November 2008 that it was clear that several groups were querying the need for a simplified IVA and in evidence to the Business and Enterprise Committee in

The limits of the protocol were demonstrated in *Mond v MBNA*.[140] This was a test case brought against MBNA, which was perceived by David Mond (a leading insolvency practitioner[141]) and others as engaging in practices subverting the protocol and diverting debtors to lengthy individual debt management plans rather than an IVA or bankruptcy.

In this case a 23-year-old man with five financial institution debts of £18,969, a monthly income of £1,083 and outgoings of £860 proposed an IVA to pay £223 a month over five years. He had rejected the initial advice of Clear Debt, the intermediary, to declare bankruptcy (perhaps because of the stigma). The total fees charged under the proposal would be the nominee's fee of £1,500 and the supervisor's fee of 15 per cent of all payment realisations, resulting in an overall fee of about £3,200.[142] The total estimated dividend payable to creditors would amount to 46p in the £. MBNA held more than 25 per cent of the debt and refused to accept this offer, citing 'high fees' (later withdrawn) and 'disposable income available for a DMP [debt management plan]'. MBNA contacted the debtor and arranged for an individual DMP of £70 a month until the debt was paid off (with interest frozen). This approach was based on internal MBNA guidelines that a DMP was more appropriate than an IVA where the debt could be paid off within 10 years. Mond requested a declaration that MBNA was bound by the protocol and had contravened terms of the protocol, including the requirement of giving reasons for refusal of an offer.

2009 indicated at para 20 that 'The Service decided in November 2008 to withdraw its proposals to introduce a SIVA by means of a Legislative Reform Order. This decision reflected both our developing experience of the operation of the protocol as well as concerns about (a) whether the desired policy outcome could be achieved by non-legislative means, (b) whether it removed burdens and (c) whether it was clear that it would not add new burdens. Business and Enterprise Committee—Sixth Report, *The Insolvency Service* Session 2008-09 HC 198 (London, The Stationery Office, 2009).

[140] *Mond v MBNA Europe Bank* [2010] EWHC 1710 (Ch).

[141] David Mond is described in para 5 of the judgment as a 'senior partner of Hodgsons Chartered Accountants, a firm which Mr Mond describes in his first witness statement as "one of the leading independent business rescue and corporate personal insolvency specialists in the North West of England". Mr Mond states that he has specialised in personal and business insolvency and related matters for about 40 years. He has been a member of several professional and other bodies concerned with insolvency law and practice, especially in the field of business recovery, and with projects for the review and reform of the law and its practical implementation. Those bodies include the Council of the Association of Business Recovery Professionals, the Debt Resolution Forum, the Consumer Finance Forum, and the Joint BBA/Insolvency standing committee on the Protocol (whose functions are, among others, to monitor and review the operation of the Protocol and to communicate and consult on its future development). He is also the founder and chief executive of the second claimant, ClearDebt, which, according to Mr Mond's first witness statement, "is a provider of debt solutions for individuals, whether IVAs (in accordance with the Protocol or otherwise) or debt management plans (DMPs)".'

[142] In addition, 3.15% of the monthly contribution would be paid to Clear Debt as a premium for insurance to indemnify C against being unable to work owing to accident, illness, or unemployment during the period of the IVA.

The Court held that the protocol was not a legally binding document and that although the protocol did require a reason to be given for refusal of the offer, in doing so the bank could act to maximise its self-interest. The fact that the 10-year rule might not be a good reason was not relevant. While the Court had sympathy for the debtor it indicated that it was up to the drafters of the protocol to insert the necessary amendment or for Parliament to amend the IVA rules.

The result in *Mond* would have been different if the proposed simplified Individual Voluntary Arrangement (SIVA) had been in force as MBNA would not have had a blocking vote. The deference shown by the judge to the private ordering process of the protocol committee assumed a balance of power between debtor and creditor interests in achieving an optimal balance of interests. But this seems fanciful given the composition of the standing committee, the low visibility of the work and the need for technical knowledge. Undoubtedly, insolvency practitioners may act as proxies for debtor interests as in the *Mond* litigation. But creditors in the committee could block any reform proposals that went beyond the high level of consensus required by a Legislative Reform Order.

The terms and conditions of IVAs reflect, therefore, 'good practices' as developed by private intermediaries and creditors. This process of development has been one of primarily private lawmaking with changes to standardised terms on IVAs negotiated in low-visibility committees where financial institutions and insolvency professionals dominate.[143] The existing terms of IVAs, such as equity contributions and five-year plans, may be optimal from the point of creditors and intermediaries but whether they are optimal from a public policy perspective in ensuring financial rehabilitation and a fresh start is not clear. No studies exist of the overall costs and benefits of IVAs.

If section 13 of the Courts and Legal Services Act had been implemented a different balance of public and private regimes might have emerged. The absence of adequate court-based schemes stimulated the growth of the informal advice agency alternatives, which in turn were spotted as a possible market niche by private providers. An element of contingency exists, therefore, in the present system in England and Wales. The existing system was also partly a result of one government department, the Lord Chancellor's Office/Ministry of Justice, being unwilling to invest in the costs of managing the administration order. Other government departments were happy to permit increased private handling of debt cases through the IVA since it reduced government costs and fitted with the ideology of privatisation of many services in the UK.

[143] See discussion in J Spooner and I Ramsay, 'Submission to Insolvency Service, Insolvency Proceedings: Debt Relief Orders and the Bankruptcy Petition Limit' (October 2014) (on file with author) and see Green, 'New Labour' (n 96) 408–09. For a judicial discussion of the IVA protocol see *Mond v MBNA Europe Bank* (n 140).

VI. Relief for the Deserving Poor: The Debt Relief Order

The most recent innovation in English debt relief is the DRO,[144] a low-cost administrative process of means-tested debt relief which provides individuals who have limited assets and income the possibility of discharging most unsecured debts after one year.[145] This legislation was a transplant from New Zealand, which pioneered the idea of the no-asset procedure in a government paper published in 2002.[146] The objectives of the order are both to provide relief for those 'who cannot pay their debts and are unable to access current procedures of debt relief' and to promote 'financial inclusion'.[147] Other Anglo states (eg New Zealand, Ireland) associated with neo-liberal economies have introduced such a procedure and the International Monetary Fund (IMF) in its work with the troika has recommended this procedure as good practice for countries in structural adjustment (Cyprus, Greece).[148]

In England and Wales the process involves an online application to the Insolvency Service through a limited number of primarily publicly subsidised[149]

[144] See Part 7A of the Insolvency Act 1986 c.45.

[145] The Tribunals, Courts and Enforcement Act 2007 enacted the debt relief order with the legislation being implemented in 2009. The background to the introduction of the English and Welsh procedure can be traced to a 2004 document 'A Choice of Paths' in which the Ministry of Justice (then Department of Constitutional Affairs) put forward this alternative, proposing that it be aimed at '[t]he type of person at whom the scheme is aimed [who] cannot pay even a portion of their debt within a reasonable timeframe. Such people are often living on very low incomes, and whilst at the time they borrowed the money they had every intention of paying it back, they simply lack the means to do so.' See Department of Constitutional Affairs 'A Choice of Paths: Better Options to Manage Over-indebtedness and Multiple Debt' (2004) CP23/04. In 2005 the Insolvency Service published a consultation paper 'Relief for the Indebted—An Alternative to Bankruptcy' (London, The Insolvency Service). Subsequently a working group developed proposals that were inserted in the Tribunals, Courts and Enforcement Act 2007.

[146] See NZ Ministry of Economic Development, No Asset Procedure Paper (Wellington, Ministry of Economic Development, 2002).

[147] 'Part 5 … solutions seek to promote financial inclusion and are targeted, in particular, at those who are disproportionately affected by debt and are generally least able to deal with a range of creditor demands' (HL Deb 29 November 2006, vol 687, col 766). Part 5 included a package of solutions to address individuals with short term over-indebtedness (through an enforcement restriction order), individuals who could repay a portion of their debts (through a reformed administration order) and those with no repayment capacity (through the debt relief order') and who are unable to access current procedures of debt relief. Only the debt relief order has been brought into force.

Financial inclusion can be defined in a variety of ways. Lavinia Mitton defines it in a 2008 review as 'the inability, difficulty or reluctance to access appropriate, so-called mainstream, financial services'. See L Mitton, *Financial Inclusion in the UK: Review of Policy and Practice* (London, Joseph Rowntree Foundation, 2008) 1. See also HM Treasury, *Promoting Financial Inclusion* (London, Treasury, December 2004).

[148] See Greece Memorandum of Understanding between EU and Greece (2015) 18–19, http://ec.europa.eu/economy_finance/assistance_eu_ms/greek_loan_facility/pdf/01_mou_20150811_en.pdf. For Cyprus, see Insolvency of Natural Persons (Personal Repayment Plan and Debt Relief Order) Law of 2015.

[149] Citizens Advice is the major intermediary. Citizens Advice services are 'to provide the advice people need for the problems they face' and secondly 'to improve the policies and principles that affect

'approved intermediaries'[150] (see Table 3.2) who act as screening agencies and check the eligibility of the debtor, using, for example, credit reference data.[151] Access is limited to individuals with non-exempt assets below £1,000, a vehicle valued at less than £1,000, unsecured debts less than £20,000 and no more than £50 in surplus income defined by reference to the reasonable household needs of a lower income individual, which is generally calculated by reference to the Common Financial Statement, a standard developed though negotiations between the British Bankers Association and debt advisers.[152] Individuals must

people's lives', a research and campaigns agenda known as 'social policy'. But Citizens Advice is not permitted to campaign on welfare issues. Citizens Advice is a registered charity. It receives the majority of its funding from central government and each local bureau may also receive funds from institutions such as the National Lottery. A central office provides expertise, but it also relies heavily on volunteers in local bureau. According to its website:

> 'Citizens Advice Bureaux deliver advice services from over 3,300 community locations in England and Wales, run by 338 individual charities. Citizens Advice is the national body for bureaux and is a registered charity in its own right. Together we make up the Citizens Advice service. Of the 28,500 people who work for the service, over 22,000 of them are volunteers and nearly 6,500 are paid staff.
>
> Through the training, information systems and operational support it provides, Citizens Advice equips bureaux to deliver the highest quality advice to their local residents. In turn, client evidence submitted by bureaux alerts Citizens Advice to widespread problems that require action at a national level.'

https://www.citizensadvice.org.uk/about-us/how-citizens-advice-works/who-we-are-and-what-we-do/introduction-to-the-citizens-advice-service/.

[150] See Debt Relief Orders (Designation of Competent Authorities) Regulations 2009, regulation 3(2)(b)(i).

[151] Data indicate that about 1% of applications are rejected by the Insolvency Service with further information requested in about 5% of cases. This compares with the high number of rejections (approximately 20%) in the NZ scheme.

[152] The Schedule defines 'monthly surplus income' as 'the amount by which a person's monthly income exceeds the amount necessary for the reasonable domestic needs of himself and his family', Sch 4Z(2). The Insolvency Service Technical Manual states at para 46.33 that '[t]his is generally calculated using the Common Financial Statement which is an electronic form devised by the Money Advice Trust and created using data obtained from the Family Expenditure Survey (now called Costs and Food Survey [CFS]) produced by the Office for National Statistics. The form contains "trigger" points to show up areas where the debtor's expenses might exceed those considered normal and is accepted as a standard tool in the debt advice sector. It is the responsibility of the intermediary to ensure that the debtor's expenses do not exceed the trigger points. To maintain the integrity of the CFS, the levels of the trigger points are not widely circulated.' (https://www.insolvencydirect.bis.gov.uk/technicalmanual/Ch37-48/chapter46/Part%201/Part%201.htm#46.33)

The Common Financial Statement was first developed by the Money Advice Trust (a debt charity) and the British Bankers Association in November 2002. The Money Advice Trust is funded primarily by the private financial sector (66%) with some government contribution and self fundraising. See Money Advice Trust www.moneyadvicetrust.org/whoweare/Funding/Pages/default.aspx.

The Money Advice Service, a statutorily appointed body funded by government, has developed in association with financial institutions and debt advisors a 'Standard Financial Statement' which will be used from 2017 by all debt advisors funded by the agency and will replace the common financial statement. This standard will also use the Costs and Food Survey and 'Levels of expenditure observed among typical households within the bottom income quintile in the UK'. See Money Advice Service, *The Standard Financial Statement: A Consultation* (2014) and see Press Release: Standard Financial Statement, 'Money Advice Service announce start date for vital initiative to bring greater consistency to debt advice sector' (27 July, 2016) https://www.moneyadviceservice.org.uk/en/corporate/

pay for the service (£90) with £10 going to the approved intermediary.[153] Access is barred to individuals who have entered into a transaction at an undervalue or given a preference within the previous two years,[154] and debtor behaviour can be sanctioned through a DRO.[155] This continues the restrictions associated with an undischarged bankrupt after discharge for a period of 2 to 15 years. A debtor can only use the order once every six years. A debtor must inform the Insolvency Service of any change in their financial status, eg increase in income) during the one-year period.[156] The use of the term 'debt relief' rather than 'bankrupt' is intended to avoid the stigma of bankruptcy, which might deter some applicants.[157]

Table 3.2: Competent authorities, their intermediaries, and the volume of DRO applications, 2013–14

	intermediaries	applications
Advice UK	140 (8%)	827 (3%)
Baines & Ernst	7 (0%)	229 (1%)
Christians Against Poverty	7 (0%)	1,097 (4%)
Citizens Advice	1,337 (72%)	14,520 (53%)
Debt Release Direct	1 (0%)	120 (0%)
Insolvency Practitioners Association	2 (0%)	225 (1%)
Institute of Money Advisers	287 (16%)	3,703 (14%)
National Debtline	12 (1%)	1,227 (4%)
Payplan	12 (1%)	269 (1%)
Shelter	10 (1%)	40 (0%)
Stepchange Debt Charity	31 (2%)	4,962 (18%)
Think Money	5 (0%)	106 (0%)
Total	**1,851**	**27,329**

Source: Insolvency Service, Insolvency Proceedings: Debt Relief Orders and the Bankruptcy Petition Limit—Call for Evidence (2014) 5.

press-release-standard-financial-statement. Scotland has conferred statutory force on its use as the exclusive tool for determining surplus income. See Bankruptcy and Debt Advice (Scotland) Act 2014 asp 11 s 3.

153 The modest £10 fee to the intermediary is based on the assumption that the existence of the DRO saves the advisor's resources in negotiating with creditors.

154 The explanatory notes indicate that the rationale for this prohibition is 'to avoid a situation where the debtor has disposed of his assets in order to meet the permitted criterion for obtaining a debt relief order and to protect the position of creditors'.

155 A restriction order may be made either through the court or an undertaking by the debtor to the Insolvency Service. A broad discretion exists to make such an order where it is appropriate, and structured by a list of factors such as 'incurring, before the date of the determination of the application for the debt relief order, a debt which the debtor had no reasonable expectation of being able to pay'. See Sch 4ZB(2)(h).

156 Insolvency Act 1986. S251J(5).

157 This was proposed in a 2004 research paper on administration orders where the authors noted that 'some of the people we interviewed were very resistant to the idea of bankruptcy, and were deterred

The DRO, initially proposed by the Ministry of Justice, had the advantage of taking low-value cases out of the court system and transferring responsibility for the order to the Insolvency Service within the Department of Business. It was also promoted as reducing pressure on debt advice agencies such as Citizens Advice by providing a resolution for long-term debt clients and freeing up resources for other advice work.[158]

Preliminary research indicates that the majority of debtors are female[159] and many are sole parents. The majority are unemployed. They owe debts to central and local state creditors and public utilities as well as private creditors.[160] No systematic survey of the experience of debtors using the DRO has been conducted or the long-term outcomes of the DRO. However, a government review in 2014–15 gathered useful information from approved intermediaries and others on the effects of a DRO. The conclusion was that the 'current system is working well'.[161] Clients of intermediaries indicated that the DRO had improved their mental and physical health. The DRO also had a positive impact on a debtor's relationship with their family.[162] Sixty-one per cent of debtors in a non-random online survey indicated that they had not wished to access credit after the DRO, with one commenting that the experience of the DRO has 'taught them a lesson about borrowing in the future'.[163]

This remedy reflects a residual state role similar to a neo-liberal welfare model with the state providing means-tested relief to deserving debtors.

VII. The Great Recession and Personal Insolvency Law

The Great Recession and the payment protection insurance scandal had a significant impact on credit law, with the increased powers for the new Financial

by the stigma they would face given the relatively small sums of money they owed … A simplified debt procedure would therefore seem more appropriate for people on very low incomes that are unlikely to increase. This could be called something other than bankruptcy, to overcome the stigma that people feel and differentiate it from the full bankruptcy procedure. Kempson and Collard, *Managing Multiple Debts* (n 82) 76.

[158] Eg an advisor would no longer have to write a letter to a creditor every six months indicating that an individual client was still unemployed.

[159] Also in France, where 59% of debtors on *rétablissement personnel* are female.

[160] An early survey by the Insolvency Service noted that the profile of debtors accessing the DRO system was primarily 'low income, predominantly unemployed individuals with an average of six creditors; over 53% of debt was owed to banks, building societies and credit card companies'. See Insolvency Service, *DROs Initial Evaluation Report* (London, Insolvency Service, 2010). More informal data since the recession suggest that public creditors may now be more significant. See eg. A Pardo, J Lane, P Lane, and D Hertzberg, Citizens Advice, *Unsecured and Insecure* (Citizens Advice, 2015). This report argues at p 3 that over the past five years [since 2009] there has been a significant shift in problems 'away from mainstream credit issues towards problems with arrears on council tax, rent and energy bills. Five years ago, credit cards were the main debt issue we saw. Now council tax arrears top the list.'

[161] See Department of Business, Innovation and Skills, *Insolvency Proceedings: Debt Relief Orders and the Bankruptcy Petition Limit—Call for Evidence; Analysis of Responses* (London, DBIS, 2015).

[162] ibid 14. The Insolvency Service conducted a non-random survey. Of the respondents, 72% had been through the DRO process.

[163] ibid 18.

Conduct Authority, the development of norms of responsible mortgage lending, and the introduction of price controls on payday lending. It did not, however, stimulate any major rethinking of personal insolvency law. Protections were enhanced for over-indebted homeowners against foreclosure but not within the insolvency regime. The coalition government in 2011 conducted a consultation review of credit and insolvency regulation. It concluded that 'the overall view is that the current options [for debt relief] do provide a balance between debt write-off and relief and reasonable/fair levels of debt repayment … and while the current range of debt solutions is not seen as perfect, little strong evidence has been offered to suggest that a complete overhaul is required or would bring substantive benefit'.[164] Measures to make bank accounts more accessible to bankrupts were proposed to increase greater financial inclusion. In 2015 the Treasury appeared set to review the legal framework of debt administration but it is unlikely that any comprehensive review will transpire.[165]

VIII. Discussion

England and Wales presents a picture of public drifting and private conversion. Private professionals converted a statutory remedy designed for businesses into a mass-produced partial-repayment remedy for consumers, and a public and private over-indebtedness advice industry now flourishes. Government ministries concerned with reducing costs seek to keep consumer bankruptcy away from the courts, and neither judges nor lawyers demonstrate an interest in personal insolvency, as illustrated by the drifting public policy development of the administration order procedure.[166] The banks as long-term repeat players have been influential not only through their lobbying of MPs, government departments and specialist committees, but also through their political action in the IVA marketplace and influence over the use of appropriate living standards for debtors as enshrined in the common financial statement.

England and Wales, unlike France or Sweden, entered the 1980s to face the problem of the consumer debtor with existing methods of writing down debt, such as the administration order and the possibility of a bankruptcy discharge for non-traders. The failure to follow through with the Cork Committee reforms

164 See DBIS and Treasury, *Consumer credit and personal insolvency review: summary of responses on consumer credit and formal response on personal insolvency* (2011) paras 5.33, 5.47 https://www.gov.uk/government/uploads/system/uploads/attachment_data/file/31840/11-1063-consumer-credit-and-personal-insolvency-responses.pdf

165 See HM Treasury, *The Government's Response to the Independent Review of the Money Advice Service* (London, Treasury, 2015).

166 Michael Green suggested that if effective change was to come about then 'a locus within a trade-orientated ministry, rather than, say, justice, is desirable' (n 96) 415.

to the court-based administration order opened the door to the development of the mass-produced IVA. The process of development in England and Wales might be described as pragmatic adjustment, celebrating the ability of the law to meet the needs of a changing society. English insolvency law seems to have settled around an equilibrium of insolvency alternatives with few interest groups or ministries interested in substantial review or change. The policy preference for income repayments by consumers as a condition of obtaining debt relief with swift relief provided for a residual category of debtors under the DRO probably satisfies the interests of most policy actors. These preferences are supported by a contemporary public narrative of can pay should pay. This policy equilibrium is unlikely to change in the near future.

It is difficult to state whether this equilibrium is optimal, given the limited systematic knowledge of the operation of the insolvency system. Debtors can influence the system through their market choices (although behavioural economics might raise questions about the long-term rationality of these choices) but debtors have had little influence on policy development. The regulation of personal insolvency in the UK underlines the important role of policy communities and networks in the development of contemporary public governance. There are advantages to such communities which can draw on expertise and permit the development of trade-offs and consensus building, and provide legitimacy to any measures which emerge from working groups, committees and consultations. Legislative time can be saved. At the same time the tendency towards privatisation of policy making on topics such as the IVA reduces the transparency of policymaking where the often technical nature of the relevant knowledge may confer power on insiders and have results which are not necessarily in the public interest.

4

France: Contingency, the Role of Narratives, and the New *Droit Social*

C'était un peu la fin du monde, l'institution de quelque chose d'absolument nouveau et de juridiquement scandaleux: le droit à ne pas payer ses dettes.

Emmanuel Carrère, D'autres vies que la miènne (Paris, PL, 2009) 167[1]

I. Introduction

The French system of over-indebtedness regulation is remarkable for students of stability and changes in policy regimes. Since its introduction in 1989, changes have occurred in the goals of the system, the understanding of the nature of the problem addressed by the policy and the techniques adopted. A temporary law, intended to ensure effective recovery of debts has metamorphosed into a consumer insolvency law portrayed by some authors as an international model for the administration of over-indebtedness.[2] Over-indebtedness has become a field

[1] Describing the response of Étienne Rigal's professor at the National Judges College (École Nationale de Magistrature) to the passage of the loi Neiertz in 1989. 'It was almost the end of the world: the introduction of something completely new and legally outrageous: the right not to pay one's debts.'

[2] See eg London Economics, *Study on Means to Protect Consumers in Financial Difficulty: Personal bankruptcy, datio in solutum of mortgages and restrictions on debt collection abusive practices* (London, 2013) 190; J Kilborn, 'Still Chasing Chimeras but Finally Slaying Some Dragons in the Quest for Consumer Bankruptcy Reform' (2012) 25 *Loyola Consumer Law Review* 1; H Fraisse and P Froute, 'Household Debt Restructuring: Evidence from the French Experience' (Bank of France, Working Paper no 404, 2012) (stating at 1 that 'French … bankruptcy laws are theoretically considered close to optimum'). For accounts of the development of the French regime in English see J Kilborn, '*La Responsibilisation de l'Economie*: What the United States Can Learn from the New French Law on Consumer Overindebtedness' (2004–05) 25 *Michigan Journal of International Law* 619; I Ramsay, 'A Tale of Two Debtors: Responding to the Shock of Over-Indebtedness in France and England—A story from the trente piteuses' (2012) 75(2) *Modern Law Review* 212. For an excellent sociological account of the French system see S Plot, *Les enjeux d'une mise en risque. La construction du surendettement comme problème public (1989–2010)* (Thesis, University of Paris-Dauphine, 2011).

of law with its own distinct actors, institutions and constructions of debtors and creditors.[3]

The French developments illustrate several themes. The first is the institutional context of policymaking and administration and the role of French ministries and technocrats in attempting to cautiously and pragmatically reform the over-indebtedness system[4] before being disrupted in these efforts by a political intervention in 2003. The second theme is the construction of influential narratives about debtors that attempt to give meaning to over-indebtedness policy and administration. The state managed these narratives in France; the 'war of ideas' which characterised the US debates leading up to the Bankruptcy Abuse and Consumer Protection Act (BAPCPA) did not occur. Third, it reveals that an element of contingency exists concerning a central aspect of the French regime, the role of the Bank of France in the over-indebtedness system. Fourth, it shows that the French *Cour de Cassation* had to convert the 1989 law into a workable form, notwithstanding the official ideology that the court does not make law. Finally, there is the paradox of a law characterised by substantial local autonomy and difference—characteristics not associated with French administrative values of uniformity, hierarchy and expertise.

II. Over-indebtedness Regulation in Context

Treatment of over-indebtedness in France is part of the overall regulation of the French credit market. The institutional structure of French credit regulation is characterised by certain features:[5] limited credit data sharing of negative information through a register maintained by the central bank; detailed price ceilings on credit; limited possibilities for home equity lending; and relatively restrictive home mortgage lending criteria. These may contribute to the historically lower levels of household debt-to-income in France compared with other European countries, although France now has overtaken Germany in levels of household debt (Figure 4.1). At the same time, the lending practices of French banks (preferring those with long-term income security and family stability) mean that lower-income individuals borrow more from high-cost sources of revolving credit.[6]

[3] See discussion in L Lacan and J Lazarus, 'A Relationship and a Practice: On the French Sociology of Credit' (2015) MaxPo Discussion Paper No 15/1, 19.

[4] See M Prasad, *The Politics of Free Markets: The Rise of Neoliberal Economic Policies in Britain, France, Germany, and the United States* (Chicago, University of Chicago Press, 2006) ch 4, 275: 'The most prominent source of innovations in France … is the technocracy.'

[5] See further I Ramsay, 'Culture or Politics? Models of Consumer Credit Regulation in France and the UK' in T Wilson (ed), *International Responses to Issues of Credit and Over-Indebtedness in the Wake of Crisis* (Farnham, Ashgate, 2013) 80.

[6] Lacan and Lazarus, 'A Relationship and a Practice' (n 3) at 6 state that 'members of the working class use revolving credit to a greater extent … while, overall the use of credit is most common among middle-income families, cases in which consumer credit … is the only option used are primarily correlated with blue collar workers, non-managerial white collar workers, and female-headed single-parent households'.

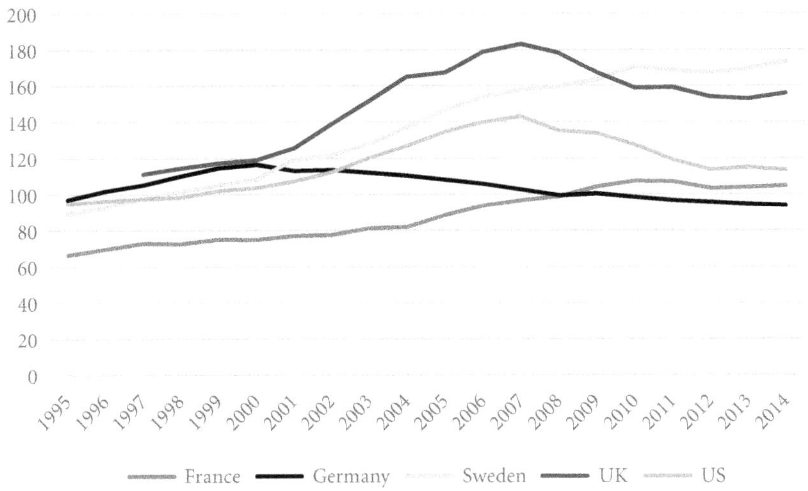

Figure 4.1: Household debt-to-income, selected countries, 1995–2014 (UK 1997–2014)
Source: OECD, National Accounts at a Glance: Household Debt to net disposable income.

These institutional barriers to credit extension might suggest a cultural distrust of credit as a potentially dangerous product and a concern for protection of individuals from the market rather than facilitating access to the market.[7] Gunnar Trumbull argues that this historical narrative of credit reflected a political coalition of conservative family pressure groups and the labour Left in France who distrusted credit as undermining workers' wages.[8] This coalition established a status quo that has placed a burden on market liberalisers.

Neo-liberalism and the idea of using private credit as a lever of growth, so-called 'privatised Keynesianism',[9] has however been influential in France notwithstanding stereotypical views of France as the representative of a 'social model'.[10] Vivien

[7] See eg A Chatriot, 'Protéger le consommateur contre lui-même: la régulation du crédit à la consommation' (2006) *Vingtième siècle. Revue d'histoire* 95. The English writer John Lanchester perceives 'an entirely different culture of money and borrowing and debt'. J Lanchester, *Whoops! Why Everyone Owes Everyone and No One Can Pay* (London, Penguin, 2010). 'The French tradition … protects the consumer against himself' and 'the majority of French society is distrustful of credit', C Taffin and B Vorms, *Élargir l'accès au crédit au logement des emprunteurs atypiques* (no page numbering) (Agence Nationale pour l'Information sur le Logement (ANIL), 2007).

[8] See G Trumbull, *Consumer Lending in France and America: Credit and Welfare* (Cambridge, Cambridge University Press, 2014).

[9] C Crouch, 'Privatised Keynesianism: An Unacknowledged Policy Regime?' (2009) 11(3) *British Journal of Politics & International Relations* 382.

[10] See F Denord, *Neo Liberalisme, Version Française* (Paris, Demopolis, 2007); S Audier, 'Is There a French Neoliberalism?' in R Geenens and H Rosenblatt (eds), *French Liberalism from Montesquieu to the Present Day* (Cambridge, Cambridge University Press, 2012); and discussion in M Prasad, 'Why is France so French? Culture Institutions and Neo liberalism, 1974–1981' (2005) 111 *American Journal of Sociology* 357. See generally B Amable, E Guillard, and S Palombarini, 'Changing French Capitalism: political and systemic crises in France' (2012) 19 *Journal of European Public Policy* 1168.

Schmidt describes French neo-liberalism as 'state managed' neo-liberalism,[11] with attempts in the 1970s, 1980s, and again in the early 2000s, to harness consumer credit as a vehicle of growth.[12] A government report in the early 1990s argued that the French were 'under-indebted'.[13] The government of Nicolas Sarkozy initially promoted a greater role for consumer credit in the economy, facilitating the use of home equity, for example, through the introduction of the *hypothèque rechargeable*. Jean Louis Borloo looked to the US 'fresh start' model of bankruptcy in justifying *faillite civile* in 2003. Reforms in 2005 eased strict regulation of offers of '*crédit gratuit*' (interest free credit). Nicolas Sarkozy, speaking as President of France, stated in 2008 to the UK Parliament that 'the UK has shown that there was a way in the global economy to attain strong growth, full employment and solidarity'.[14] The Great Recession of 2007–09, however, muted this admiration, so that by late 2008 Sarkozy stated: '*Laissez faire*, this is over. The almighty market which is always right, this is over.'[15] France emerged relatively unaffected by the sub-prime crisis with very low rates of housing repossession.[16] However, consumer credit may be increasingly being used to address stagnant wages and cutbacks in the social security system. The loi Lagarde of 2010 attempts to 'protect consumers without discouraging consumer credit', recognising that consumer credit is a useful method of budgeting and contributes to maintaining economic growth during a period of crisis. The changing nature of French capitalism since the 1980s and the tensions between neo-liberalism and 'the social' provides a backdrop to the approach to the treatment of over-indebtedness.

III. The Development of the Over-indebtedness Regime

In the 1980s the socialist Mitterand government in a *volte-face* began removing lending controls, inaugurated increased privatisation and liberalisation of the financial sector and permitted the existence of derivative markets.[17] The French household debt-to-income ratio increased from 35 per cent in 1984 to 47 per cent

[11] V Schmidt, 'French Capitalism Transformed, Yet Still a Third Variety of Capitalism' (2003) 32(4) *Economy and Society* 526.

[12] See I Rey-Lefebvre, 'La croissance par l'emprunt?' *Le Monde* (12 January 2004); C Mausson, 'Faut-il s'endetter plus?' *Libération* (13 June 2007). The Barres regime in the 1970s promoted new home ownership by subsidising borrowers rather than building more state housing. See discussion in P Bourdieu, *The Social Structure of the Economy* (Cambridge, Polity, 2005).

[13] J Bourdin, *Accès des ménages aux crédit en France* (London, Senate, 2006).

[14] Speech before two houses of Parliament UK, London (26 March 2008).

[15] Nicolas Sarkozy, 25 September 2008, Discours de Toulon quoted in Amable, Guillard, and Palombarini, 'Changing French Capitalism' (n 10) 1183.

[16] See discussion in W Schelkle, 'A Crisis of What? Mortgage Credit Markets and the Social Policy of Promoting Homeownership in the United States and Europe' (2012) 40 *Politics & Society* 59.

[17] See discussion in B Eichengreen, *The European Economy since 1945: Co-ordinated Capitalism and Beyond* (Princeton, Princeton University Press, 2007) ch 11; G Gloukoviezoff, *L'exclusion Bancaire* (Paris, Presse Universitaire, 2010) 58–60.

in 1989—a significant increase, although substantially less than the increase in the UK.[18] The French Economic and Social Council mentioned the topic of over-indebtedness for the first time in 1983. Trumbull argues that the French banks embraced the new freedom to lend directly to consumers but blundered in this initial foray, making poor risk assessments and incurring substantial bad debts.[19]

Consumer credit legislation in France had been modernised in 1978 by the loi Scrivener, inspired partly by the English Consumer Credit Act 1974, focusing on pre-contractual information obligations and cooling-off periods. Further concerns about impulsive purchasing on credit resulted in strict regulation of offers of 'free credit' in 1984.[20] In 1985, the government also prohibited charging any fee for debt management services,[21] thereby preventing the rise of private debt management companies.

Consumer credit was increasingly being used to compensate for pressures on purchasing power. However, the effects of disinflation (from 13 per cent in 1981 to 3 per cent in 1988) on progressively increasing mortgage repayments for new homes in the suburbs which were losing value—a French mini sub-prime crisis related to the neo-liberal policies of the Barres government—provided the trigger for public action.[22] In 1989, there was no bankruptcy law in France which provided a discharge of debts. Limited provisions did exist in the civil code permitting the rescheduling of debts. However, in 1877 during the occupation of Alsace-Moselle the German government had introduced German bankruptcy law in the region.[23] When this area was reoccupied by France after the First World War, French civil and commercial law were reintroduced. However, certain local laws including bankruptcy law were retained, and in 1924 the commercial law on *faillite civile* was extended locally to non-traders, ultimately permitting in 1985 a discharge of debts by a process not dissimilar to Anglo-Saxon insolvency procedures. The law retained different entry criteria for traders and non-traders: the latter were required to demonstrate *insolvabilité notoire*, interpreted by the courts as 'irremediably compromised'. This law would play a significant symbolic role in subsequent French policy development.

Consumer groups supported the introduction of *faillite civile* as a response to the perceived problem of over-indebtedness. The Consumer Ministry proposed

[18] The UK debt-to-income ratio grew from 21% in 1981 to 68% in 1988. See National Consumer Council, *Credit and Debt: The Consumer Interest* (London, TSO, 1990) Table III.7.

[19] See Trumbull, *Consumer Lending* (n 8).

[20] See now L 311-27 Code de la Consommation.

[21] Ibid L321-1.

[22] See discussion in V Vigneau and G-X Bourin, *Droit du surendettement des particuliers* (Paris, Lexis Nexis, 2007) 3–4; Kilborn, 'What the United States Can Learn' (n 2) 626. For discussion of the decrease in job security and increased unemployment see L Boltanski and E Chiapello, *Le nouvel esprit du capitalisme*, tel edition (Paris, Gallimard, 2011). The Hyest and Loridant report (J-J Hyest and P Loridant, *Rapport d'information no 60: Surendettement Prévenir et Guérir* (Sénat Français Paris, 1997)) describes the problematic effects of disinflation on the mortgages. For a full discussion of the context see Bourdieu, *Social Structure of the Economy* (n 12).

[23] See discussion in D Dagorne, 'La faillite civile en Alsace et Moselle' in M Gardaz (ed), *Le surendettement des particuliers* (Paris, Anthropos, 1997) 39.

in 1988 the extension of *faillite civile* as a general remedy for over-indebted consumers. Attention was also drawn to the 'fresh start' model of US bankruptcy law.[24] *Faillite civile* was immediately rejected by the more powerful Ministry of Finance, concerned about its impact on the banking sector. The credit industry also organised opposition to the introduction of *faillite civile*. With a new government in 1989, Veronique Neiertz, the socialist Consumer Minister acting as a policy entrepreneur, mobilised a media campaign with claims that there were more than 200,000 over-indebted consumers. Neiertz rejected the possibility of *faillite civile* as too costly and stigmatising, leading to social exclusion and undermining payment morality and the sanctity of promises in French civil law. The objective of the 1989 law was precisely to avoid social exclusion by permitting debtors to exit from a 'spiral which leads to … social exclusion'.[25] She canvassed foreign solutions such as the US Chapter 13 and repayment programmes in Quebec[26] but concluded that the US straight discharge procedure was too extreme and that it would be economically and socially costly. According to Neiertz, Anglo-Saxon ideas were not directly transplantable. New concepts adapted for French law and the French *mentalité* were necessary.[27] But the Ministry of Consumer Affairs did not have the resources to introduce a new mechanism to aid over-indebted consumers. An out-of-court conciliation procedure was proposed which would permit individuals to come to an agreement with their creditors to reschedule their debts over a period of time, initially 10 years.[28] This would not only prevent a 'spiral into social exclusion' but would also avoid placing further burdens on an overloaded court system. But who would conciliate and administer the procedure?

The law[29] established over-indebtedness commissions in each department, presided over by the prefect, which was the political representative of the central state. It was comprised initially of representatives of public administration creditors and a representative of consumer and financial institutions, with Bank of France employees acting as the secretariat. Since 2003 the commissions have also included a lawyer and social worker. The Bank of France was considered ideal for this role

[24] For an account of the interest groups involved in the original French law see D Salomon, 'Quand une politique Publique en cache une autre … La Loi Neiertz comme réponse politique et acte opportuniste des organes de tutelle' in Gardaz, *Le surendettement des particuliers* (n 23) 13.

[25] Présentation de la loi du 31 décembre 1989 par le secretaire d'État à la consommation (Brochure DGCCRF 1990).

[26] See the Loi Lacombe in Quebec. Neiertz visited Quebec to understand the operation of the programme.

[27] Projet de loi du 5 septembre 1989.

[28] Reduced in 2010 to eight years and from 2016 to seven years.

[29] Loi no 89-1010 du 31 décembre 1989 relative à la prévention et au règlement des difficultés liées au surendettement des particuliers et des familles. The current provisions are now located in Book III, Title III of the Code de la Consommation. For official background see L Lamier, *Projet de la loi relatif à la prévention et au règlement des difficultés liées à l'endettement des particuliers* Avis no 43 (1989–90); J Simonin (1989–90) *Rapport no 40* (Commission des Affaires Économiques, Paris). The creation of the over-indebtedness commissions was part of a consumer protection package that included the introduction of a register of individuals making application to the new over-indebtedness commissions and a modernisation of usury laws.

since it already had offices in each department that could provide the physical site for conciliation. It could also provide legitimacy for the commissions when dealing with financial institutions.

Why would a central bank take on such a role—a unique role worldwide for a central bank? Several explanations have been put forward. Danielle Salomon argues that the law provided an opportunity for more powerful groups, such as the Ministry of Finance, to achieve prudential goals by monitoring more closely the lending practices of banks that had not properly assessed the risks of expansion in the consumer credit market. Second, more cynically, there was the issue of surplus staff due to bank restructuring. French labour laws provided strong redundancy protection and employment on over-indebtedness could avoid confrontations with the labour unions. However, a further factor was an overarching assumption in the Bank of France that this was a temporary function. Indeed the initial law was described as 'experimental', with a requirement to report on its operation within two years. This overcame the Bank's reluctance to take on this role.[30] The Bank has therefore become locked into a role which it did not really want and which does not carry high status within the bank. However by 2010, 12 per cent of the Bank's personnel (1,570 employees) were involved in processing over-indebtedness dossiers.

The over-indebtedness regime was modified in 1995, 1998, 2003, 2007, 2010, 2013, and 2014—a remarkable number of changes for this area of law—primarily to liberalise relief and to reduce the costs associated with judicial processing of debt cases. It has also been characterised by a large number of parliamentary and committee reports[31] and its implementation by several regulations, decrees and circulars. The initial 1989 law was not at all similar to an insolvency procedure and was not intended to permit the discharge of debts but, rather, to facilitate repayment through negotiation.[32] There was no automatic stay of creditors' actions while an application was being considered and the property of the debtor did not pass to a trustee. The legislation provided little guidance on the ground rules for conciliation, such as the relative priority of debts.[33] The commissions could determine the

[30] Based on correspondence with a senior employee of the Bank of France.

[31] See eg R Leron, *Rapport sur l'application de la loi no 89-1010 du 31 decembre 1989 relative a la prevention et au reglement des difficultes liees au surendettement des particuliers et des familles* (Paris, Senat, 1991); Hyest and Loridant, *Rapport d'information no 60* (n 22); J-C Le Duigou, *Rapport sur l'endettement et surendettement des ménages*. Avis et rapports du Conseil Économique (Paris, La documentation française, 2000); JJ Hyest, *Projet de loi d'orientation et de programmation pour la ville et la rénovation urbaine*. Avis no 404 (2002–03) (Paris, Sénat, 2002–2003); G Canivet, *Rapport du comité de suivi de l'application des dispositions relatives au surendettement de la loi no 2003-710 du 1er août 2003* (Paris, Cour de Cassation, 2005); Le Médiateur de la Republique, *Le malendettement, nouvelle urgence sociale* (Paris, 2006); Conseil Économique et Social, *Le surendettement des particuliers* (Paris, 2007); Cour des Comptes, *La lutte contre le surendettement des particuliers; une politique publique incomplete et insuffisante pilotee* (Paris, Cour des Comptes, 2010); M Dini and A-M Escoffier, *Crédit à la consommation et surendettement: une réforme ambitieuse à completer* (2011–12 Senate Report no 602).

[32] It is misleading therefore to describe the 1989 Act as introducing 'a civil personal bankruptcy procedure in France'. Trumbull, *Consumer Lending* (n 8) 201.

[33] Certain debts were excluded from a plan: alimentary debts (see Code Civil arts 203, 205, 207 and Code de l'action sociale et des familles art L132-6), reparations for crimes, and criminal fines. L 333-1. Fiscal debts were privileged until 2003.

priority and amount of repayment, taking into account the conduct of the creditor in granting the loan so that irresponsible lending could be sanctioned.[34]

The Commission, rather than the courts, now dominates the French system, providing a free 'one-stop shop' for debtors which ranges from moratoria, through repayment plans typically lasting five years, to the possibility of a discharge of debts. Discharge through *rétablissement personnel* for individuals who are 'irremediably compromised'[35] now permits the Commission, since 2010, to recommend an immediate discharge without any process of liquidation: the courts merely provide formal approval. The treatment of over-indebtedness has become a legal field.

A. The Phases of French Reforms: From Debt Repayment to Debt Discharge[36]

Figure 4.2 indicates the relentless rise in the number of individuals using the over-indebtedness commissions since their introduction in 1990. Many potential reasons exist for this increase, such as increased credit, increased uncertainty in employment and so on. French policymakers view the increase as a problem since it suggests that the general over-indebtedness policy of reducing those in default is failing. Figure 4.3 indicates the decline of the conciliated plan which normally lasts five years and the rise of imposed plans and, since 2003, the *rétablissement personnel* procedure which permits a full discharge of unsecured debts. This last procedure, intended to be a subsidiary procedure of last resort, is now the most common remedy.

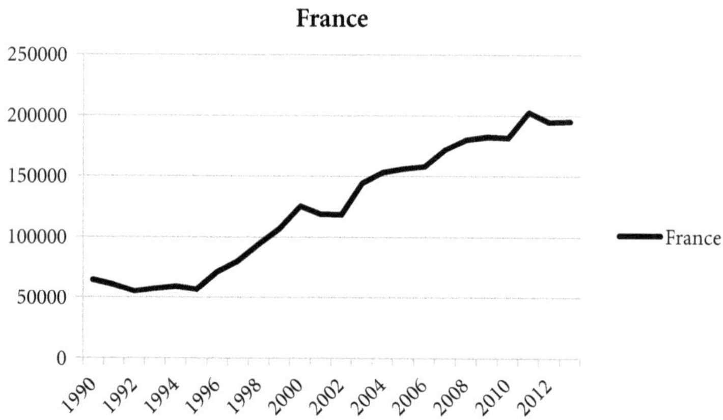

Figure 4.2: Applications to the Overindebtedness Commission, 1990–2013
Source: Bank of France.

[34] L 331-7. See for example Civ 1er 24 February 1993 D 1993, where the court wrote down the deficiency on the forced sale of a home on the basis that the creditor must have known that the debtor was at high risk of financial difficulties.

[35] Generally the inability to develop a repayment plan, including the possibility of some writedown of debt, within eight years (seven years from 2016). It is not necessary to have no repayment capacity. See Cass 2e civ, 22 May 2008, *Revue de Droit Bancaire et Financier* No 6, November–December 2008, 49.

[36] See generally Plot, *Les enjeux d'une mise en risque* (n 1) ch 2.

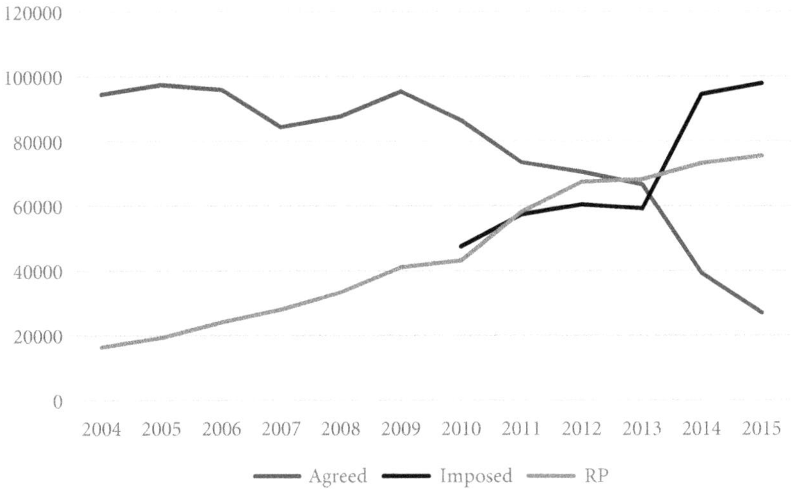

Figure 4.3: Agreed and imposed repayment plans and *rétablissement personnel*, 2004–15
Source: Bank of France, Statistics on activities of Overindebtedness Commissions https://www.banque-france.fr/fileadmin/user_upload/banque_de_france/La_Banque_de_France/statistiques-commissions-surendettement-2015.pdf (imposed from 2004).

From 1990 French policymaking cautiously moved towards the possibility of a debtor obtaining a discharge of debts. Drawing on a legitimating narrative that many debtors had little repayment capacity, the 1998 reforms introduced the possibility of a commission entering a moratorium of two years for those who were permanently insolvent and at the end of this period writing down some or all of the debts under an 'extraordinary' procedure. However, government reports throughout the 1990s continued to reject the introduction of *faillite civile* as a solution. The Hyest and Loridant report in 1997 concluded that *faillite civile* was a false solution likely to lead to fraud by debtors and excessive costs.[37]

The 2003 loi Borloo, however, layered onto the existing debt adjustment law an insolvency procedure with liquidation of assets, supervision by a trustee and a discharge. *Faillite civile* was transplanted internally, with some minor modifications, to the rest of France. Described as *rétablissement personnel* to distinguish it from the negative associations of *faillite civile* it permitted the possibility of the discharge of all debts if an individual was 'irremediably compromised', incorporating the test from the initially rejected Alsace-Moselle law.[38] This reform is difficult to explain given that the Consultative Committee on Credit, which includes financial, consumer, labour and family groups[39] had concluded in 2002 that the

[37] Hyest and Loridant, *Rapport d'information no 60* (n 22).

[38] Defined as the 'manifest impossibility of putting in place treatment (repayment) measures'. *Code de la consommation* (Consolidated Version, 2016) L724-1 available at https://www.legifrance.gouv.fr/affichCode.do;jsessionid=9BE150823077EBBF8F0CE9965774D177.tpdila18v_3?cidTexte=LEGITEXT000006069565&dateTexte=20161115.

[39] Comité Consultatif du Conseil National du Crédit et du Titre, *Rapport 2002–2003*, 43 et seq.

1998 reforms, properly applied by the commissions, would adequately address the problems of individuals with little or no repayment capacity. Some consumer groups on the Committee had proposed the introduction of *faillite civile*,[40] but neither the Justice Ministry nor the Economics Ministry had wished to introduce further legislation.

The issue of over-indebtedness was foregrounded in the election of 2002 after the high-profile story of *Les Époux Cartier*.[41] An over-indebted couple with overwhelming credit card debts had attempted to kill their five children and then commit suicide. This focused substantial media attention on over-indebtedness. Jean Luis Borloo, although a Minister in the Union pour la Majorité Presidentielle (UMP) and on the right of the political spectrum, was a populist, and his ministry was the social window of the conservative Raffarin government. He was also a corporate lawyer with experience and knowledge of US insolvency law,[42] and he was critical of what he termed the sclerotic nature of the French state and the world of the *Énarques* (the technocratic elites in the various ministries). His Ministry was outside the traditional ministry structure and the over-indebtedness policy community dominated by Bercy (Economy and Finance) and the Ministry of Justice. Sebastien Plot argues that Borloo wanted the high-profile media benefits of being seen to introduce a 'new procedure', doing something for the 'ordinary hard working person'.[43] Armed with evidence that *faillite civile* in Alsace appeared to be effective and did not result in recidivism by debtors, Borloo argued that a discharge of debts existed in the US, and France was out of line with modern developments. With support from the judges' association, the promise that the procedure would not overrun the courts, and the approval of President Sarkozy, his draft rather than Bercy's was enacted by Parliament in a package of measures on social solidarity and social exclusion directed at the *quartiers sensibles* and *quartiers difficiles*, which are sites of substantial social exclusion.[44] He also succeeded in reducing the preferential status of the tax authorities in over-indebtedness procedures, a reform traditionally opposed by the Ministry of Finance. An outsider had, at least in the short term, ousted the traditional policy community on over-indebtedness.

The parliamentary reports on the Bill justified the law by the supposed 'new face' of over-indebtedness, with an increase in passive over-indebtedness,[45] the

[40] 'Faillite civile: les consommateurs font pression sur le gouvernement' *Les Echos* (4 February 2003) 20.

[41] See 'L'affaire des époux Cartier' *La Croix* (29 August 2002). The couple were subsequently charged and imprisoned. P Robert-Diard, 'Les dérives d'un couple, du surendettement à l'infanticide' *Le Monde* (19 October 2005). The following section draws on Plot's account (n 1).

[42] Plot, *Les enjeux d'une mise en risque* (n 1) 111–18.

[43] See Plot, *Les enjeux d'une mise en risque* (n 1) 112.

[44] 'Les professionnels s'accommodent de la procédure de rétablissement personnel' *Les Echos* (7 August 2003).

[45] See Hyest, *Avis de M Jean-Jacques Hyest, au nom de la commission des lois, no 404* (Paris, Senate, 2002–2003).

need to fight social exclusion,[46] along with the newly discovered virtues of the Alsace-Moselle law. The Senate report emphasised however the subsidiary nature of *rétablissement personnel.* It was 'an escape hatch for the most desperate cases and should only be instituted if the traditional methods of addressing over-indebtedness were impracticable or their operation would be clearly destined to fail'.[47] Bankruptcy law for consumers was, therefore, introduced for consumers without using the term bankruptcy.

Some commentators were not convinced that the 2003 law represented in substance a large difference from a purposive application of the 1998 law and noted that a liquidation of assets procedure might be detrimental for debtors. The Ministry of Justice, feeling that it had been dispossessed of the Bill by Borloo, had managed to insert the requirement that an individual be 'irremediably compromised' before using the law—a more extreme state than the definition of 'insolvency' in the 1998 amendments—which would therefore limit its scope. The creation by the law of different entry requirements for a conventional repayment plan which promised a partial write-down of debts and access to *rétablissement personnel* rendered the law more complex,[48] and legal commentators relished pointing out the *volte-face* on the *faillite civile* procedure, described in 1989 as stigmatizing and leading to social exclusion,[49] but now lauded as effective and a positive model for France.

The commissions acted as initial gatekeeper to the new process, but the courts returned to centre stage in opening and supervising the insolvency. Contrary to Borloo's promises, the new procedure resulted in a 20 per cent increase in the work of the courts, with delays, and significant costs borne by the state.[50] The Canivet Commission concluded in 2005 that the new procedure was too cumbersome, had often been restrictively interpreted by lower courts, and had not provided the expected benefits.[51] As a consequence of this report in 2007,[52] amendments were made enabling a judge to close the insolvency procedures immediately if it was clear that the individual had no assets.

[46] *Avis No 405 de M Éric Doligé, fait au nom de la Commission des finances, du contrôle budgétaire et des comptes économiques de la Nation (2002–2003)* (Paris, Commission des Finances). See also E Sander, 'La faillite civile: l'experience alsacienne, un succes' *Les Echos* (28 May 2003).The 2009 Annual Report of the Cour de Cassation comments that 'Because the profile of over-indebted debtors has changed, the objectives of the over-indebtedness procedure evolves. The social dimension and a concern to integrate it within a more global fight against exclusion, assuring social cohesion, takes precedence over the purely procedural aspects' (translation by the author). Rapport Annuel Cour De Cassation, *Les personnes vulnérables dans la jurisprudence de la Cour de cassation, Contributions de la deuxième chambre civile de la Cour de cassation* (Paris, 2009) 146.

[47] Hyest report (n 45).

[48] See discussion in G Paisant, 'La réforme de la procedure de traitement du surendettement par la loi du 1er août 2003 sur la ville et la rénovation urbaine' (2003) *Revue trimestrielle de droit commercial* 671, 673.

[49] See Decl Neiertz in Journal Officiel Sénat (CR) 31 October 1989, 2833, quoted in Paisant, 'La réforme de la procedure' (n 48) 673.

[50] See the Canivet review, *Rapport du comité* (n 31).

[51] ibid.

[52] Loi no 2007–1787 2007 inserting a new art L.332-6-1 into the *Code de la Consommation.*

In 2010 the loi Lagarde introduced a further package of reforms to credit and over-indebtedness regulation, as part of the implementation of the EU 2008 Credit Directive.[53] These included measures to reduce the costs of *rétablissement personnel* and ensure easier re-entry of the debtor to the credit market.[54] In nearly all cases courts will only be involved if this is required to provide formal approval of commission decisions to write off debts or impose a *rétablissement personnel*.[55] Repayment plans are limited to eight years, and an individual is listed on the public *fichier* for five rather than eight years. An individual may be provided with social or budgetary advice.[56] In addition, those who are over-indebted will not be deprived of access to bank accounts. Further reforms in 2013 and 2014 reduced the length of plans to seven years and encouraged greater cooperation between public housing agencies, social agencies such as the *Caisses d'allocations familiales*, and the commissions.[57] The French procedures now resemble more closely an Anglo-Saxon insolvency with an automatic stay on creditors' actions on acceptance of a dossier and freezing of interest from the date of confirmation. Many of these reforms responded to criticisms of, for example, the limited assistance provided to debtors when dealing with the Commission. This suggests a 'social learning' rather than a 'social power' approach to policymaking. However the French reforms also reflect the significance of political context where Borloo, a maverick and charismatic minister, with the backing of the President and a majority in Parliament, was able to enact a significant change—the introduction of *rétablissement personnel*—over the opposition of the technocracy and financial interests, represented by Bercy.

IV. Legitimating Narratives: From Active to Passive Debtor to …?

A valuable aspect of the French system are the official statistics of the Bank of France on the demographics of the users of the over-indebtedness commissions

[53] Directive 2008/48/EC on credit agreements for consumers; loi no 2010-737 2010 (Journal Officiel 2 juill).

[54] For a summary of the reforms see V Vigneau and A Lauriat, 'La réforme du droit du surendettement des particuliers par la loi du 1er juillet 2010' (2010) 39 *Receuil Dalloz Chroniques* 2593–2602.

[55] L 331-7 and L331-7-1. Béguery claims that 80% of plans are now confirmed by the courts. See M Béguery, 'Le dispositif de traitement des situations de surendettement des particuliers: les principaux effet de la loi Lagarde' (2010) *Bulletin de la Banque de France* (No 182).

[56] See L 331-3.

[57] See Circulaire 22 Jul 2014 Ministre des Finance et des Comptes Publics, *Circulaire relative a la procedure de traitement des situations de surendettement des particuliers*; Ministry of Justice, *Circulaire du 12 mars 2014 de présentation des dispositions de la loi no 2013-672 du 26 juillet 2013 de séparation et de régulation des activités bancaires relatives au traitement des situations de surendettement et du décret no 2014-190 du 21 février 2014 relatif aux procédures de traitement des situations de surendettement des particuliers.*

and the reasons for over-indebtedness. Table 4.1 indicates the socio-professional categories of debtors[58] applying to the commissions between 1990 and 2007 and Table 4.2 illustrates the demographics since 2010.

Table 4.1: Socio-professional category of applicants to Overindebtedness Commission, 1990–2007

	1990	2001	2004	2007	2007 (rp)	2007 France
Artisans, self-employed		0.3	0.3	0.3	0.3	7.5
High-level manager		1.1	1.1	1.0	0.3	13.1
Technician and associated professionals	8	3	2.3	2.1	0.9	16.1
Employees	27	31	32.6	31.7	23.7	11.6
Manual Worker	27	24	22.3	21.2	14.1	22.2
Retired	3	8	8.0	8.0	11.4	24.2
Others	5	2				
Unemployed and inactive	30	32	34	35.7	49.3	

Source: Bank of France, *Enquête Typologiques, rp=rétablissement personnel*, Insée. An analysis of French socio-occupational categories can be found at A Desrosières, 'Socio-occupational categories', http://www.insee.fr/fr/ffc/docs_ffc/cse15b.pdf.

Table 4.2: Socio-professional categories of applicants, 2010–13

	2010	2011	2012	2013	rp 2013	France 2012
Artisans, self-employed	0.4	0.4	0.4	0.4	0.3	4.4
High level managers	1.0	1.0	1.1	1.0	0.3	9.6
Technicians and associated professionals	2.6	2.8	2.9	2.8	2.7	13.3
Employees	33.8	35.1	35.7	34.8	27.8	16.0
Manual workers	24.1	24.5	24.8	25.1	22.7	12.4
Inactive having worked	10.7	10.9	10.0	9.8	9.7	26.5
Others without a professional activity	27.5	25.3	25.0	26.1	37.8	17.7

Source: Bank of France, Insée. *rp=rétablissement personnel.*

[58] The classifications are based on French methods of classifying socio-economic position. See C Brousse, 'ESeC: The European Union's Socio-Economic Classification Project' (2009) 15 *Courrier des Statistiques* 27, 29.

Debtors are not representative of the French population. Skilled and unskilled blue-collar workers (ouvriers) are now over-represented as are white collar female employees who dominate the category of *employé* in France.[59] Unemployed and economically inactive individuals are disproportionately represented compared with the general population. In 2012, 26 per cent of debtors were unemployed. Almost 80 per cent of debtors rent rather than own, in a country with a home ownership rate of approximately 65 per cent.[60] They receive significantly more state support than the general population. Single persons, including divorced and separated individuals are over-represented, as are women, particularly in the *rétablissement personnel* category. In 2004, 31 per cent of debtors had no repayment capacity; in 2013, 54 per cent had no repayment capacity and 71 per cent less than €250 per month. Although this change in payment capacity may be partly explained by an increase in the determination of their ability to make repayments (the so-called '*reste à vivre*'), the French debtors do not appear to fit the middle-class image of the US bankrupt, although they are not all poor.[61]

The conventional wisdom in official documents in France is that there has been a change in the profile of debtors and reasons for over-indebtedness since the early 1990s. Initially used by middle-class debtors who had over committed themselves on housing loans, individuals in a more precarious economic position now use the process. The early phase from 1990 to 1993 was associated with the phenomenon of homeowners suffering negative equity and being unable to maintain mortgage repayments. First-time homebuyers were over-represented among applicants to the commissions in the early 1990s.[62] In 1992, three reasons were identified for over-indebtedness: a home loan (41 per cent); consumer credit (55 per cent) and insufficient income (11 per cent).[63]

The Duigou report in 2000 summarised the changes in the nature of over-indebtedness, including the feminisation of over-indebtedness:

> [I]n the early 1990s, the indebtedness of households affected more frequently those in the middle life cycle, fairly large households, usually economically active—while

[59] See Institut national de la statistique et des études économiques (INSEE) socio-professional categories, http://www.insee.fr/fr/methodes/default.asp?page=nomenclatures/pcs2003/n1_5.htm.

[60] Some uncertainty existed in jurisprudence as to whether a homeowner could take advantage of the loi Neiertz on the theory that debtors were not over-indebted if they could sell the home and after deducting the costs of rehousing repay their debts. This approach was often not followed by commissions and some courts. The 2010 law clarifies that being a homeowner does not prevent an individual being characterised as over-indebted. See art L330-1.

[61] Further investigation into an individual's route into bankruptcy might reveal more about the individual's social status. Compare the profile of individuals in *rétablissement personnel* with those using the English debt relief order (see ch 3 above).

[62] Hyest and Loridant, *Rapport d'Information no 60* (n 22) 3 (38% to 20% in the general population).

[63] See E Leser, 'Le rapport annuel du comité des usagers: La loi sur le surendettement est inefficace pour régler les problèmes des faibles revenues' *Le Monde* (4 August 1992). The 1997 Senate report identified the effects of liberalised measures intended to increase homeownership in France as one cause for increased recourse to the over-indebtedness commissions. These included variable rate mortgages which increased over time; a variety of loans which qualified for a housing deposit [PAP], undercutting the need for a real financial contribution by the borrower; and subsidies to the purchase of new

individuals with more modest incomes, people suffering exclusion, without access to bank credit, were rather less prominent …

More recent work [indicates] individuals with limited qualifications, and larger risks of unemployment who have recently suffered from a sharp degradation of their financial situation and have also had to face unexpected expenses which they cannot manage with their current budget so that … use of an overdraft is the only solution. … Over-indebtedness seems to occur more and more to single parents … with two or three children … Women are most often affected.[64]

Studies of debtors' dossiers by the Bank of France drew a distinction between 'active' and 'passive' over-indebtedness[65] and documented a change from overspending (active indebtedness) to passive indebtedness caused by circumstances outside the control of the debtor. A standard legal text indicates that a law originally enacted to address individual debt mismanagement (see Table 4.3) now addresses individuals in a more marginal position and that the regime has moved from treating active to passive over-indebtedness.[66] This active/passive distinction has played a crucial narrative role in justifying the liberalisation of the conditions for discharging debt. First, passive over-indebtedness allocated responsibility for over-indebtedness to external conditions beyond the debtor's control. It absolved both creditor and debtor groups for responsibility and provided common ground between creditor and consumer groups. The former could argue that it was external circumstances subsequent to credit granting which had caused over-indebtedness. The French bankers association used this argument in 2013 to oppose a proposal that they should contribute to financing the over-indebtedness commissions.[67] Conceptualising themselves as victims of exogenous events such as unemployment and pointing to their support for the work of the over-indebtedness commissions, the

homes which artificially inflated their prices but made them difficult to sell. For a full discussion of the sociology of this era of housing development see Bourdieu, *Social Structure of the Economy* (n 12).

[64] Duigou, *Rapport sur l'endettement et surendettement des ménages* (n 31) 69–70. See also B Bertrand, *Le Monde* (16 February 2002): 'En dix ans, la pauvrete est devenue la premiere cause du surendettement; Familles monoparentales ou celibataires, chomeurs ou bas revenus: le profil sociologique des personnes criblees de dettes a evolue depuis le vote de la loi Neiertz, en 1989. Parmi ses causes, l'usage compulsif du credit a peu a peu cede la place aux accidents de la vie.' (In ten years, poverty has become the primary cause of overindebtedness; single individuals or one parent families, the unemployed and low income: the social profile of overindebted individuals has evolved since the loi Neiertz in 1989. Credit overextension has given way to accidents of life as the main cause of overindebtedness.)

[65] The distinction between active and passive over-indebtedness originates in the Comité Consultatif Rapport du Groupe de Travail sur l'endettement et le surendettement des ménages (July 1989) and a report in that document by L Arondel and D Kessler.

[66] See F Ferrière and P-L Chatain, *Surendettement des Particuliers*, 3rd edn (Paris, Dalloz, 2006).

[67] See Response of the French Banking Federation to the 2013 report of the Cour des Comptes. 'Cette proposition est particulièrement surprenante et peu compréhensible après l'analyse du surendettement par la Cour qui montre pourtant que ce phénomène est pour l'essentiel une consequence d'événements sociaux, économiques et personnels extérieurs et postérieurs à l'octroi de credit' ('This proposal is particularly surprising and difficult to understand given the analysis by the Cour which demonstrates however that this phenomenon is primarinly a consequence of economic, social and personal events subsequent to the granting of credit'). Cour des comptes, *La lutte contre le surendettement des particuliers: des progrès encore trop limités*, Annual Report 2013, 260–61.

banking association argued that it would be unjust for them to contribute to the cost of the commissions. As a social problem it was properly the responsibility of the state. Consumer groups, comprised often of labour and family pressure groups, argued that the increases represented failures in the French social safety nets and employment protections.[68]

Table 4.3: Principal causes of over-indebtedness, 1990 (percentage)

Excess of debt without modification of resources	48
Unemployment	24
Illness	4
Separation or death	9
Loss of reduction in social subsidies	2
Other	13

Source: Bank of France, 1990.

Table 4.4: Principal causes of over-indebtedness 2001–07 (Bank of France)

		2001	**2004**	**2007**	**2007 (rp)**
ACTIVE	Too much credit	19.4%	14.6%	13.6%	5.4%
	Poor management	7.7%	6.4%	6%	2.4%
	Housing costs	3.1%	1.2%	1.2%	0.9%
	Excess charges	2.2%	1.4%	1.3%	1%
PASSIVE	Unemployment/ job loss	26.5%	30.8%	31.8%	32%
	Separation/ divorce	15.5%	14.7%	14.7%	14.5%
	Accident/illness	9.1%	10.8%	11.3%	18.8%
	Lowered resources	6.9%	6.2%	6.2%	7.3%
	Death	2.5%	2.4%	2.5%	3.6%
	Other	7.1%	11.5%	11.4%	14.1%
	Total	100%	100%	100%	100%

Source: Bank of France, *Enquètes Typologiques.*
Note: rp=*rétablissement personnel.*

[68] S Plot, 'Du Flambeur au Victime? (From Big-Time Gambler to Victim): Vers une problématisation consensuelle du surendettement' (2009) *Sociétés Contemporaines* 67, 82.

French official reports and documents repeatedly draw on the active/passive distinction, using the passive debtor model to justify greater leniency of treatment for debtors.[69] Laure Lacan and Jeanne Lazarus note the instrumental use of these categories in the administration of over-indebtedness policy so that the actively indebted 'should be forgiven and helped', while the passive debtor represents the 'contemporary incarnation of the deserving poor'.[70] Notwithstanding the limited nature of these essentialising typologies, they continue to influence policymaking.

The active/passive dichotomy seems an elegant dichotomy but a cursory reflection reveals its oversimplification of the reasons for over-indebtedness. There may often be a combination of circumstances. Individuals may experience an exogenous shock such as divorce but then try to maintain a lifestyle through credit, hoping that their situation will improve. Does one classify this as active or passive over-indebtedness? It may often be difficult for those making the classification to allocate a single reason for the over-indebtedness, and classifications may reflect the approach or ideology of the individuals making the classification.[71] Sebastien Plot suggests that employees of the Bank of France preferred to use a passive category rather than stigmatise debtors as being actively over-indebted.[72] In 2010, the French National Audit Office (*Cour des Comptes*) delivered a withering critique of the Bank of France's methodology for classifying individuals into distinct categories, pointing to the fact that the Bank seemed to automatically classify a divorced individual as passively over-indebted however long that individual had been divorced.[73] This had a dramatic effect on the Bank of France, which stopped publishing an analysis of the reasons for debt or making any reference to the active/passive distinction.

The Bank recently published an empirical study of paths into over-indebtedness that acknowledges the complexity of reasons for debt.[74] Four typologies are identified: unemployment or reduced employment (23 per cent); budget constrained (17 per cent); routine use of credit (14 per cent); and the largest percentage (41 per cent) representing a conjuncture of events such as a change of circumstances

[69] See eg Hyest and Loridant, *Rapport d'Information no 60* (n 22), Duigou, *Rapport sur l'endettement et surendettement des ménages* (n 31), Dini and Escoffier, *Crédit à la consommation et surendettement* (n 31). The Parliamentary Report preceding the introduction of the 2003 Bill comments: 'L'enquête de la Banque de France met en lumière une évolution de la nature du surendettement, avec une prépondérance des situations de surendettement "passif", qui concernent plus de 64% des dossiers. Les causes principales de ce surendettement passif sont le chômage (26.5% des cas) et une séparation ou un divorce (16%).' ('The Bank of France research highlights the development of the nature of overindebtedness with a preponderance (64%) of "passive" overindebtedness. The principal causes of this form of overindebtedness are unemployment (26.5%) and separation or divorce (16%).') See Avis Houillon doc AN NO 1001 12.

[70] Lacan and Lazarus, 'A Relationship and a Practice' (n 3) 21.

[71] See discussion of narratives in ch 1.

[72] See Plot, *Les enjeux d'une mise en risqué* (n 1) 256.

[73] See Cour des Comptes, *La lutte contre le surendettement des particuliers: une politique publique incomplete et insuffisament pilotée* (Paris, 2010).

[74] *Étude des Parcours Menant au Surendettement* (Bank of France, 2014) 7–8.

but also some individuals who had not adjusted their budgets effectively to these changes (see Table 4.5). A comparison group of similar individuals who had not accessed the Commission seemed to manage their budgets and savings slightly more effectively—'confronted with recent difficulties, they seemed better protected against over-indebtedness because of a more responsible budget management and monitoring of their budget, by a more prudent use of credit and by the existence of a savings fund which permitted them more easily to face their temporary difficulties'.[75] This picture of the responsible subject of credit—similar to Lazzarato's indebted man 'who should learn to exploit credit markets appropriately'[76]—has been used by the Bank[77] to justify greater financial education and literacy to prevent over-indebtedness as well as earlier intervention and greater use of microfinance. This new narrative of individual responsibilisation gives coherence to the work of the Bank, even if the reality of over-indebtedness is more complex.[78]

Table 4.5: Principal causes of over-indebtedness, 2014

	%
Unemployment or degradation of employment	23
Budget constrained	17
Routine use of credit	14
Conjuncture of events	41
Intergenerational assistance	5

Source: Bank of France, *Study of Paths leading to Over-Indebtedness* (2014) 7–8, https://www.banque-france.fr/fileadmin/user_upload/banque_de_france/La_Banque_de_France/study-of-paths-leading-to-over-indebtedness.pdf.

The discourse of social exclusion has also been an important narrative in French legal[79] and policy documents of over-indebtedness. In 2013 over-indebtedness was included in the inter-ministerial plan to fight poverty and social exclusion. The concept of social exclusion was developed initially in France during the 1970s[80] as a substitute for a discourse focused on class inequality and income redistribution. It provided a blueprint for reforms of the welfare state that might appeal to both the right and the centre-left, for example justifying measures to link unemployment

[75] ibid 11.

[76] M Lazzarato, *The Making of the Indebted Man: An Essay on the Neoliberal Condition* [*La fabrique de l'homme endetté: Essai sur la condition néolibérale*] (Cambridge MA, MIT, 2012).

[77] See Banque de France, *Étude des parcours menant au surendettement* (paris, 2014).

[78] See L Lacan, 'Les dossiers de contentieux des banques: observatoire privilégie de l'endettement' (2010) 2 *Entreprises et histoires* 122.

[79] 'Legislation on over-indebtedness "draws its justification in safeguarding individuals from social exclusion"', Vigneau and Bourin, *Droit du surendettement des particuliers* (n 22) 16. The Annual Report of the Cour de Cassation 2009 (n 46) at 146 refers to the objective of 'the social dimension and a concern to integrate it within a more global fight against exclusion'.

[80] See R Lenoir, *Les Exclus: un Francais sur dix* (Paris, Editions du Seuil, 1974).

benefit to the promotion of active participation in the labour force. The protean nature of the concept is illustrated by its use both to justify a refusal to introduce *faillite civile* in 1989 and, then, to introduce it in 2003. Daniel Béland argues that social exclusion 'legitimizes modest policy reforms entirely compatible with moderate understandings of economic liberalism and ultimately unable to fight the social evils this idea refers to'.[81]

V. The Changing Institutional Landscape: Commissions, Courts, and the Law in Action

The French story of over-indebtedness regulation is one of the increased dominance of the commissions, primarily because of the delays in access to the overburdened lower courts in a 'chronically underfunded'[82] justice system and a Ministry of Justice interested in diverting debt cases from the courts. However, the original law failed to divert cases from courts,[83] with 15-month delays for court hearings being experienced. Initially, the lower judiciary were not always sympathetic to their new role in managing debt problems, which differed from the traditional role of pronouncing on the law (*dire le droit*), with some ideological resistance on the behalf of judges to a law which undermined the binding nature of promises.[84] The 1995 reforms, which made the commissions the pivot of the process,[85] was promoted by the Ministry of Justice as a method of reducing costs. The Ministry supported a complete transfer of jurisdiction to the commissions, a position not supported by consumer and business groups. The 1995 compromise therefore retained the role of the courts in providing formal approval to commission recommendations where conciliation failed.[86]

The commissions are free-standing administrative institutions, not part of a national hierarchy. They are not conceptualised as an administrative tribunal, subject to the jurisdiction of the administrative courts for errors in decision-making.[87]

[81] See D Béland, 'The Social Exclusion Discourse: Ideas and Policy Change' (2007) 35 *Policy and Politics* 123.

[82] See generally A Knapp and V Wright, *The Government and Politics of France* (London, Routledge, 2006) 330–38.

[83] See generally Kilborn, 'What the United States Can Learn' (n 2); D Laniet, B Munoz-Perez, P Pailler, and E Serverin, 'Le traitement amiable et judiciaire des situations du surendettement' 37 *Infostat Justice* (May 1994) 3; Hyest and Loridant, *Rapport d'information no 60* (n 22).

[84] See the empirical study, D Saudane de Olivera, 'La réticence des juges face à l'application des lois sociales' (1999) 42 *Droit et Société* 421 and P Ancel, 'La pratique française du redressement judiciaire civil' in Gardaz, *Le surendettement des particuliers* (n 23) 55.

[85] In the event of a failure of negotiation, the Commission could recommend a plan for approval by a judge.

[86] See L 332-1 and L332-2.

[87] The Cour de Cassation has held that Commissions are not subject to rules such as Article 6(1) of the European Convention on Human Rights. See Cass 2e civ, 18 December 2003 Bull Civ II no 397. And see decision of Conseil D'État CE 18 June 1997, no 170824, inédit au *Recueil Lebon*.

They are managed by the Bank of France under a contract with the state. Presided over by the *préfet*, the departmental representative of the state,[88] creditors' representatives are drawn from large financial organisations, consumer representatives from consumer and family organisations.[89] Employees of the Bank of France, as secretary of the commissions, play a key role in ensuring the organisation and disposition of the dossiers. This includes making initial decisions on whether the dossier can be accepted, corresponding with creditors and debtors and informing the national *fichier* of the application. Straightforward cases are not addressed in detail by the Commission, which usually meets twice a month. Social agencies may assist debtors in preparing an application and the secretary of the Commission may conduct an interview with the debtor where they are informed of the consequences of the over-indebtedness process (for example, being recorded in the *fichier*).[90] Decision-making is consensual: recourse to a vote is an exceptional event. Both parties can appeal against the initial decision to the *juge d'exécution* but debtors rarely do this and creditors do so in less than 10 per cent of cases.[91] The Commission may hear anyone who has an interest in the dossier and since 1998 the debtor has had a right to a hearing before the Commission, although this is hardly ever exercised. Many plans follow a relatively standardised process with little negotiation and most large creditors have routinised their interactions with the Commission. It is a relatively impersonal process.

The composition of the commissions poses the question of the influence of different groups on decision-making and whether they are captured by particular groups.[92] Public and private creditors dominated the initial composition of the commissions. Sebastien Plot has claimed that it was often difficult to find active consumer representatives, with a resultant imbalance of representation.[93] The large financial institutions represented on the commissions are well-organised repeat players who monitor the results of different commissions to assess whether they are more, or less, debtor friendly. When the law was initially introduced, creditors were often reluctant to cooperate with the commissions but subsequently realised that the state system might actually reduce their collection costs. The Bank

[88] The complexities of the contemporary role of the *préfet* are described in J Loughlin, *SubNational Government—The French Experience* (London, Palgrave, 2007) ch 7.

[89] For example, CETELEM the largest consumer financier provides representation on about 30 Commissions while UNAF (the Union Nationale Des Associations Familiales) through its departmental organizations (UDAF) also has substantial representation on the Commissions. See N Revenu, 'L'accompagnement social, pratique de l'institution familiale' (2010) 91 *Réalités Familiales* 44.

[90] Discussion with the Bank of France suggests that interviews occurred in about 50% of cases. See also Ferrière and Chatain, *Surendettement des particuliers* (n 66) 23.22.

[91] See Conseil Économique et Social, *Le surendettement* (2007) (n 31).

[92] The regulation on over-indebtedness (see R331) require that the members are appointed by a decision of the local prefect from lists supplied by creditors and consumer groups. The legal representative is nominated by the local president of the court of appeal, and must have three years' legal experience.

[93] Plot, *Les enjeux d'une mise en risque* (n 1) 276–77. Filling the legal post on the Commission after 2003 was often difficult since it was unpaid.

of France secretariat—the *instructrices* who prepare the dossiers—are dominated by women. Working on over-indebtedness is viewed within the Bank as a second class role. Consumer groups critiqued the Commission in the early 2000s for creditor bias in being unwilling to use its power to partially write down debts.

The decentralised nature of the commissions initially led to wide variations in application of the law, with differing approaches to debtors and the determination of their ability to make repayments (the '*reste à vivre*'). The *Cour des Comptes* drew attention to this absence of consistency in its 2010 report. These substantial local differences pose challenges to French administration values of uniformity, hierarchy and expertise. Greater transparency and accountability was imposed on the commissions in 2010 and the Bank of France attempts through circulars to ensure common treatment.[94] The *Cour des Comptes* continued its critique of local differences in its 2013 report and its lack of coordination with other social agencies. Legal amendments in 2013 required greater liaison between the commissions and the commissions on tenant evictions and the family assistance networks (*Caisse d'allocation familiales*).[95]

Those who implement policies may also convert or subvert policies.[96] Studies demonstrate that Bank of France employees vary in their approaches to determining whether to grant moratoria.[97] The commissions also have discretion on how to allocate repayments and prioritise debt repayments (usually rent, family, utilities, then consumer credit) so that the application may not be one of simple *pari passu* allocation. The decision whether to channel an individual to '*rétablissement personnel*' (personal recovery) is certainly not mechanical, and commissions differ in their exercise of this discretion.[98] Again the Bank of France provides guidance on priorities, through circulars and attempts to bring together the different partners (commissions, courts and so on), in order to ensure consistency in treatment.

A. The Role of the Courts: High Law and Low Law

Although the French over-indebtedness system is increasingly conceptualised as an administrative system, the courts played a significant role in the development.[99] The French Cour de Cassation played an important role in policy development,

[94] See eg the extensive circular of 22 July 2014.

[95] See loi no 2014-366 24 March 2014. This responded to critiques in the Dini and Escoffier Report of 2012, *Crédit à la consommation et surendettement* (n 30).

[96] See Sebastien Plot's discussion of the Bank of France employees as street level bureaucrats (n 1) 25–29.

[97] See Fraisse and Froute, 'Household Debt Restructuring' (n 2).

[98] The Cour des Comptes noted these differences in its 2013 report on the management of over-indebtedness by the Bank of France. They note that 'some commissions are more favourable to a discharge of debts and substantially different interpretations of the jurisprudence on this topic are adopted by the various commissions'. Cour des Comptes, *La lutte contre le surendettement des particuliers: des progrès encore trop limités* (Paris, 2013) 230.

[99] French lower courts still hear a reasonable number of cases categorised as surendettement. and in 2012 55,082 cases addressing surendettement were heard by the Tribunaux d'instance, comprising

particularly in the early years of the law. Vincent Vigneau and Guillaume-Xavier Bourin argue that *le droit du surendettement* is largely the creation of the Court of Cassation.[100] The Court dealt with hundreds of cases initially,[101] concerning issues such as the requirement that a debtor be in good faith as a condition of entry to the system,[102] the ability of individuals with both business and non-business debts to use the procedure,[103] and whether individuals with no repayment capacity could access the system.[104] The approach of the court was to maintain liberal access and to provide some relief for those with no repayment capacity, whom the political compromise of 1989 had failed to protect.[105] It attempted to give coherence to a vague 'Swiss cheese' law which left many issues to the *pouvoir souverain des juges du fond* (the power of the first instance judge to decide issues of fact), which permits significant judicial equity by lower courts. The Court limited the potential effect of good faith as a barrier to entry by instead requiring creditors to prove bad faith, preventing lower courts raising the issue of their own motion. The Court did, however, leave interpretation of substantive good faith to the *pouvoir souverain* of the first instance judge but indicated that negligence by a debtor is not equivalent to bad faith.[106] The Court held that it was improper for the Court to speculate on the debtor's future prospects to justify restricting access to the commission.[107] It required a file to be opened even if an individual had no repayment capacity and permitted courts to grant successive reschedulings of periods of five years, refusing to follow the approach of the majority of Cours d'appel.[108] This effectively resulted in court-imposed moratoria; the Cour de Cassation also approved courts freezing interest to 0 per cent, notwithstanding that the legislative

9% of their caseload, 10,513 cases before the Tribunaux de grande instance (1.5%) of its caseload and 7,772 before the courts of appeal (comprising 3.8% of its caseload).

[100] See Vigneau and Bourin, *Droit du surendettement des particuliers* (n 22) 16. For a commentary on its role see the 2009 Annual Report of the Cour de Cassation (n 46).

[101] See G Paisant, 'La Jurisprudence de la cour de cassation et la question de la réforme de la loi sur le surendettement des particuliers' (1994) *Dalloz Chronique* 173. See also B Bouloc (1991) Cass Civ 1991 D 1991 307 note Bouloc.

[102] See Cass 1ère civ 4 Avr 1991 (Bull civ 1 no 123). The Court limited the effect of the good faith requirement by requiring creditors to prove bad faith and prohibiting lower courts raising the issue on their own motion. The Court also indicated that negligence was not the equivalent of bad faith. 1ère civ 31 mars 1992, Bull 1992, I no 107, arrêt no 3, pourvoi no 91-04.032.

[103] The Court permitted professional debts to be included in a plan if non-professional debts were sufficient to render an individual unable to pay her debts. See discussion of cases in Vigneau and Bourin, *Droit du surendettement des particuliers* (n 22) 85–92.

[104] Bracq Bull Civ I no 41, arrêt n 2: D 1993.343 note Bonthoux.

[105] See G Paisant (1993) *Revue trimestrielle de droit commercial* 368, 370. The Court also held that it was improper for the lower courts to speculate on the debtor's future prospects to justify restricting access to the Commission. 1ère civ 31 mars 1992, Bull 1992, I no 107, arrêt no 3, pourvoi no 91-04.032.

[106] Cass 2e civ, 20 October 2005. G Henaff, (2006) Note, *Receuil Dalloz* 870. Leaving the issue of good faith to the determination of the lower courts was criticised by Bouloc who thought that the court should have given greater guidance since the new procedure challenged classical conceptions of contract.

[107] Iere civ 31 mars 1992, Bull 1992, I no 107, arret no 3, pourvoi no 91-04.032.

[108] See Paisant (1993) *Revue trimestrielle de droit commercial* 368, 370.

provisions referred only to 'reducing' the interest, and wiping out deficiencies on the sale of a home—again the law referred only to a power to reduce interest. The legal scholar Gilles Paisant critiqued these decisions as the Court going beyond its classical role of 'completing the law' to one of 'rewriting it', substituting 'equity' for the rigour of the terms of the law.[109] The Court also permitted business debts to be included in plans if non-business debts were sufficient to render individuals unable to pay their debts.[110] This was significant for those in liberal professions, such as doctors, architects, and lawyers, who were unable to access commercial insolvency procedures until 2005. Paisant described these as 'audacious' interpretations of a law designed for consumers, which perhaps might be better dealt with through the power of the Cour de Cassation to recommend legislative reforms in its annual report.[111]

After the introduction of *rétablissement personnel* in 2003 the Cour de Cassation again provided a liberal interpretation to the concept of 'irremediably compromised', disapproving interpretations by lower courts which refused to grant relief to younger debtors.[112] In a re-run of the initial response to the loi Neiertz, the Court issued an *avis*—a form adopted where there are conflicting lower court decisions—which limited *rétablissement personnel* to situations where an individual had almost no repayment capacity.[113] Comparative lawyers have drawn attention to the paradoxes in the role of the Cour de Cassation; *jurisprudence* is supposedly not a source of law and does not create binding precedents, yet the reality appears to be quite different.[114]

In France the relationship between 'high law' and 'low law' is mediated by the principle of the *pouvoir souverain des juges du fond* which confers substantial discretion on lower court judges to decide factual issues in a system where the Cour de Cassation addresses issues of law. The Cour de Cassation is *une cour régulatrice* concerned with the consistent application of the law. Lower courts varied in their

[109] See G Paisant, 'La jurisprudence de la cour de cassation et la question de la réforme de la loi sur le surendettement des particuliers' (1994) *Dalloz Chronique* 173. The 1995 reforms changed the terms of the law to 'treatment' rather than 'settlement' of debts.

[110] 1ère civ, 16 juin 1993, Bull 1, pourvoi no 92-04.113; Cass 1ère civ 2 décembre 1992 (Bull civ 1, no 302). These decisions and the approach of the court of cassation to business debts are discussed in Vigneau and Bourin, *Droit du surendettement des particuliers* (n 22) 85–92.

[111] Paisant (n 108) 374. See Cour de Cassation, *Contributions de la deuxieme chambre civile de la cour de cassation, troisieme etude* (n 46) 140.

[112] In a sample of cases between December 2003 and 2005 the juge d'execution refused to open a *retablissement* personnel in 33% of cases. More than 30% of these cases represented situations where the court thought that the debtor's position might improve, 26% on the basis that the revenue and assets were sufficient to make some form of repayment, and 8% gave the reason that the debtor was too young to make an application. See the empirical study of cases between 2003 and 2005. C Bourreau-Dubois, B Chopard, and Y Ziane, 'Plans de redressement et procédure de rétablissement personnel: une analyse du traitement du surendettement des particuliers' (2010), http://congres.afse.fr/docs/2010/865526predetprpuneanalysedutraitementdusurendettementdesparticuliers.pdf.

[113] See Cass civ Avis no 0050001 10 January 2005. See the opinion of M Benmakhlouf.

[114] For a general discussion see J Bell, *French Legal Cultures* (London, Butterworths, 2001) 66 et seq; M Mitchel de S-O-l'E Lasser, *Judicial Deliberations: A Comparative Analysis of Transparency and Legitimacy* (Oxford, OUP, 2009).

handling of cases. Emmanuel Carrère, in his novel *D'autres vies que la miènne*, describes the judicial equity exercised by judges Étienne Rigal and Philippe Flores in the *tribunal d'instance* of Vienne and Niort. These 'red judges' struck down credit contracts through formalistic interpretations of credit law and adopted liberal interpretations of the loi Neiertz.[115] Rigal was likened to the 'bon juge Magnaud' who in a celebrated judgment of 1898 refused to convict a young woman who out of necessity had stolen bread to feed her child.[116]

French legal writers have conceptualised the field of over-indebtedness as a new *droit social*, inspired by ideas of *solidarisme contractuel* and the amelioration of social exclusion. It represents *un droit d'exception—un droit social* with '*une logique sociale de solidarité envers les plus faibles*' ('an exceptional law representing social solidarity towards the weakest individuals'),[117] reviving the ideas of the late nineteenth century writers who stressed social interdependence and inequality in social relations in contrast to the atomistic individualism of nineteenth century liberalism embodied in the will theory of contract.[118] The nineteenth-century justifications for protection of the worker casualties of industrialisation were transplanted to the consumer casualties of contemporary credit society. However, just as the initial casualties of industrial capitalism often faced labyrinthine processes in order to achieve compensation from the new bureaucracies of the social state, so individuals are subject to the discretion of commissions determining whether they are merely insolvent or 'irremediably compromised' and deserving a full discharge. The 'process is the punishment'[119] might be an appropriate description from the viewpoint of the debtor. Conceptualising discharge as an exception to full contractual enforcement for the benefit of 'the weak' is a socially conservative reading of the new *droit social*,[120] a reading suggested above by Lacan and Lazarus,[121] and discharge of debts through *rétablissement personnel* is a modest form of redistribution reducing the need for state welfare.[122]

[115] See eg Trib Inst Vienne 25 November 2002 *Revue trimestrielle de droit commercial 2003* 174, note Paisant discussed by Kilborn, 'What the United States Can Learn' (n 2) 653.

[116] Judicial equity by 'low law' courts is documented in common law. See eg D Cowan and HE Hitchings, '"Pretty Boring Stuff" District Judges and Housing Possession Proceedings' (2007) 16 *Social and Legal Studies* 363–82. M Finn, *The Character of Credit* (Cambridge, Cambridge University Press, 2003).

[117] 2009 Annual Report of the Cour de Cassation (n 46) 129.

[118] These writers included Francois Gény, Emmanuel Gounot, and Leon Duguit. See MC Belleau, 'The "Juristes Inquiets": Legal Classicism and Criticism in Early Twentieth Century France' (1997) *Utah Law Review* 379; D Kennedy, 'Two Globalizations of Law & Legal Thought 1850–1968' (2003) 36 *Suffolk Law Review* 631, 648 et seq. Kennedy emphasises at 650 the disparate legitimating narratives of the 'social'. 'The Social, then, could be based on socialist or social democratic ideology (perhaps Durkheimian), on the social Christianity of Protestant sects, on neoKantian "situational natural law", on Comtean positivism, on Catholic natural law, on Bismark/Disraeli social conservatism, or on fascist ideology.' See also J Cedras, 'Le Solidarisme contractual en doctrine et devant la cour de cassation' in *Cour de Cassation Rapport Annuel 2003*.

[119] The reference is to M Feeley, *The Process is the Punishment: Handling Cases in a Lower Criminal Court* (New York, Russell Sage Foundation, 1992).

[120] See A Supiot, 'Grandeur and Misery of the Social State' (2013) 82 *New Left Review* 99.

[121] Lacan and Lazarus, 'A Relationship and a Practice' (n 3).

[122] See Gloukoviezoff, *L'exclusion bancaire* (n 17) 229–30.

VI. Discussion

The French experience demonstrates the significance of institutional context for political change, the role of narratives, and the long-term consequences of initial events, in this case the role taken by the Bank of France as manager of the process. A vague temporary law was saved from failure partly by the Bank of France and partly by expansive judicial interpretations. Prasad's analysis of French policy innovation indicates three sources of change: backlashes against previous government policy, imitation of other countries and the technocracy.[123] She argues that the most significant influence is the technocracy—the various French executive institutions that act cautiously and pragmatically, with critiques often coming from within the technocracy.[124] The main players in the development of the over-indebtedness regime were the Ministries of Justice and Finance and the Bank of France, which cautiously adapted the law, attempted to manage policy through Consultative committees such as the Consultative Committee on consumer finance and responded to internal criticisms. The Ministry of Justice wished to get debt cases out of the courts and the Ministry of Finance acted as the conduit for financial interests. The gradualist approach of the French technocracy to change was disrupted in 2003 by the *loi Borloo*. The French technocracy were aware of foreign models of over-indebtedness regulation such as the US. They initially rejected an internal transplant, the Alsace-Moselle law of *faillite civile*, linking it to extreme positions such as the US straight discharge. The subsequent adoption of the Moselle law could, however, be justified as a French rather than Anglo-Saxon solution.

The *Cour Des Comptes* (National Audit Office) has maintained a continuing critique of the work of the Bank in managing over-indebtedness. In 2005 it argued that this was not a proper role for a central bank; in 2010 it delivered a stinging critique of many aspects of the Bank's management of over-indebtedness including basing policy on an inadequate and unreliable evidence, high costs,[125] mediocre performance by commissions, whose approaches to central issues varied widely, and an absence of monitoring of the debtor after a plan was agreed. There seemed to be little central coordination of over-indebtedness policy or attempts to link the work of the commissions with other social agencies.[126] Its 2013 report continued the critique.[127]

The Bank has attempted to respond by conducting further studies, developing links with other agencies and ensuring greater consistency in commissions

[123] Prasad, Why Is France So French? (n 10).

[124] See Prasad, *The Politics of Free Markets* (n 4).

[125] The Cour des Comptes estimated that each dossier cost €1,035 to process.

[126] See Cour des Comptes, *La lutte contre le surendettement des particuliers: une politique publique incomplete et insuffisament pilotée* (Paris, 2010).

[127] Cour des Comptes, *La lutte contre le surendettement des particuliers: des progrès encore trop limités* (Paris, 2013).

through detailed circulars. But the attitude of the bank to the management of over-indebtedness is revealed in its response to the 2010 report, exhibiting hostility to the suggestion that it should monitor the implementation of repayment plans. It pointed out that its unique role in over-indebtedness management was costly and not fully compensated by the state. It could not therefore accept further extensions of its responsibilities.[128]

The unique role of the Bank of France might be explained by the literature on legal origins.[129] This argues that French civil law and common law represent 'different styles of social control of economic life' with the French civilian tradition supposedly less hospitable to facilitating credit, more willing to protect debtors and more likely to intervene in market failures with centralised regulation. While legal systems are not hard-wired to particular solutions, they may introduce centralised regulation during a crisis, which is then not abolished after the crisis. This last proposition on legal origins might aid in explaining the unique role of the Bank of France in regulating over-indebtedness. However, other French civilian countries, while following the mediation model have linked it to court supervision rather than involving a central bureaucracy. The initial role of the bank seems therefore to have been a contingent event, but one with long-term effects.

State management of narratives about debtors and over-indebtedness is a characteristic of French policymaking in a knowledge regime dominated by the state.[130] This contrasts with the US 'war of ideas' between different policy paradigms that vied for dominance. There was no overt war of ideas in France. The state continues to manage the narrative through the studies conducted by the Bank of France. Law professors in France do not adopt techniques of policy analysis such as interdisciplinary empiricism or the theoretical framework of law and economics.[131] Their critiques focus primarily around the conceptual integrity of the law. Sociologists in France increasingly study debt, credit, and over-indebtedness as a sociology of domination, primarily through detailed ethnographies of credit.

Veronique Neiertz initially rejected *faillite civile* as a general remedy for consumers as not fitting the French *mentalité*, which seemed to be equated with the importance of *pacta sunt servanda*.[132] This raises the question whether the reluctance to introduce an insolvency discharge is explained by French legal culture which celebrates the strength of the binding force of contract embedded in the ideology of article 1134 of the French civil code. Did French policymakers take the sanctity of credit contracts, and concerns about the detrimental consequences for

[128] ibid at 494.

[129] See R La Porta, F Lopez-de-Silanes, and A Shleifer, 'The Economic Consequences of Legal Origins' (2008) 46 *Journal of Economic Literature* 285.

[130] See J Campbell and O Petersen, *The National Origins of Policy Ideas: Knowledge Regimes in the United States, France, Germany, and Denmark* (Princeton, Princeton University Press, 2014).

[131] See R Colson and S Field, 'Socio-legal Studies in France: Beyond the Law Faculty' (2016) 43 *Journal of Law and Society* 285.

[132] It was important to 'not let French people think that they could contract debts and not repay them'. Decl Neiertz Jo An (CR) 8 December 1989, 6109.

the credit market of introducing consumer bankruptcy, more seriously than US policymakers did in 1978[133] or English policymakers in 2002?

The French choice in 1989 was quite different from the US enactment of the Bankruptcy Reform Act 1978. The absence in 1989 of access to a bankruptcy discharge for individuals in France placed high political costs to be overcome by any group attempting to justify such a major change in policy with little evidence of the potential effects. US bankruptcy law in 1978 was already well established and experience suggested that it had only a modest effect on credit granting. The law and economics focus on the *ex ante* effects of bankruptcy did not exist at this time. In England and Wales in 2002, the more liberal bankruptcy discharge procedures were not intended for consumers and were not part of a discourse of consumer (as opposed to entrepreneurial) risk-taking.

Elite policymakers in the Ministry of Finance and the Bank of France were probably genuinely concerned about the impact of writing down debt, as were all European policymakers who introduced debt adjustment systems around this time. References to the importance of maintaining credit discipline in French debates are not reducible solely to the pursuit of self-interest by creditors. The introduction of these systems throughout Europe was often accompanied by the rhetoric that they were not intended to challenge the norm of *pacta sunt servanda.*[134] Concerns about the impact of debt relief on the sanctity of promises exist also in common law countries. When debt relief orders were introduced in 2009 for debtors with no income or assets and no repayment capacity, it was emphasised that this posed no threat to the credit system. It was a remedy for 'vulnerable people trapped in debt'.[135] *Pacta sunt servanda* is not therefore a peculiarly French obsession, part of a French *mentalité.*[136]

France is sometimes portrayed as the representative of a social model in contrast to a dominant Anglo-Saxon neo-liberalism, where consumption credit drives the economy. Increasingly, reference is being made in official documents to the social role of the over-indebtedness commissions, over-indebtedness law as *droit social*, and the central idea of social exclusion, with the state taking responsibility for managing over-indebtedness. It is however a conservative conception of the social with discharge reserved for the 'irremediably compromised', generally

[133] Trumbull, *Consumer Lending* (n 8).

[134] See eg Netherlands, 'It is a starting point in our legal system that a debtor should honour its obligations. The present proposal does not offer an easy escape for people who ... lead a loose life and irresponsibly pile one debt upon another' quoted in J Apeldoorn, 'The 'Fresh Start' for Individual Debtors: Social Moral and Practical Issues' (2008) 17 *International Insolvency Review* 57.

[135] See Parliamentary Under Secretary of State for Business, Innovation and Skills (Mr Edward Davey) HC Deb 9 November 2010 c7-8WS. See also DTI Insolvency Service, *Relief for the Indebted—An Alternative to Bankruptcy* (London, Insolvency Service, 2005).

[136] The limited effects of changed circumstances on contract validity in French civil law may owe more to historical accident. See J Gordley, 'Comparative Law and Legal History' in *The Oxford Handbook of Comparative Law* (Oxford, Oxford University Press, 2007) 764. Gordley argues that the failure to include relief for imprévision in the Civil Code was an 'accident'.

the vulnerable poor. It could be described as a modest form of need-rationality welfarism in private law.[137] The link to social exclusion has not resulted in substantial social intervention to support individual debtors.[138] A patchwork of decentralised charitable and social organisations provide advice and support to debtors.[139] There is no equivalent to the national system of Citizens Advice Bureaux found in the UK. The 2010 reforms, which make it easier for an individual to get back into the credit market, could be interpreted as compatible with neo-liberal ideas, along with the recent financial literacy initiatives. These provide a 'hand up rather than a hand out'.[140] Whether it provides a long-term solution for the precarious situation of individuals using *rétablissement personnel* remains unclear.

The French welfare system, based on a Christian democratic model, has traditionally favoured families over individuals, insiders with secure employment over those unable to secure employment and passive labour market policies which did not encourage individuals to return to work. It was often financed through regressive measures.[141] The system changed substantially during the 1980s and 1990s, attempting to compensate for the effects of neo-liberalism and high levels of unemployment.[142] It now increasingly targets the excluded through state-financed measures such as the RMI (*Revenu Minimum d'Insertion*), which 3 per cent of the French population received in 2009.[143] There remains concern in contemporary France for the 'excluded' and those inside society whose positions are not secure. Individuals may also fear that they will slip from 'insider' to 'outsider'. Over-indebtedness may therefore function as a symbolic site for discussions of *déclassement*, breakdown in social and family solidarity and inequality.

[137] See T Wilhelmsson, 'Varieties of Welfarism in European Contract Law' (2004) 10(6) *European Law Journal* 712.

[138] See Dini and Escoffier, *Crédit à la consommation et surendettement* (n 31) 72; Cour des Comptes, *La lutte contre le surendettement* (Paris, 2013) 233–34 (referring to the weak relationships between the commissions and social services).

[139] For a discussion of the large role of the third sector and the decentralised nature of social services in France see E Archambault, 'Social Services in France: A Public Private Partnership' in P Herrmann and S Herrenbrueck (eds), *Changing Administration –Changing Society. Challenges for Current Social Policy* (New York, Nova, 2006) 223.

[140] See discussion in R Gaillard, 'Échec Annoncé de la Lutte Contre le Surendettement des Particuliers en France? Sociologie d'une Forme d'Assistance' (2014) 1–2 *Revue Française des affaires sociales* 78.

[141] See J Levy, 'Vice into Virtue? Progressive Politics and Welfare Reform in Continental Europe' (1999) 27 *Politics and Society* 239.

[142] See M Vail, *Recasting Welfare Capitalism* (Philadelphia, Temple University Press, 2010).

[143] See B Palier and K Thelen, 'Institutionalizing Dualism: Complementarities and Change in France and Germany' (2010) 38(1) *Politics and Society* 119, 134. The RMI will be altered through the progressive introduction of the RSA.

5

Sweden: The Quality of Mercy *is* Strained

I. Introduction

Sweden is often regarded as a paragon of economic and social progress. 'Swedes are some of the most highly educated people in the world, take the longest vacations, have one of the best health care systems, live the longest, are exposed to very low levels of crime and enjoy one of the highest standards of living in the world.'[1] Commentators note that it survived the Great Recession of 2008 relatively unscathed.[2] Sweden's debt restructuring system is sometimes characterised as part of a welfare state or social orientation,[3] and its administrative debt enforcement system is cited as a model of best practice.[4] But my research suggests that it remains a relatively strict, creditor-oriented system more compatible with ordoliberal ideas of personal responsibility Several commissions and reports have considered reform of the debt restructuring system since its introduction in 1994. These have resulted in changes designed primarily to reduce costs and achieve more efficient enforcement. The Swedish politics of compromise has resulted in a 'balance' that places more weight on the perceived importance of a 'good payment culture' than the economic and social benefits of a fresh start for debtors.

Sweden is not a socialist state. There is a low level of public ownership of production and it has historically combined a (neo-)liberal market approach with a universalist social safety net based on a social insurance model rather than a 'welfare' system.[5] Industry has traditionally been concentrated into a few major

[1] S Steinmo, 'Sweden: The Evolution of a Bumble Bee' in S Steinmo, *The Evolution of Modern States: Sweden, Japan and the United States* (Cambridge, Cambridge University Press, 2010).

[2] See G Schnyder, 'Like a Phoenix from the Ashes? Reassessing the transformation of the Swedish political economy since the 1970s' (2012) 19(8) *Journal of European Public Policy* 1126.

[3] J Niemi, 'Constructions of Debtors and Creditors in Consumer Bankruptcy' in J Niemi, I Ramsay, and W Whitford, *Consumer Bankruptcy in Global Perspective* (Oxford, Hart Publishing, 2003).

[4] See London Economics, *Study on means to protect consumers in financial difficulty; personal bankruptcy, datio in solutum of mortgages, and restrictions on debt collection abusive practices* (2012) 190.

[5] Sven Steinmo describes it as a 'social–liberal' political economy to 'describe the unusual system that combines enormous social protection for the individual with a remarkably liberal economy'. S Steinmo, *The Evolution of Modern States: Sweden, Japan and the United States* (Cambridge, CUP, 2010) 41.

enterprises, including the financial system which is dominated by an almost oligopolistic banking system of four major banks. Sweden is known historically for its politics of compromise and also for an elite corporatism where political problems are often conceptualised as technical questions. This is reflected in the 'SOUs',[6] which are official committees appointed by the government in anticipation of legislation. Sweden has also been associated with a progressive Nordic consumer law[7] which takes into account the needs of the weaker party and focuses on the general fairness of contractual outcomes.

Since the banking crisis of the early 1990s, the Swedish economy and social protections have changed significantly. Small and medium enterprises (SMEs) have been encouraged and grown, doubling in number between 2003 and 2013. Sweden has embraced the new knowledge economy. Government policies encourage entrepreneurialism, and this is reflected in recent proposals for insolvency reform.[8] The social safety net has changed. Sweden has had education loans for many years[9] but unemployment insurance fees have risen since 2006 with more workers dropping out of the plans, health insurance benefits have decreased and are being more strictly policed, and temporary employment has increased. Unemployment remains relatively high.[10] The Hedborg report in 2014 suggested that these factors create a higher risk of individuals becoming over-indebted.[11]

Sweden has a high ratio of household debt to disposable income (see chapter one, Figure 1.1).[12] Since 1995, the aggregate household debt to disposable income ratio has increased from 90 to 179 per cent of disposable income in 2015 and is expected to continue to increase.[13] Mortgage credit represents the great majority of debt with consumer credit a mere 10 per cent of disposable income. The tax

[6] Statens offentliga utredningar (SOUs). These are government commissions of inquiry that take evidence from different groups of stakeholders in anticipation of legislation.

[7] 'In the 1970s and 1980s Sweden was a leader in the field of consumer protection … [T]he consumer perspective is still a characteristic feature of Swedish private law'. See R Dotevall, 'Sweden' in J Smits, *Elgar Encyclopeadia of Comparative Law* 2nd edn (Cheltenham, Edward Elgar Publishing, 2012) 849–50.

[8] See SOU 2014: 44 *An Opportunity for a Fresh Start for Serious Entrepreneurs.*

[9] The modern system dates from 1965. Tuition is free in Sweden but the great majority of Swedish students take out educational loans in addition to grants, graduating with an average debt of US$19,000. The amortisation period is 25 years and is written off at the age of 67. However, the government is proposing to raise this age and tighten enforcement against those in arrears. See M Phillips, 'The High Price of a Free College Education in Sweden. Here's why Swedish college students still graduate with a ton of debt' *The Atlantic* (31 May 2013), www.theatlantic.com/international/archive/2013/05/the-high-price-of-a-free-college-education-in-sweden/276428/. See also 'Students to keep paying off debt beyond 67' *The Local* (20 April 2014), www.thelocal.se/20140420/students-to-keep-paying-off-debt-beyond-67.

[10] See IMF, *Article IV Consultation on Sweden* (2014) 4. Eight per cent unemployment rate compared with pre-recession of 6.5%.

[11] See SOU 2013:78 *Over-indebtedness in the Credit Society*? ('the Hedborg report') (under the direction of Anna Hedborg, a social democrat politician and ex-government minister), http://www.regeringen.se/49bb85/contentassets/7d6ed04741ab4b9badd089ed01fd3039/overskuldsattning-i-kreditsamhallet-sou-201378-hela-betankandet.

[12] Other Nordic countries (Denmark and Norway) also have high rates of debt to income compared with other European countries. They are also higher than current US rates.

[13] See Riksbank's *Financial Stability Report* 2016:1, 11.

regime encourages mortgage debt since interest is deductible:[14] a Swedish joke is that the state finances the purchase of a home. Little incentive exists for individuals to amortise debt swiftly, and many mortgage loans are interest only.[15] If analysis is restricted to those who hold household debt then the ratio is over 300 per cent, with the highest debt ratios among low- and middle-income consumers.[16] Lower-income consumers hold substantially less mortgage credit and significantly more consumer debt (ie credit card debt, instalment loans and educational loans).[17] A conflict of opinion exists as to the distribution of problematic levels of debt among the population. The Hedborg report argues that it is concentrated among lower-income consumers and that debtors registered with the *Kronofogden* (KFM) the state enforcement agency are generally less well educated, single and living in rented accommodation.[18] The Bank of Sweden, in contrast, argues that potentially problematic levels of debt exist throughout society. The Bank describes the situation as worrying given the potential detrimental effects of this level of debt on the Swedish economy and the hardship to consumers who might default.[19]

The high levels of household debt in Sweden and other Nordic countries initially seems odd since high levels of household debt-to-income are usually associated with economies such as the UK and the US, where household debt maintains high levels of private consumption in the face of uncertain or stagnating wages. Many consumer services are provided by government in Nordic countries and private consumption constitutes a lower level of gross domestic product (GDP). Different social classes in Sweden may be using credit for distinct purposes, with the middle classes geared towards capital acquisitions and poorer individuals

[14] 'Mortgage interest costs up to 100,000 kronor (approximately £8,500) can be deducted at a 30% income tax rate, with amounts over that deducted at a 21% rate.' IMF, *Article IV Consultation on Sweden* (n 10) at 9. Interest is also deductible on the purchase of yachts.

[15] *Financial Stability Report* (n 13) 24. See 'Swedes Doomed to Die with Mortgage' *The Local* (7 May 2014), www.thelocal.se/20140507/swedes-doomed-to-die-with-mortgages-central-bank.

[16] See C Skingsley, 'Household Debt under the Microscope', www.riksbank.se/Documents/Tal/Skingsley/2014/tal_Skingsley_140508_eng.pdf. See also J Winstrand and D Olcer, 'Economic Commentary: How indebted are Swedish households?'(Riksbank, 2014).

[17] G Alfelt, M Bos, and K Roszbach, 'Online Intermediation and the Terms of Consumer Credit' (2014) *Sveriges Riksbank Economic Review* 1, 2, www.riksbank.se/Documents/Rapporter/POV/2014/2014_1/rap_pov_artikel_3_140306_eng.pdf.

[18] Hedborg report (n 11) para 2.6, 112 'Over-indebtedness among households for those who have debts with the Kronofogdemyndigheten … do not have post-secondary education, are single and live in rented dwellings to a greater extent in the population in general.' They also speculated that individuals registered with the KFM might have loans that were not registered on the credit register, such as payday loans.

[19] See Skingsley, 'Household Debt' (n 16). See also IMF, *Article IV Consultation* (n 10) at 6, noting that the high household debt has potential dangers for financial stability. For an argument that high debt levels are not problematic because they are held by high-income groups, see L Svensson, 'The Riksbank's new study of household debt—misleading conclusions, or deliberate disinformation?' ['Riksbankens nya undersökning av skulderna—missvisande slutsatser, eller medveten desinformation?'], http://larseosvensson.se/2014/05/12/the-riksbanks-new-study-of-household-debt-misleading-conclusions-or-deliberate-disinformation.

using it for everyday consumption.[20] Changes in the welfare state affecting the latter groups may increase recourse to debt.

II. Swedish Regulation of the Consumer Credit Market

Sweden has a relatively liberal approach to consumer credit regulation. Credit information is extensive and Swedes live in a 'goldfish bowl' of information where all information maintained by the government is public (tax returns and so on). Credit reports compiled by UCAB[21] contain detailed information on an individual's sources of income and property ownership and provides risk scores to lenders. UCAB claims to have a 100 per cent coverage of individuals over 16 years of age and include both positive and negative data, but less positive data than a US credit report.[22] Negative data such as 90 days arrears remains on file for three years, and debt restructuring information for five years, the period of the plan.[23]

Swedish consumer credit law is not more protective of consumers than a country such as the UK, and implementation of the EU consumer and mortgage credit directives have reduced significant differences. Creditors must make *ex ante* assessments of debtors' ability to sustain repayments. Interest rate ceilings do not exist in Sweden although excessive rates might be attacked as unreasonable. A current debate and ongoing investigation is the possible application of a ceiling to payday loans.[24] The general unreasonableness clause in section 36 of the Contracts Act (added in 1976) confers discretionary power on the courts to protect consumers, conceptualised as being in a weaker position in the market. Controversy exists as to the extent to which this envisaged the introduction of welfarist ideas into contract law or was primarily a response to market failures.[25] Thomas Wilhelmsson argued in 1990 that a concept of *social force majeure*, which might be used to adjust obligations where one party was subject to an unforeseen change such as illness

[20] See the discussion in C Crouch, 'Employment, Consumption, Debt and European Industrial Relations Systems' (2012) 51 *Industrial Law Journal* 389.

[21] This is the Swedish Business and Credit Information Agency, which is owned by the four Swedish banks.

[22] Swedish credit reports contain more detail on individual incomes than in other countries. They do not seem to include payment profiles (pays on time, misses one payment etc) that are standard in US reports.

[23] Thus a Swedish debtor will have a 'clean' credit record before a US consumer where a bankruptcy may stay on file for 10 years.

[24] See discussion in AH Persson and A-S Henrikson, 'Regulation of Instant Loans and Other Credits in Swedish Law' (2014) 22 *Juridica International* 57. The UK has now introduced price controls on 'payday loans'.

[25] See U Bernitz, 'Swedish Standard Contracts Law and the EC Directive on Contract Terms' (2000) 39 *Scandinavian Studies in Law* 13 (section 36, primarily addressing market failures); T Wilhelmsson, 'Varieties of Welfarism in European Contract Law' (2004) 10 *European Law Journal* 712.

or unemployment which prevented performance, could be discerned in specific Nordic statutes and decisions.[26] This represents a need-based welfarism, responding to the situation of a weaker party. A narrative in Sweden of protecting consumers *from* credit, as in France, does not seem to exist, except in the situation of young consumers who may be thought to be more prone to being taken advantage of by 'instant loans' available online or via mobile phone. Swedish consumers express significant dissatisfaction with banking and financial services markets primarily in terms of a lack of transparency.[27] The most recent Hedborg report expresses similar concerns to UK reports on consumer credit: lack of transparency, irresponsible marketing of credit and exorbitant interest rates on payday loans.

The Swedish debt enforcement system is relatively swift and efficient from a creditor's viewpoint. If a consumer is overdue with a payment then a business may pass the account to the KFM which triggers an administrative process of enforcement with the burden on the debtor to raise any defences to the claim. The agency does not have any responsibility here and a widespread belief is that, through inertia, many individuals with legal defences do not raise that defence.[28] However Sweden does not rank highly in the World Bank *Doing Business* reports. It is twenty-first in the ease of enforcing contracts and sixty-first in terms of 'getting credit'. This places it below France and Germany but above the UK in the enforcement of contracts indicators. Both Germany and the UK rank higher in terms of the ease of 'getting credit'.[29] These data relate to business credit but may be useful indicators for consumer credit.

III. The Development of the Swedish Debt Restructuring System[30]

Sweden deregulated its financial system during the 1980s. This strategy arguably contributed to the subsequent banking crisis in the early 1990s when several banks

[26] See T Wilhelmsson, '"Social Force Majeure" A New Concept in Nordic Consumer Law' (1990) 13 *Journal of Consumer Policy* 1. Wilhelmsson clarified the concept of social force majeure to mean 'obstacles to performance' since phenomena such as unemployment are not unforeseeable. See T Wilhelmsson, *Critical Studies in Private Law; A Treatise on Need-Rational Principles in Modern Law* (Springer, 1992) ch VII.

[27] See Konsumentverket, *Swedish Consumer Report 2014*, 58.

[28] Hedborg report (n 11).

[29] World Bank, *Doing Business 2015: Going Beyond Efficiency* (World Bank, 2014). These data relate to business but there are overlaps with consumer credit in terms of rankings of credit information systems.

[30] For an overview of the Swedish developments up until 2013, see A Persson, 'The New Swedish Debt Relief Act' in W Backert, S Block-Lieb, and J Niemi (eds), *Contemporary Issues in Consumer Bankruptcy* (Berlin, Peter Lang, 2013). See also the excellent article by J Kilborn, 'Out with the New; In with the Old: As Sweden Aggressively Streamlines its Consumer Bankruptcy System, Have U.S. Reformers Fallen off the Learning Curve?' (2006) 80 *American Bankruptcy Law Journal* 435.

failed. The Swedish Debt Adjustment system was introduced in 1994 in the wake of these events, as many individuals and small businesses faced substantial debt problems. The introduction of the Debt Adjustment Act (*Skuldsaneringslagen*) followed the recommendations of a government Commission which canvassed alternatives and assessed comparative approaches.[31]

Gertrude Lennander, an expert member of the Commission and future Justice of the Swedish Supreme Court, in 1991 set out the background to and objectives of the proposed legislation. These ideas still remain important in understanding the Swedish Debt Adjustment Act. The proposed Act was a 'pragmatic response' to the problem, drawing on Denmark's experience and the English administration order.[32] The US straight discharge was rejected because it did not take account of the debtor's future ability to pay. An adjustment scheme with some payments by a debtor would satisfy both creditors, who would obtain more than they could in bankruptcy, and debtors, who would avoid the stigma of bankruptcy. It was intended to address both consumer debt and the problems of small business persons who had failed and incurred large personal debts. It sought a 'middle way' between the long seven-year requirements of the German law and the US-style discharge procedure. Intended for individuals without seizable assets, the process was designed to be low cost and efficient

The objective was 'economic rehabilitation'. It was not intended to be a 'panacea' for social problems and was only to apply in situations of social *force majeure*, where because of radically altered circumstances or unforeseen events individuals were unable to repay. Lennander argued that this development did not challenge *pacta sunt servanda*; it simply represented the counterprinciple *rebus sic stantibus* and, in any event, the new legislation would only permit adjustment under strict conditions—a requirement of permanent insolvency and a reasonableness requirement which permitted the court to examine the conduct of the debtor and the nature and age of the debts. At the same time, the Debt Adjustment Act would discharge tax and student loans at the end of the repayment period. The procedure should be court supervised but 'quick, simple and inexpensive'.[33]

The legislative history of the Debt Adjustment Act emphasised that debt relief should not challenge *pacta sunt servanda*, and that debt relief was an exception, but that it should be quick and simple. Access to debt restructuring was limited to individuals in permanent insolvency and was subject to a reasonableness test

[31] See G Lennander, 'Debt Adjustment for Private Individuals' (1991) 5 *Stockholm Institute for Scandinavian Law* 1129 (SOU 1990:74).

[32] Referring to the Swedish proposals, Lennander states that 'the closest pattern is the Danish procedure, which in turn was inspired by the Anglo-American equivalents' (administration order and Chapter 13). Lennander, 'Debt Adjustment' (n 31) 137.

[33] ibid 141.

(see discussion below). The original legislation divided the process into three stages. Initially, with the assistance of the municipal counselling services the debtor would attempt to negotiate a settlement with her creditors. If this was not successful, then she would attempt to reach a settlement with the enforcement office. Ultimately, a binding decision on debt restructuring could be made by a district court. The Act established a norm for repayment of five years, with the possibility of a discharge of debts at the end of this period.

Initial reviews of the Debt Adjustment Act found long processing times, few voluntary settlements, and a lack of clarity in the roles of the enforcement service and the municipality. Reforms in 2006 following a review in 2004 abolished the initial stage and conferred power on the KFM to impose a binding decision subject to the possibility of appeal to a district court. The KFM is an ancient institution in Sweden, originally a tax collection agency, but now an autonomous agency related to the Ministry of Finance which collects all government and private debts. It includes both an enforcement and prevention arm and has offices throughout the country. It is intended, like the English Insolvency Service, to be a 'neutral intermediary' and thus it does not provide advice to debtors about the validity of their debts.

The KFM had in the past an image of being a tough enforcer but since the late 2000s it has been trying to change its image. A clear policy to encourage officers to be generous in permitting access was found by Bengt Larsson and Bengt Jacobsson in 2010. This reflected the political goals for the agency of decreasing 'turnover time, increase[d] productivity and mak[ing] it easier to get debt relief'.[34] The most recent SOUs (discussed below) propose a more active role for the KFM in publicising the existence of debt restructuring (particularly to individuals who may be 'eternity debtors'), providing more advice and co-ordinating with debt counsellors.

Figure 5.1 indicates the substantial increase in applications for debt restructuring since 2006, partly a consequence of the streamlining of the process,[35] but Sweden still has a relatively low rate of applications per capita compared with other European countries with developed personal insolvency systems. The high entry barriers to the Swedish system may underestimate the number of individuals who could benefit from debt restructuring, just as the private alternatives in England make the bankruptcy statistics seem modest. They may also make it harder for debtors to reach informal settlements with creditors.

[34] B Larsson and B Jacobsson, 'Discretion in the "Backyard of Law": Case Handling of Debt Relief in Sweden' (2013) 3(1) *Professions and Professionalism* 1, 8 (an observational study conducted in 2011).

[35] The large increase after 2006 is attributed to the abolition of the 'first-stage' requirement of an attempt at voluntary settlement. This often proved to be a fruitless and costly process.

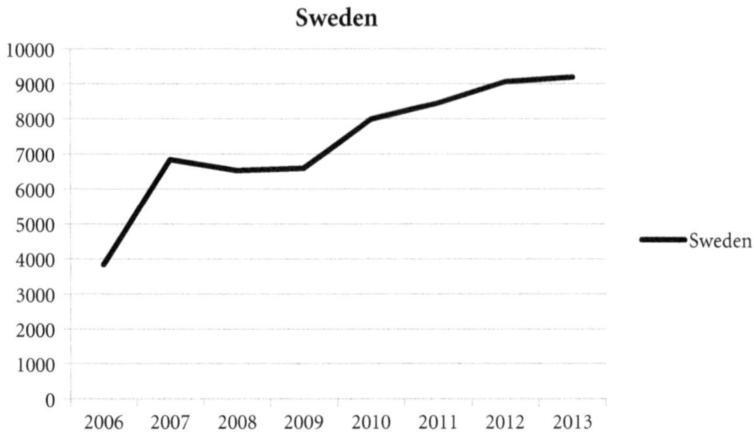

Figure 5.1: Applications for debt restructuring in Sweden (x axis= year, y axis, number of applications)
Source: KFM Annual Reports.

The Debt Adjustment Act has been subject to several reviews since its inception.[36] Legislative revisions have reduced the role of the courts and made the process simpler and faster. A recent report proposes a simple internet application form for debtors.[37] The process was extended to small individual businesses[38] (as originally intended) in 2011 as part of the promotion of entrepreneurialism. But fundamental aspects of the process—the requirements of a five-year plan for all debtors who must live on a subsistence income during this period—and high entry barriers have changed little so that the Swedish system remains a tough creditor-oriented system.

Many debtors have little or no repayment capacity[39] after taking into account a minimum level of subsistence;[40] such debtors must wait for five years before being discharged, even if they are on a zero-repayment plan. In addition, they will only have gained entry to the system if they have demonstrated no likelihood of being

[36] See eg Swedish Consumer Agency, *Assessment of the Debt Relief Act 1995* (this consumer agency report criticised the qualified insolvency test and proposed more realistic evaluations of the ability of a debtor to get back into the housing market); National Tax Board Report 2001; SOU 2004: 81 *A Step Towards a Simpler and Faster Debt Settlement Procedure*; SOU 2008: 82 *The Road Back for the Over-indebted*; Swedish Enforcement Authority, 2008: *Everyone Must Pay Their Fair Share*; SOU 2013: 72 *Out of the Debt Trap*; SOU 2013:78 *Over-Indebtedness in the Credit Society* (n 11); SOU 2014: 44 *An Opportunity for a Fresh Start for Serious Entrepreneurs.*

[37] SOU 2013:72 *Out of the Debt Trap*, 21.

[38] Which are 'simple to investigate', Debt Restructuring Law 2006: 548 as amended 2011, s 4.

[39] See V Nordenanckar, 'The Swedish Debt Relief Act' ECDN Money Matters (2007). SOU 2013: 72 *Out of the Debt Trap* in 2014 states that 36% of the debtors have no repayment capacity and the balance repay under 20% of the debt.

[40] Disposable income is determined by reference to the wage attachment provisions in the Enforcement Code, s 74. This establishes the reserve amount for the debtor.

able to meet their debts over the next 15 years. Sweden has no swift procedure for the NINA (no-income no asset) debtor similar to the *rétablissement personnel* in France or the debt relief order in England and Wales. Official reports repeatedly worry about the impact of any liberalisation of debt relief on Sweden's 'good payment culture' and credit granting. A recent report suggests the possibility of less than a five-year plan only for 'heavily indebted old-age pensioners and debtors who are seriously ill'.[41] The quality of mercy does indeed seem strained!

An emerging issue during the mid 2000s concerned the 'eternity debtor'—individuals who had no possibility of paying their debts in the foreseeable future—but who were not applying to the KFM for debt restructuring. Policy-makers estimated that there were approximately 50,000 eternity debtors.[42] They wished to encourage these individuals to undertake debt restructuring for both economic (reduction in state costs) and humanitarian concerns.[43] Eternity debtors may have been registered with the KFM for many years and subject to wage assignments for over a decade. The European Court of Justice in 2011 provided an example of an 'eternity debtor'. The case concerned a Swedish national working for a Swedish company in Belgium. His small business had gone bankrupt in 1996 (presumably in the wake of the banking crisis) and he had been subject to a wage attachment order since 1997, a period of over 12 years, when he applied for debt restructuring.[44] The KFM refused his application because he was not resident in Sweden. The Court of Justice of the European Union (CJEU) struck down this requirement, holding that it contravened the free movement of workers in the EU treaty and was not justified by the arguments put forward by the Swedish state.

The 2008 report[45] considered the issue of the eternity debtor at some length and proposed a reduction in plan length to three years and modification of the strict entry requirements. This report concluded that such a change would not affect credit granting or payment behaviour. However, while there was a modest modification of the entry requirements in 2011, the five-year plan remained as did the problem of the eternity debtor. Two further reports appeared in 2013. *Out of the Debt Trap*[46]—authored by the same judge as the 2004 SOU—proposed some modest changes to the debt restructuring regime (see below), the latter Hedborg report[47] was a more wide-ranging study, entitled *Overindebtedness in the credit society*. In addition to extensive statistical material, the report was a 'wake up call' for the administration of the debt restructuring system in Sweden, and the development of a strategy on over-indebtedness. Both reports agreed that debt restructuring was a neglected area of public policy with a low public visibility and a poor evidence base for public policy.

41 SOU 2013: 72 *Out of the Debt Trap* at 23.
42 Source: Swedish Consumer Agency.
43 See SOU 2013: 72 *Out of the Debt Trap*, para 4.3.1.
44 Case 461/11 *Ulf Kazimierz Radziejewski v Kronofogdemyndigheten I Stockholm* EU:C:2012:704.
45 SOU 2008: 82 *The Road Back for the Over-indebted.*
46 SOU 2013: 72.
47 SOU 2013: 78.

IV. Who Accesses the Swedish Debt Restructuring System?

An early report suggested that the typical Swedish over-indebted person was a single woman aged 45 with limited education, renting her home, and without children.[48] Table 5.1 indicates that 62 per cent of debtors granted debt restructuring are over 50 and one-third are over 60. They are not representative of the Swedish population and their age profile contrasts sharply with other countries such as France[49] and England and Wales (see Table 5.2). Much higher percentages of debtors in Sweden are over 50 and few debtors are under 40. Debtors involved in restructuring, as shown in Table 5.1, also differ from the age profile of individuals registered with the KFM, or against whom individual enforcement action has been taken. The latter group are over-represented in the 25–54 group.[50]

Table 5.1: Age of debtors granted debt restructuring 2009–12(%)

Age	2009	2010	2011	2012
20–29	0.5	0.9	0.9	1.6
30–39	6.5	7.9	8.7	10.3
40–49	29.1	27.5	24.7	25.3
50–59	31.9	31.9	30.5	28.9
60+	32	31.8	35.2	33.9

Source: SOU 2013:72 *Out of the Debt Trap*, 170, Table 8.3.

Table 5.2: England and Wales Insolvencies 2012

Age	Per cent
<25	4.1
25–34	23.1
35–44	29.6
45–54	26.3
55–64	11.9
65+	4.9

Source: Insolvency Service, *Insolvencies by age, gender, and region 2009–2013*, https://www.gov.uk/government/statistics/insolvency-statistics-individual-insolvencies-by-region-2013. Percentages not adding to 100% due to rounding.

48 B Carlsson and D Hoff, 'Dealing with insolvency and Indebted Individuals in respect to law and morality' (2000) 9 *Social & Legal Studies* 293, 296 quoting the 1996 Report of the National Board for Consumer Policies.

49 See above, ch 4.

50 See the Hedborg report (n 11).

The main sources of income of debtors in 2012 was long-term disability/health insurance payments (32 per cent), or pensions (21 per cent).[51] Those who are unemployed seem less likely to be accepted for debt restructuring. The Hedborg report notes that debtors registered with the KFM are generally less well-educated, single, and living in rented accommodation.[52]

A recent study of debtors on repayment plans confirms the atypical nature of Swedish debtors.[53] The average age was 58, 50 per cent were no longer gainfully employed, and only 25 per cent owned their home. Under 10 per cent had attended university. Over 80 per cent had a total household income under about £29,000 with 45 per cent earning under £17,500. This study examined the effects of debt restructuring, interviewing individuals three years after they had completed restructuring. One-third thought that debt consolidation had given them a fresh start, while 34 per cent did not. Almost a fifth of the subjects had been excluded from access to a bank account. In general, their standard of living had not improved from the period before debt restructuring and their physical and mental health had deteriorated. The conclusions are a mixed endorsement of the programme but deserve comparison with recent research on the effects of the fresh start in the US.[54]

The demographics of those using the debt restructuring system are partly an artefact of the high entry requirements. Approximately 40 per cent of applications for debt restructuring are refused.[55] This is a high level of refusal compared with similar systems such as France, and one wonders about the level of advice that is given to prospective applicants. Table 5.3 indicates the grounds for refusal between 2009 and 2012.

Table 5.3: Grounds for refusal (percentage) 2009–12

	2009	2010	2011	2012
Formal	3	3	3	3
Qualified insolvency	24	37	40	35
Unreasonable	73	60	57	52

Source: SOU 2013:72 *Out of the Debt Trap*. p 170, Table 8.2.

The categories of 'qualified insolvency'—that 'an individual is not likely to have the ability to pay their debts within the foreseeable future'—and 'unreasonableness'

[51] See SOU 2013: 72 *Out of the Debt Trap*, Tables 8.4, 8.5 p 171.

[52] Hedborg report (n 11).

[53] See R Ahlstrom, S Edstrom, and M Savemark, 'Over-Indebtedness as a Risk Factor for Inequality in Health and Life Quality among Swedes—A Survey of Debts, Health and Living Conditions among Over-Indebted Households in Sweden' (Stockholm, Swedish Consumer Agency, 2014).

[54] See ch 3 at 66 (n 192).

[55] See Table 8.1 in SOU 2013: 72 *Out of the Debt Trap*.

confer significant discretion on decision makers.[56] These requirements were intended to prevent those who were temporarily insolvent from using the process and also address concerns about moral hazard both before and after a debtor experiences financial difficulty.

The 2013 report *Out of the Debt Trap* provides an overview of the limited case law on qualified insolvency and suggests significant variation in practice outside those cases[57] where individuals are retired or on long-term disability. The lack of clarity from the courts stimulated the KFM in 2008 to provide guidelines stating that decision makers should not speculate beyond a period of 5 to 10 years. Bengt Larsson and Bengt Jacobsson studied how the case officers (who may be individuals with a legal qualification) approach the general clauses of qualified insolvency and reasonable behaviour.[58] They found divergences in practice, with some officers more generous to debtors than others. They concluded that the guidelines, and computer programmed case handling procedures, reduced discretion but that significant discretion still existed as to the selection and interpretation of information in an applicant's file which could meet the broad standards of reasonableness. Officers claimed that case law provided limited guidance[59] and they relied more heavily on the guidelines which concretised 'the foreseeable future' in terms of the inability of an individual to repay.[60]

However, in 2010, the Swedish Supreme Court held that a 47-year-old social worker working part time who had accrued substantial debts during the 1990s while unemployed, with a monthly salary of approximately £1,500, debts of about £30,000 (much of which represented accrued interest), and student loan debt of £25,000 (but not yet due) and offering repayments of about £400 a month (which would pay down over 80 per cent of the non-student debt), did not meet the test of qualified insolvency, because in the long run she could potentially find full-time work until retirement, and become debt free (apart from the student loan) in 15 years.[61] This adoption of a 15-year period overturned the earlier guidance by

[56] Article 4 of the Debt Adjustment Act defines qualified insolvency as a situation where a debtor is 'so in debt that he or she is not likely to have the ability to pay their debts within the foreseeable future' and 'it is reasonable having regard to the debtor's personal and economic conditions that debt settlement is granted to him or her'. In determining 'reasonableness', 'special consideration shall be given to the circumstances of the liabilities' inception, the efforts the debtor has made to fulfill its obligations and the way in which a debtor has been involved in handling of the case of debt settlement'. This section no longer includes 'the age of the debts' which was viewed as restricting debt settlement to individuals who had incurred debts several years before an application for debt settlement.

[57] 'There are a large number of reported court cases on the issue of qualified insolvency but few statements about what is to be considered a foreseeable time.' SOU 2013: 72 *Out of the Debt Trap* at 8.5.

[58] Larsson and Jacobsson, 'Discretion in the "Backyard of Law"' (n 34).

[59] They quote one officer stating 'There is extremely little to stand on in the legislation. The legal cases are—or individual debtors are—as different as night and day'. Ibid 6. Larsson and Larsson also draw attention to the idea that in 2010 there was 'an unspoken policy at the SEA encouraging officers to be generous … and not to "over-investigate" before initiating a case', ibid 6–7.

[60] Although the KFM handbook states that 'the calculation of insolvency is not an absolute truth but only an approximation', ibid at 10.

[61] See *Nytt Juridiskt Arkiv* (NJA) 2010, s 496 discussed in SOU 2013: 72 *Out of the Debt Trap* s 8.3.

the KFM, but the Court backpedalled in a 2013 decision, indicating that a court must make an individualised decision in all the circumstances.[62] Meanwhile the government commissioned another SOU in 2012[63] and social democratic and Christian democratic politicians in Parliament pressed the government to accelerate reforms to reduce the qualified insolvency period and the length of the plans. However the consequences are clear in the statistics on debt settlement which indicate the underrepresentation of individuals under 50. This could be accounted for by other factors, but it is surprising that unlike other countries there is not an over-representation of debtors between 30–50, traditionally the period in the life cycle when individuals have the heaviest debt burdens.

The latter 'reasonableness' test invites an assessment of the debtor's character and handling of the debt. The decline in refusals on this ground may be attributable to the deletion of the 'age of the debts' in section 2 of the Debt Adjustment Act which often limited debt adjustment to situations where an individual had carried a debt for a long time.

V. Debt Counselling and the 'Enabling Welfare State'[64]

One image of Nordic debt adjustment is that of the debt counsellor acting as part of an 'enabling welfare state' providing economic rehabilitation for the citizen debtor. The enabling welfare state provides services to permit individuals to rejoin in the labour market rather than receive cash transfers.[65] Cutbacks have occurred during the past decade in these services and debt counselling may have been one casualty of these cuts.

Legal aid was available initially for lawyers to assist debtors but lawyers do not now play a role in providing assistance. Municipalities must offer budget counselling services,[66] but it is not a mandatory requirement to seek counselling before applying for debt restructuring. Approximately 75 per cent of debtors do so in preparing their application to the KFM.[67] Advice is desirable as the applicant must

62 *Nytt Juridiskt Archiv* (NJA) 2013, s 28, discussed in SOU 2013: 72 *Out of the Debt Trap* s 8.3.

63 Which became SOU 2013: 72 *Out of the Debt Trap*.

64 See P Kristensen, 'Developing Comprehensive Enabling Welfare States for Offensive Experimentalist Business Practices' in P Kristensen and K Lilja (eds), *Nordic Capitalisms and Globalization* (Oxford, Oxford University Press, 2011) 220, discussed in Schnyder, 'Like a Phoenix from the Ashes?' (n 2) at 1134.

65 ibid 1134.

66 The latest provision (s 2) is more extensive in imposing an obligation to 'provide advice and guidance in the budget and debt issues to indebted people. This obligation also applies during debt settlement procedure and duration of a payment plan'. Earlier versions simply require the municipality to 'provide advice and instructions to indebted people' (s 1).

67 SOU 2013: 72 *Out of the Debt Trap* notes, at para 7.4.1, that 'more than seven out of ten of the debt settlement applications lodged in 2012 received help from a budgetary advisor'. Advice does not seem to guarantee acceptance. Sixty-six per cent of those rejected had received advice. Ibid.

complete a relatively long application[68] which includes questions related to the likelihood of future employment. This application will be used by the KFM staff to determine acceptability for debt restructuring and, given the discretionary nature of this decision, advice from knowledgeable individuals on how to frame the relevant information is likely to be important. The structure of debt counselling follows the Swedish model of social welfare which attempts to reconcile principles of universalism and local autonomy. Policy is established at national level and implementation is the responsibility of 'highly independent' local authorities.[69] A problem with this model is that the benefits of local counselling may accrue to national programmes such as the social insurance agency and public healthcare in the form of reduced costs, providing little incentive for municipalities to invest in budget counselling.[70]

The Hedborg review in 2014 provided a scathing critique of the existing system of counselling. A few municipalities had no counsellor and many had only one counsellor who worked one day a week. Long waiting times existed for appointments. An average waiting period of six weeks existed, followed by an average of four months from consultation to the debt restructuring application.[71] The KFM generally takes about two months to determine whether to accept a file and then another five months until debt restructuring is granted. This last period allows the KFM to check official records to verify the information provided by the debtor. More than a year may elapse from the initial contact with the budget adviser to the commencement of the debt-restructuring plan. This is a longer process than in England or France.

The Hedborg report found that little preventive work was being undertaken and contact occurred rarely between advisers and debtors once debtors were on a plan. Variations existed in the level of professionalism of counsellors, with distinct approaches evident among different municipalities. Hedborg expressed concern that incorrect advice may have been provided to debtors and that little assessment was made of the legal validity of debts. No thorough investigation of counselling services seemed to have been undertaken for many years, leaving it the 'Cinderella' of social services. The Hedborg report concluded that radical change was necessary to make counselling services work satisfactorily throughout the country.[72] The central Swedish Consumer Agency will in future have a much greater role in

[68] 'The requirements for the content of the application are extensive and will probably lead to people refraining from applying for debt settlement.' Ibid.

[69] See G-B Trydegard and M Thorslund, 'One Uniform Welfare State or a Multitude of Welfare Municipalities? The Evolution of Local Variation in Swedish Elder Care' (2010) 44(4) *Social Policy and Administration* 495.

[70] See I Nilsson and E Nilsson Lundmark, 'Budget and Debt Counselling—A Huge Cost or a Profitable Social Investment', paper prepared for Swedish Consumer Agency 2011.

[71] SOU 2013: 72 *Out of the Debt Trap*, 133. Substantial variations existed, ranging from no waiting time to over a year.

[72] Hedborg report (n 11) 235–37.

supporting and providing guidance to municipalities[73] and in training counsellors with the central state providing greater basic financing for counselling.[74]

VI. The Five-Year Plan

The law requires a five-year repayment plan as a condition of discharge unless special reasons exist to justify a shorter period of time. This almost never occurs. In 2013 only 25 or 30 of 4,637 cases resulted in a repayment period of less than five years. The appropriateness of this period has been a continuing topic in discussion of the law, particularly since substantial numbers of debtors have no repayment capacity. Little incentive exists to develop a payment capacity during the five years since any surplus will go to creditors. In 2002, the Swedish Consumer Agency suggested that the period be reduced to three years on the basis that debtors would have often been in financial difficulties for many years and a shorter period would induce further voluntary settlements. The 2004 report reviewed the five-year requirement but took the view that five years was the established period.[75] In 2006 the possibility of a period longer than five years was excised from the Act. The 2008 report recommended a shortened period of three years, partly based on the argument that it would promote entrepreneurship.[76]

The government did not adopt this proposal in the 2011 amendments citing the fear of its impact on payment culture, as well as a concern that it would lead to an increase in the number of debt applications. The SOU 2013 *Out of the Debt Trap* surveyed different stakeholders and ultimately decided to leave the term at five years, but with the possibility of discretion for a shorter period, for example for those in retirement or who are seriously ill. The report recognised the costs of living with over-indebtedness and the importance of early economic rehabilitation so that individuals can become productive. However, it also cited losses to creditors from a reduction in plan length, the need for debtors to have time to learn how to manage a budget, the general effect on overall payment habits, and the need to maintain a high level of confidence among the public. Moreover, the consultations with stakeholders indicated no strong demand for a reduction in the five-year period.

The 2013 report recognised that Sweden might be out of line with international trends towards a reduction in the debt repayment period but it could find no domestic need for it. It was not clear, however, who represented the interests of debtors in the process of stakeholder consultation. Debt counsellors were not united on the value of a shorter period. Some argued that a five-year period is

[73] See now Debt Restructuring Act, 2006 as amended s 2.
[74] See Hedborg report (n 11) 237.
[75] SOU 2004: 81, s 235.
[76] SOU 2008: 82, s 135.

necessary for an individual to get back on track. Credit groups generally opposed a shortening of the period. The Commission concluded with a compromise, recommending the possibility of two 'payment holiday' months each year. This maintained the appearance of a five-year plan but would effectively reduce it to four years and two months.

A further issue concerns the implementation of the plan. Surprisingly, no institution monitors or checks that a debtor is maintaining repayments and an individual must make separate payments monthly to each creditor. While this might be justified by its educational effect on the debtor, it often involves debtors in complex calculations. Proposals for a collection account operated by a bank creditor were rejected by the banks as too expensive, as was administration by the KFM. By 2013 all groups regarded the current design of payment plans as unsatisfactory and the 2013 report recommended a central payment service.

A further report in 2014 investigated the need for a special discharge regime for entrepreneurs. The original proposals for debt relief in the early 1990s would have included small businesses within its scope, but it was only in 2011 that small businesses with simple debts were included. They have represented only a tiny percentage of cases (69 cases in total) from 2011–13. The report proposes that a new procedure be developed for 'serious entrepreneurs' providing a discharge after three years.[77] Entrepreneurs will still be required to make payments over a three-year period at a higher rate (minimum 5,000 Swedish kronor each quarter). Criteria for identifying honest or serious entrepreneurs have been identified and the 'reasonableness' entry requirement will be maintained. As if to confirm that entrepreneurs are not receiving favourable treatment over consumers, the three-year period will have no payment holidays. The report suggests that their proposals will have important symbolic consequences in signalling that Sweden is entrepreneur friendly.

Although the report draws inspiration from the ideology of the US swift fresh start as a promoter of entrepreneurialism, the preconditions for the Swedish entrepreneurial fresh start are much higher. The report justifies these by playing what might be described as 'the cultural card'. The report argues that over-indebtedness is seen differently in Europe and the US. In Europe 'overindebtedness is regarded as a social and moral problem and … the debtor is expected to bear more of the risk. … The European approach is characterised by not making debt restructuring available to everyone and not letting it be perceived as an "easy way out"'.[78]

[77] See SOU 2014: 44 *An Opportunity for a Fresh Start for Serious Entrepreneurs*. The three years was chosen to be in line with the 2014 European Recommendation. See Commission Recommendation on a New Approach to Business Failure and Insolvency C(2014) 1500. The Commission has now proposed a Directive on Business Failure and Insolvency. See below, ch 6.

[78] 'In the US system, writing off liabilities is regarded as an efficient way to distribute risks. Over-indebtedness is seen as a market failure and is explained as a failure of the market to assess the risks. With this approach, it is logical to regard debt restructuring as a means of efficiently tackling problems of over-indebtedness so as to enable the individual to rapidly return to the market as a con-

Sweden may, however, have to modify its stance in the light of the 2016 EU Directive on Insolvency discussed in chapter six which requires jurisdictions to reduce barriers to access to insolvency for entrepreneurs, as part of a European strategy of promoting entrepreneurialism.

VII. Protection Against Home Eviction and Mortgage Foreclosure

Sweden has a relatively high level of home ownership (70 per cent). Housing is both a market asset and a form of welfare, often providing rent-free accommodation in old age. Sweden facilitates home purchases through the tax system and mortgages are often long term, with variable interest rates. This form of *ex ante* universal 'welfare' is generally regressive in its impact. Since the Great Recession of the late 2000s the Central Bank has demonstrated concern about Sweden's high mortgage debt levels and there has been an increase in foreclosures, doubling between 2007 and 2011.[79]

The Central Bank has regulated access to housing mortgages through maximum (85 per cent) loan to value requirements. This *ex ante* protection for consumers is also designed to protect bank capital. Sweden has not instituted any programmes to protect homeowners in financial difficulty. Foreclosure and sale procedures are relatively swift, providing limited protection to a homeowner. Annina Persson, Ann-Sofie Henrikson, and Karin Lundstrom conclude that 'despite the home being a tremendously central factor in the lives of Swedes generally, it is in many ways poorly safeguarded in Swedish law'.[80] This contrasts with the 'neo-liberal' UK which instituted a wide range of subsidies, procedures and regulations to address the problems of over-indebted homeowners in the wake of the Great Recession.[81] These were often targeted at more vulnerable consumers.

sumer and borrower. It has been pointed out that in Europe overindebtedness is regarded as a social or moral problem and that the debtor is expected to bear more of the risk. Debt restructuring for private persons, which is known as "personal bankruptcy" in the US, where it became available in 1978, was only introduced in Europe in the 1980s and 1990s. The European approach is characterized by not making debt restructuring available to everyone and not letting it be perceived as an "easy way out".' SOU 2014: 44 *An Opportunity for a Fresh Start*, 34.

[79] See discussion in H Haber, 'Regulation as Social Policy: Home Evictions and Repossessions in the UK and Sweden' (2015) 93(3) *Public Administration* 806.

[80] A Persson, A-S Henrikson, and K Lundstrom, 'Household Credit, Debt and Insolvency' (2013) 3 *European Review of Private Law* 795, 813.

[81] I discuss them in I Ramsay (2015) 'Two Cheers for Europe: Austerity, Mortgage Foreclosures and Personal Insolvency Policy in the EU' in HW Micklitz and Irina Domurath (eds), *Consumer Debt and Social Exclusion in Europe* (Farnham, Ashgate, 2015). For further discussion of this contrast see generally Haber, 'Regulation as Social Policy' (n 79).

VIII. Discussion

The strictness of the Swedish regime has been modified slightly since its inception in 1994. This outcome might be accounted for by reference to the political power of the concentrated banking sector, but I am not convinced that this provides a full explanation. Certainly one question concerns the representation of debtor interests on the various commissions. Labour groups (who might speak on behalf of debtors) seem absent from discussions and debt counsellors do not seem to be a well-organised constituency. Unlike the US, debt relief is not conceptualised as a benefit that might be used by a broad cross-section of the population. It does not fit the traditional Swedish form of universalist benefit which might garner support from middle-class consumers. They are more likely to be worried about the impact of debt relief on the cost of credit. Sven Steinmo cites statistics that demonstrate that Swedes are less supportive of needs-based programmes such as housing allowances or social assistance.[82]

Household debt restructuring does not fit neatly into welfare state models of redistribution through subsidies and social spending. Sweden subsidises *ex ante* the purchase of homes, which has traditionally been conceptualised as a 'middle-class' perk, but provides little legal protection for homeowners in difficulty. Sweden has institutions and policies regarded as inefficient and potentially destabilising, such as generous tax relief for mortgages and interest only mortgages with long amortisations. The very high level of household debt which individuals may carry into old age is considered potentially dangerous by international agencies and the Central Bank, but seems to be embedded in Swedish practice. The argument that it is matched by asset accumulation is not completely convincing since this was the standard retort in the UK to concerns about household debt before the Great Recession.

The state takes responsibility for enforcement and counselling, and individual debtors do not have to pay to access debt restructuring. In that sense, debt restructuring does seem to fit a more 'social' model of debt relief. There is not a strong narrative in Sweden, like France, of protecting individuals from the market through price controls. Pre-contract controls on the granting of credit do not differ markedly from those of a supposedly neo-liberal state such as the UK. The recent proposals in the Hedborg report for a strategy against over-indebtedness (better counselling and education, adjustment of exorbitant interest rates and experiments with 'remediation loans') are similar to UK initiatives.

The politics of compromise seem to have resulted in a gridlock on further progress in liberalising the Swedish individual regime. Legislative politics may be relevant, with a centre-right coalition government in power since 2006 less sympathetic to the provision of debt relief. The technical analyses in the various SOUs attempt to 'balance' the different viewpoints. Social science knowledge has had limited impact in testing the empirical questions of the effects of reforms on

[82] Steinmo, 'Sweden: The Evolution of a Bumble Bee' (n 1) 83.

credit granting and Sweden's 'payment culture'. The strict limits on debt discharge may be resulting in an overextension of credit and, possibly, many individuals struggling to maintain repayments rather than applying for debt restructuring. Nor is there any guarantee that the profits made by financial institutions in this situation are passed on to consumers, given the quasi-oligopolostic nature of the Swedish banking system. These are of course hypotheses which remain to be tested.

The difficulty of regulating household debt is complicated by the division of jurisdiction in this area between state agencies and municipalities, reluctance to invest state resources, and the absence of private actors such as lawyers who might act on behalf of debtors. Debtors are conceptualised as individuals with needs rather than rights. The 2014 reform proposals may result in greater attention being paid to over-indebtedness policy: a central conclusion of *Out of the Debt Trap* was the 'low visibility' of debt restructuring.[83] The Swedish response is to make the state more efficient, through more effective coordination between the different public agencies (KFM, municipalities, Konsumentverket). There is little enthusiasm for harnessing the private sector, as in England, to address debt problems.

The emphasis on maintaining a 'good payment culture' resonates with the US rhetoric of 'personal responsibility' which drove the enactment of the Bankruptcy Abuse Prevention and Consumer Protection Act 2005.[84] The narrative of maintaining Sweden's 'good payment culture' is a recurring theme and cannot be simply reduced to the interests of the financial industry. It seems to be a shared narrative. The most recent SOU investigation of entrepreneurship states:

> It is important that we keep a high standard of payment behaviour in both business and private life. Business relations and trade benefit if actors are confident that contracts will be kept and invoices paid, and this is also crucial to the smooth functioning of society and a high degree of social trust.[85]

Data cited by an EU commissioned study of over-indebtedness suggest that Sweden does have currently a lower level of arrears on mortgage and rent payments than most states in the EU, with the exception of Germany. Swedes are also, according to the study, less likely than other Europeans to be unable to face unexpected financial circumstances, make ends meet or to feel at risk of being over-indebted.[86] Perhaps Sweden does have a good payment culture but the idea of a good payment culture as an artefact of strict insolvency laws may overestimate the role of law in shaping behaviour or moulding a shared morality.[87]

[83] 'Society currently knows little about debt reconstruction.' SOU 2013: 72 *Out of the Debt Trap*, 20.

[84] See discussion above, ch 3.

[85] *An Opportunity for a Fresh Start for Entrepreneurs* (n 36) 42.

[86] See Tables 7, 13, 14, and 16 in Civic Consulting, *The Over-indebtedness of European Households: Updated Mapping of the Situation, Nature and Causes, Effects and Initiatives for Alleviating its Impact Final Report* (Brussels, 2014).

[87] The idea of a shared morality may harken back to the idea of a 'good society'. Per Albin Hansson, 'in a good society there is equality, care, co-operation and willingness to help', quoted in R Goksor 'Jurisprudence of Protection of Weaker Parties in European Contracts Law from A Swedish and Nordic Perspective' (2006) 6 *Chicago-Kent Journal of International and Comparative Law* 184.

6

After the Crisis: Towards an International 'Common Sense' in Personal Insolvency Law?

'To the wind that will blow tomorrow'

Charles Baudelaire, Review of Salon des Refusés 1845

I. Introduction

This chapter documents a step change in regional and international policymaking on personal insolvency after the Great Recession of 2008. Crises can be transformative because they raise questions about existing knowledge and expertise, providing opportunities for new diagnoses and policy remedies.[1] The perceived international significance of household debt and insolvency after the Great Recession accelerated transnational narratives and policy scripts about the nature and role of personal insolvency. The policy process in several European countries was in some cases dramatically shortened under the pressure of international institutions and the EU.[2] Convergence in legal institutions may result from several sources. These include similar responses by countries to common problems, imitation,[3] the imposition of rules by powerful countries on other countries, harmonisation, regulatory competition, and 'transnational communication'.[4] A further phenomenon is the spillover effect when reform in one topic prompts reform of an adjacent topic. Reforms of corporate and business insolvency may stimulate a state

[1] '[C]risis also often raises questions about the limits of technical knowledge and practice: in many crises the medical expert either does not know what will work reliably or even what to expect next.' E Engelen et al, *After the Great Complacence: Financial Crisis and the Politics of Reform* (Oxford, Oxford University Press, 2011) 160.

[2] See generally on the acceleration of policy, J Peck and N Theodore, *Fast Policy: Experimental State-Craft at the Thresholds of NeoLiberalism* (Minneapolis, University of Minnesota Press, 2015).

[3] Referred to by sociologists as 'mimetic isomorphism'.

[4] C Knill, 'Introduction: Cross-National Policy Convergence: Concepts, Approaches and Explanatory Factors' (2005) 12(5) *Journal of European Public* 764, 770.

to introduce personal insolvency reform. All these processes are visible in relation to individual insolvency.[5] The EU and International Monetary Fund (IMF) have required insolvency reform under loan conditionality rules. The EU under the European Semester has persuaded countries such as Spain to introduce more forgiving personal insolvency laws. The EU has proposed harmonisation of aspects of individual insolvency as part of a strategy of promoting entrepreneurialism within the single market with consumer insolvency riding on its coat-tails.[6] Transnational communication on ideas occurs through professional networks such as INSOL,[7] the Association of Insolvency Regulators and academic sites. Individual 'bankruptcy tourism' has stimulated political pressures for reform.[8] Regulatory competition even exists. Recent Scottish reforms claim to have developed a world-class insolvency system (or at least one better than that in England and Wales!).

Some writers argue that a transnational legal order[9] now exists in relation to corporate insolvency and that this emerged after the Asian financial crisis of the late 1990s, when a modified Anglo-American 'rescue culture' was internationalised as part of the international financial architecture of economic development. A small close-knit community of global actors situated in distinct organisations (clubs such as G7, IFIs, associations of professionals, international governance organisations and core nations), with the belief that an effective bankruptcy law played a central role in a market economy, shaped global bankruptcy law making through the development of international norms such as the UNCITRAL legislative guide. This provides best practices for assessing a state's insolvency law by

[5] In relation to corporate bankruptcy, see T Halliday and B Carruthers, *Bankrupt: Global Lawmaking and Systemic Financial Crisis* (Stanford, Palo Alto, 2010). Globalisation efforts in corporate insolvency have resulted thus far in convergence at a level of principle, but there remains substantial local variation at the level of enactment and implementation. Ironically, the international model for corporate rescue, the US Chapter 11, no longer functions in its home country as originally intended. However the narrative of Chapter 11 continues to be influential in international reform. Carruthers and Halliday do not describe a smooth process of diffusion of global norms. States had different capacities to resist these norms and local groups demonstrated a repertoire of foiling techniques such as 'the culture hand' (388)—that the global law did not fit local conditions. Professional intermediaries (lawyers, judges, legal academics etc) often played a key role promoting or foiling international agenda in the bankruptcy arena. The outcome was not therefore a homogenization of world norms but a cycle of 'trial and error … innovation and adaptation among the global actors' (34), learning from experiences with different countries and being influenced often by the more powerful countries 'in the global financial center' (34). An element of contingency existed in the process of globalisation.

[6] See Proposal for a Directive of the European Parliament and of the Council on preventive restructuring frameworks, second chance and measures to increase the efficiency of restructuring, insolvency and discharge procedures and amending Directive 2012/30/EU COM (2016) 723 22.11.2016 and see earlier impact statement, DG Just Inception Impact Assessment DG Just (A1) 2016/JUSt/025 (2016).

[7] See the INSOL International, *Consumer Debt Report* 2001 and 2011.

[8] See below, section V.

[9] See T Halliday and G Shaffer (eds), *Transnational Legal Orders* (Cambridge, Cambridge University Press, 2015) who define at 11 a transnational legal order as a 'collection of formalized norms and associated organizations and actors that authoritatively order the understanding and practice of law across national jurisdictions' and see S Block-Lieb and T Halliday, 'Settling and Concordance: Two Cases in Global Commercial Law' in Halliday and Shaffer, ibid, where they discuss the emergence of a TLO in corporate bankruptcy.

the World Bank, and is part of structural adjustment under loan conditionality. In contrast, personal insolvency was not regarded as significant internationally in terms of the international financial architecture and it was considered that it, along with the topic of over-indebtednesss, raised social cultural and political issues best left to individual states.[10]

In this chapter the emergence of a new international narrative on personal insolvency is identified. One strand of this narrative emphasises the importance of swift deleveraging by households in the wake of debt-fuelled recessions. This overlaps with a strand linking liberal bankruptcy discharge laws to the promotion of entrepreneurialism. These narratives, however, have faced political resistance from states and agencies such as the European Central Bank which are concerned about the impact of debt discharge on 'payment culture', raising issues of moral hazard. The technocratic narratives of 'best practices' and 'cross-country experience' adopted by the IMF and the troika (that is, the European Central Bank (ECB), IMF and European Commission, an informal grouping established in 2010 during the Greece bailout) in bringing about insolvency reforms within Europe attempted to balance these conflicting strands, with different outcomes in each state, dependent partly on the balance of power between the troika and the state. An emerging European model appears to be the dominance of a repayment plan of perhaps three years as a condition of discharge with the possibility of a swift discharge reserved for the no-income no-asset debtor. It would be misleading to describe this emerging paradigm as representing a new Washington or Brussels consensus or a new 'transnational legal order' but, like all transnational paradigms, it links scholarly and political fields.

II. International Initiatives: After the Great Recession

The Great Recession transformed household debt, a peripheral aspect of finance,[11] from a parochial concern to an issue for the international financial architecture. Better prudential regulation was an immediate concern but the contribution of financial consumer protection reform to the safety and soundness of the global financial system also became relevant. International initiatives by the G20 nations

[10] Skene and Walters wrote in 2008 that 'hardly any attention has been paid at the international level to the potential global socio-economic impact of consumer over-indebtedness. This contrasts with the global interest in business insolvency and rescue'. See eg D Skene and A Walters, 'Consumer Passions: Benchmarking Consumer Bankruptcy Law Systems' in P Omar (ed), *International Insolvency Law* (Aldershot, Ashgate, 2008) 137.

[11] See K Pistor, 'A Legal Theory of Finance' (2013) 41(2) *Journal of Comparative Economics* 315, 319. Pistor argues that in terms of bail outs in the US after the Great Recession 'consumers were last in order, signifying their peripheral status. They were thrown a lifeline at long last, but primarily for political reasons (the fear that austerity might create structural unemployment or a political backlash), not because they posed an immediate threat to the financial system.'

have developed high-level principles of consumer credit market regulation that states are committed to implement.[12]

Personal insolvency law reform was not initially part of these international initiatives. Susan Block-Lieb argues that this reflects a lack of international consensus on the role of consumer credit in the economy and the significance of personal insolvency as a ground rule of the credit market.[13] International corporate rescue norms were justified as making both creditors and debtors better off, whereas relieving consumers of debt raised distributional and political conflicts between creditor and debtor, and between different groups of consumers, with non-defaulters seemingly paying for those who discharged their debts.

No authoritative international scripts for addressing individual insolvency existed in 2010. The UNCITRAL legislative guide, used by the World Bank and IMF in evaluating countries' business bankruptcy systems, and for the purpose of loan conditionality,[14] was limited in its application to individual non-trader bankruptcy.[15] No influential national model such as the US Chapter 11 existed for consumer insolvency. Indeed, the US individual bankruptcy system had a rather mixed reputation outside the US. Powerful professional groups were not promoting particular models of personal insolvency.[16] Nor was there a World Bank *Doing Business* project for consumer debt or insolvency. Many European states in the EU had introduced discharge systems for personal insolvency only towards the end of the twentieth century and many countries in the developing world did not have personal insolvency systems. Limited empirical analysis existed of the operation of individual insolvency systems. The treatment of individuals with unmanageable mortgage debt was a key issue after the recession but best practices here—for example whether to deal with secured debt within insolvency law—did not exist, and this issue continues to pose a challenge for policymakers.[17] A Washington or Brussels consensus on individual insolvency norms did not therefore exist.

[12] See OECD, *G20 High Level Principles on Financial Consumer Protection* (2011); World Bank, *Good Practices for Financial Consumer* Protection (2012). See discussion in T Williams, 'Continuity not Rupture: The Persistence of Neoliberalism in the Internationalization of Consumer Finance Regulation' in T Wilson (ed), *International Responses to Issues of Credit and Over-Indebtedness in the Wake of the Crisis* (Farnham, Ashgate Publishing, 2013).

[13] S Block-Lieb and T Halliday, 'The Micro-Economics and Macropolitics of Systemic Financial Crisis: Bankruptcy as a Point of Reference' in J Garasic and N Bodiroga-Vukobrat (eds), *Sovereign Insolvency—Possible Legal Solutions* (Springer, forthcoming).

[14] UNCITRAL 'managed to leverage its norms by linking them to institutions with the power to persuade and enforce'. Halliday and Carruthers, *Bankrupt* (n 5) 165. The UNCITRAL legislative guide on insolvency outlines 'the core issues that it would be desirable to address in that law with recommendations providing specific guidance on how certain legislative provisions might be drafted' (para 2). The guide has specific recommendations where there appears to be a 'high degree of consensus', while others outline alternatives (ibid at 158–59). The US and expert professional groups led by Americans were influential in developing this consensus along with the IMF.

[15] See UNCITRAL Legislative Guide on Insolvency at 38 Focus is 'designing an insolvency law focused on debtors engaged in economic activities'.

[16] Although INSOL, the international insolvency practitioners association had issued a guide in 2001.

[17] JR Andritzky, 'Resolving Residential Mortgage Distress: Time to Modify?' IMF Working Paper 14/226.

In 2011, the World Bank Insolvency and Creditor Rights Task Force convened a meeting with other agencies to discuss insolvency issues in the wake of the Great Recession. For the first time, the issue of insolvency of natural persons as a systemic risk was considered. Preliminary survey evidence indicated that more than half of middle-income and low-income countries had no personal insolvency system. The Bank identified the need for modernisation while recognising the 'diversity of policy perspectives, values, cultural preferences and legal traditions that shape the way countries may choose to deal with the problem of over-indebtedness'.[18] It struck an international task force to investigate the policies and principles underlying the diverse legal systems that have addressed 'consumer insolvency'. The subsequent World Bank *Report on the Treatment of the Insolvency of Natural Persons*[19] makes an economic and social case for the introduction of a personal insolvency discharge, in terms of reducing externalities from debt default (such as lost productivity, costs to family and communities), creating incentives for responsible lending and accounting practices, reducing wasteful collection costs, encouraging entrepreneurship and allocating losses to those in the best position to spread them.[20] The report drew on European ideas such as the prevention of social exclusion, as well as the promotion of a fresh start and insolvency as a form of social insurance. It argued that moral hazard was generally a small problem in existing bankruptcy systems and that a more significant problem was the problem of encouraging individuals to access bankruptcy, given the continuing stigma. It also discussed alternative institutional structures for managing bankruptcy with the central theme that bankruptcy was a 'small stakes game' where debtors often could not finance a complex process, but that an infrastructure that inspired the confidence of all parties was crucial to the success of a system.

The report underlined the economic and social significance of individual insolvency law but did not outline best practices that could be used to assess countries'

[18] This document was titled *Best Practices in the Insolvency of Natural Persons* (Susan Block-Lieb, rapporteur, World Bank, 2011). Vijay Tata (Chief Counsel, World Bank LEGPS) 'pointed out that one of the lessons from the recent financial crisis was the recognition of the problem of consumer insolvency as a systemic risk and the consequent need for the modernization of domestic laws and institutions to enable jurisdictions to deal effectively and efficiently with the risks of individual over-indebtedness … It is important to recognize the diversity of policy perspectives, values, cultural preferences and legal traditions that shape the way jurisdictions may choose to deal with the problems of over-indebtedness. Yet recent events suggest that the expansion of access to finance, the extension of modern modes of financial intermediation, and the mobility and globalization of financial flows may have changed the character and scale of the risk of consumer insolvency in similar ways in many different economies'. Insolvency and Creditor/Debtor Regimes Task Force Meeting 10–11 January 2011, Washington DC, Conference Report, Day 2 Best Practices in the Insolvency of Natural Persons.

[19] See World Bank, *Report on the Treatment of the Insolvency of Natural Persons* (World Bank, 2013) (the present author was a drafter of this report along with J Kilborn (chair), J Garrido, C Booth, and J Niemi). This was the work of a small group of academics within the context of a World Bank Task Force comprised of lawyers, government representatives, academics, judges (primarily US bankruptcy judges), and representatives of UNCITRAL.

[20] See also J Garrido, 'The Role of Personal Insolvency Law in Economic Development: An Introduction to the World Bank Report on the Treatment of the Insolvency of Natural Persons' (2013) 5 *World Bank Law Review* 111.

performance in a similar manner to the UNCITRAL guide. The report justified this position by the argument that 'personal insolvency is intertwined with social, political and cultural issues that present too many differences to be treated uniformly'.[21] Personal insolvency might differ in the context of distinct economic and social systems.[22] While these reasons have some weight, the approach taken by the report was also driven by political factors. The World Bank wished to publish a report swiftly. Any suggestion that it was enunciating best practices would raise questions of legitimacy and process, and risk the task being taken over by UNCITRAL with its relatively drawn-out procedures. The drafters of the World Bank report were careful in delineating its scope so that it did not intrude into areas which would be viewed as within the UNCITRAL standards. The report recognised the overlaps between individual business and consumer debt, arguing that it was concerned primarily with the personal rather than business aspects of insolvency.[23]

The World Bank report, following the bank's conventions, does not refer to any specific country in its discussions and recommendations. The reasons here are also political. References to influential nations such as the US could be interpreted as colonialism. The report drew primarily on developed European systems, US and Anglo-Commonwealth systems. France, for example, provided a model for a 'one-stop shop' institutional structure for managing over-indebtedness.[24] The US system often appeared within the discussions as something of an outlier.[25] European sources were a significant influence,[26] although the report was critical of European policies of mandatory requirements for attempts at voluntary settlements (which were often not cost effective), and long repayment plans imposed on individuals with no repayment capacity. This was an implicit criticism of the German system.[27] The identification of a payment plan as a general requirement for a discharge places the US, England and Canada, which recognise the possibility of a relatively swift discharge, as exceptions.

[21] World Bank (n 19) para 12.

[22] Ibid paras 28–29.

[23] Ibid para 18: '[T]he ICR Standard governs the insolvency of natural persons who are engaged in business activities (traders or merchants), this report centers its attention on the personal aspects of insolvency: these aspects are prevalent in the insolvency of persons who cannot be said to be engaged in significant business activity, but they also exist in the cases of individuals who can be classified as "traders", "merchants", or "entrepreneurs". The report avoids the use of the expression "consumer insolvency" because it would raise similar questions as to the distinction between consumers and non-consumers in numerous legal systems. Therefore, the report uses the expressions "insolvency of natural persons" and "personal insolvency" indistinctly. The report is addressed to the questions posed by the insolvency of individuals, rather than to those questions raised by the interaction of business activities and commercial credit, and it is for policymakers to determine the relevance of the analysis contained in this report to the specific circumstances that affect insolvent individuals in any particular system.'

[24] See ibid para 175.

[25] For example in the discussion of access, and the swift fresh start without the need for any attempt at repayment.

[26] See eg World Bank (n 19) para 21.

[27] See further J Kilborn, 'Reflections of the World Bank's Report on the Treatment of the Insolvency of Natural Persons in the Newest Consumer Bankruptcy Laws: Colombia, Italy, Ireland' (2014) 26(3) *Pace International Law Review* (winter 2014).

The impact of the World Bank report will depend on authority and prestige,[28] since, unlike the UNCITRAL guidelines, it is not used in the process of conditionality by the IMF.[29] The rivalry between the Bank and the IMF ensure that it is unlikely to be embraced by the IMF[30] although it may seep into reform initiatives through the work of academics, who sometimes act as 'model mongers'.

A. European Bankruptcy Reform Through Imposition and Technocratic Persuasion

The recession and eurozone crisis resulted in new EU governance actors such as the European Banking Authority,[31] the European Stability Mechanism, and the troika. The EU attained leverage over the domestic policies of countries bailed out through memorandum of understanding (MoUs) (conditionality)[32] and the European Semester[33] as part of the increased enforcement of the various stability pacts.[34]

[28] It influenced reforms in Colombia and acted as a matrix for reform in South Africa. It may also have stimulated greater action within the EU to develop norms on personal insolvency.

[29] See T Halliday and S Block-Lieb, 'Duelists: The Recursive Politics of the Text in International Trade Law' in A Perry-Kessaris, *Socio-Legal Approaches to International Economic Law: Text, Context, Sub-text* (London, Routledge, 2013).

[30] IMF documents such as Liu and Rosenberg do not cite to the World Bank report.

[31] See Regulation (EU) No 1093/2010 establishing a European Supervisory Authority (European Banking Authority) [2010] OJ L 331/12. See Article 9: the 'Authority shall take a leading role in promoting transparency, simplicity and fairness in the market for consumer financial products and services'. This includes the adoption of guidelines and recommendations for promoting 'convergence of regulatory practice' (Article 9(2)), issuing warnings (Article 9(3)), achieving a coordinated approach to regulation and supervision of product innovation (Article 9(4)); and temporarily prohibiting or restricting activities that 'threaten the orderly functioning and integrity of financial markets or the stability of the whole or part of the financial system in the Union' (Article 9(5)).

The EBA Consumer Trends report for 2014 includes 'indebtedness and responsible credit; misselling, household borrowing, and financial literacy' under 'trends and issues'. The EBA monitored the passage of the EU mortgage directive and issued two opinions in 2013 on good practices for responsible mortgage lending and treatment of borrowers in mortgage payment difficulties. The 2014 report indicates that these may be converted into guidelines.

[32] Article 136 of the TFEU specifically recognises conditionality. It is not possible in this chapter to discuss the broader implications of these governance changes. Christian Joerges remarks that 'its turn towards a community of austerity' has resulted in 'Europe riding roughshod over considerations of labour and social law' (Joerges, EUI WP 2013/09) with the troika emblematic of this more autocratic EU. See also eg W Streeck, 'The Crisis of Democratic Capitalism' (2011) 71 *New Left Review* 5; M Wilkinson, 'The Spectre of Authoritarian Liberalism: Reflections on the Constitutional Crisis of the European Union' (2013) *German Law Journal*. For an overview of the conditionality programmes see DG Internal Policies, Economic Governance Support Unit (EGOV) *Committee Study on the Troika and Financial Assistance in the Euro Area: Successes and Failures* (February 2014).

[33] In June 2013, Spain was instructed to review its insolvency framework for individuals and companies under this procedure. Council of the European Union 10656/1/13 UEM 207 *Recommendation on Spain's 2013 national reform programme and delivering a Council's opinion on Spain's stability programme.*

[34] A good discussion of these developments can be found in D Schiek (ed), *The EU Economic and Social Model in the Global Crisis* (Farnham, Ashgate Publishing, 2013).

The Great Recession and eurozone crisis provided an opportunity for the IMF to demonstrate its continuing relevance as a global problem-solver for the world financial system. The EU 'had little experience in managing severe financial problems' and the German government insisted on IMF involvement.[35] In 2007, the IMF became involved in European bailouts[36] for the first time since 1976. It committed to large loans to assist European countries compared with the loans made to countries in previous crises. It has been closely involved in reforms in Greece, Latvia, Lithuania, Ireland, Spain, and Cyprus, either through loan conditionality, technical assistance, or informal pressure through the annual Article IV consultation procedure.

The IMF has contributed to a new narrative about the macro-economic importance of a swift deleveraging of household debt after a crisis. It concluded in its 2012 World Economic Outlook that recessions triggered by household debt could result in a slower recovery than those triggered by other events.[37] An economic case existed therefore beyond relief of hardship for 'intervention' by governments to facilitate 'the writing down of household debt' and the prevention of foreclosures.[38] Measures targeted at average to lower-income consumers, with a higher 'marginal propensity to consume' could drive a recovery.[39] The IMF repeated this call for deleveraging in its 2014 report on the eurozone area. The continuing high levels of household debt constrained growth and European countries needed to provide more flexibility in 'dealing with personal and corporate bankruptcy'.[40] However, it also recognised that moral hazard by borrowers and lenders, and the need to control strategic defaults, must be considered. In addition, the distributional conflict in the establishment of individual insolvency regimes might result in 'social friction' leading to an ineffective policy or political gridlock.

Atif Mian and Amir Sufi in *House of Debt*[41]—described as possibly 'the most important book to come out of the 2008 recession'[42]—provided further

[35] See T Jost and F Seitz, 'The Role of the IMF in the European Debt Crisis' (2012) Discussion Paper no 32 9–10, www.oth-aw.de/fileadmin/user_upload/Aktuelles/Veroeffentlichungen/WEN-Diskussionspapier/wen_diskussionspapier32.pdf. The ECB opposed the request for assistance to the IMF, which it saw as a sign of weakness. This article also indicates the large size of the IMF loans in the EU in comparison to contributions to countries such as Korea during the earlier Asian crisis. For a summary of the contemporary work of the IMF in Europe see IMF factsheet, www.imf.org/external/np/exr/facts/europe.htm.

[36] IMF involvement—Hungary, 2007; Latvia, 2008; Romania, 2009; Greece, 2010; Ireland, 2010; Portugal, 2011; Cyprus, 2014; Romania, 2014.

[37] 'Household busts preceded by larger run-ups in gross household debts are associated with significantly larger contractions in economic activity.' IMF, World Economic Outlook 2012, 91.

[38] The issue of how best to address mortgage debt remains a challenge. See Andritzky, 'Resolving Residential Mortgage Distress' (n 17).

[39] IMF, World Economic Outlook 2012, ch 2.

[40] See IMF Report on the Euro Area Article IV Consultation 2013 at 10. See also F Bornhorst and M Arranz, 'Growth and Importance of Sequencing Debt Reductions Across Sectors' in M Schindler, H Berger, B Bakker, and A Spilimbergo (eds), *Jobs and Growth; Supporting the European Economic Recovery* (IMF, 2014) ch 2.

[41] A Mian and A Sufi, *House of Debt: How They (and You) Caused the Great Recession and How We Can Prevent it from Happening Again* (Chicago, University of Chicago Press, 2014).

[42] 'Atif Mian and Amir Sufi's House of Debt, despite some tough competition, looks likely to be the most important economics book of 2014; it could be the most important book to come out of the 2008

intellectual scaffolding for the 'swift writing down of household debt' narrative. They argued that the debt-fuelled housing boom in the early 2000s resulted in an artificial increase in consumer spending. The bursting of the housing bubble led to a sharp cut-back in spending as individuals became the primary 'shock absorbers' of the crisis. The 2008 recession reflected a longer historical pattern where the severity of a crisis depended on the pre-crisis levels of expansion of credit.[43] A central public policy goal should be to permit individuals to swiftly write-down debt in order to reduce the drag on spending caused by the debt overhang. This would also be distributionally progressive since homeowner debtors were generally less able to bear the risks of default than the more affluent shareholders of banks.[44]

Mian and Sufi's conclusion contradicted conventional economic wisdom—the 'bank lending' view—where the paramount policy in a recession was to recapitalise the banks and not take any measures which might threaten bank stability and lead to a collapse in lending. This premise is challenged if the problem for economic recovery is on the demand rather than the supply side for loans. While recognising that governments in a financial crisis must take some measures to protect the financial system they concluded that policymakers embraced the 'bank lending' view so strongly that excessive concern was demonstrated for creditors and shareholders of banks, rather than addressing the household debt problem.[45] They critiqued the US government for having been too concerned about protecting the banks and their ability to lend rather than addressing the household debt crisis through aggressive write-down policies. In a separate paper they concluded that financial crises are unlikely to result in significant benefits to diffuse groups such as consumers. Concentrated groups such as the financial industry are likely to be better organised and able to prevent reform.[46]

The IMF recognition that household debt was a problem for the overall economy made it a higher priority on the policymaking agenda of central banks, which now include greater discussion of household debt in their financial stability

financial crisis and subsequent Great Recession.' L Summers, 'Did the response to the financial crisis focus too much on banks while neglecting over-indebted homeowners?' *Financial Times* (6 June 2014).

[43] 'We document, to our knowledge for the first time that throughout a century or more of modern economic history in advanced countries a close relationship has existed between the build-up of credit during an expansion and the severity of the subsequent recession … [W]e show that the economic costs of financial crises can vary considerably depending on the leverage incurred during the previous expansion phase.' Mian and Sufi, *House of Debt* (n 41) 9.

[44] 'There is nothing sinister about the rich financing the poor. But it is crucial to remember that the lending takes the form of debt financing. When the rich own the stocks and bonds of a bank, they in turn own the mortgages the bank has made, and interest payments from homeowners flow through the financial system to the rich.' Ibid 21.

[45] 'When financial crisis erupts, lawmakers and regulators must address problems in the banking system. They must work to prevent runs and preserve liquidity. But policy makers have gone much further, behaving as if the preservation of bank creditor and shareholder value is the only policy goal.' Ibid 133.

[46] A Mian and A Sufi, 'The Political Economy of the US Mortgage Default Crisis' (2010) 100 *American Economic Review* 67.

reports.[47] The diffusion of this new learning is exemplified by the Swedish central bank's concerns for the high levels of Swedish household debt in its financial stability report, which caused controversy in Sweden.[48]

The IMF technical experts had the opportunity to put these ideas into practice in the bailouts following the eurozone crisis. The influential European institutions such as the ECB and Directorate General for Economic and Financial Affairs (DG) EC-FIN had little familiarity with household insolvency. However, they generally adopted a textbook analysis of insolvency as a form of insurance which therefore raised issues of moral hazard. ECB opinions on proposed insolvency reforms repeatedly refer to issues of moral hazard and 'maintaining credit discipline'.[49] DG EC-FIN in 2011 also expressed concern that the proposed Irish Personal Insolvency Law should 'avoid a deterioration of payment discipline' and 'should be carefully formulated in order to prevent an adverse impact on borrower behaviour and unintended consequences for the profitability of Irish banks'.[50] These comments contributed to changes in the Irish legislation governing access to bankruptcy and the ability to cramdown creditors. The clash of the conflicting narratives and the political influence of financial institutions resulted in a fussy and complex Irish statute. The European Commission also cautioned the Irish government not to permit parliamentary changes that might undo the safeguards. The democratic process could not be allowed to trump technocratic 'expertise'.[51]

The absence of international best practices in personal insolvency[52] reduced the bargaining power of the international agencies to require the introduction of a

[47] This theme is referenced in subsequent central bank financial stability reports.

[48] See above, ch 5.

[49] See eg in relation to Greece Opinion of the European Central Bank of 22 May 2012 on debt arrangements for over-indebted individuals. 'The ECB stresses that the proposed amendments should be accompanied by the necessary safeguards to avoid moral hazard, as it is important that the debtor has an incentive to fulfill the payment obligations determined by the court settlement procedure.' CON/2012/40, https://www.ecb.europa.eu/ecb/legal/pdf/en_con_2012_40_f.pdf. Similar comments are made in relation to Ireland in 2012. See Opinion of the Central Bank on certain measures relating to personal insolvency CON/2012/70 para 2.2 'The ECB supports the draft law's aim of lowering the cost and increasing the speed and efficiency of personal insolvency proceedings while at the same time mitigating moral hazard and maintaining credit discipline'. In 2013 the ECB commented that Greek amendments to personal insolvency law should maintain a balance: 'The ECB reiterates that the reform of the framework on debt arrangements for over-indebted individuals should ensure an adequate balance between, on the one hand, observance of the general duty of debtors to meet their payment obligations, which promotes a prompt payment culture, preserves the soundness of Greek credit institutions and prevents moral hazard and, on the other hand, the need to provide assistance to individuals in dire financial situations' (CON/2013/34, para 3.1), https://www.ecb.europa.eu/ecb/legal/pdf/en_con_2013_34_f_sign.pdf.

[50] See European Commission DG ECFIN, Economic Adjustment Programme for Ireland Winter 2011 Review 24 and DG ECFIN, Economic Adjustment Programme for Ireland Autumn, 2012 5 (2013).

[51] See DG EC-FIN Economic Adjustment Programme for Ireland Summer 2012 Review 35: 'It will be important to ensure that these safeguards are maintained as the bill progresses through Parliament.'

[52] See IMF, Republic of Lithuania, Technical Assistance Report on Proposals for Reforming the Insolvency Regime (IMF, November 2011) 5. It noted that '[t]here are no best internationally accepted practices in the area of personal insolvency'. The mission relied on 'good practices' distilled from countries where personal insolvency regimes had existed for some time (France, Germany, Japan, Latvia, Spain, Netherlands, the UK, and the US). It viewed (at 6) the main purpose of bankruptcy for

personal insolvency discharge in countries receiving assistance. Without an international standard, the introduction of a discharge was often a controversial issue within the state concerned. Politicians would demand to know the international basis for the proposed reform. 'Moral hazard' was often a significant concern. Politicians worried about the impact of reforms on voters, who might complain about their neighbours sloughing off debts under a law which permitted individuals the 'right not to pay their debts', and also the effects on the financial industry of such reforms. While outcomes varied depending on particular political structures in different states[53] it was often necessary to overcome initial resistance by sweetening the pill and assuring voters that moral hazard could be addressed.

The IMF missions appealed initially to 'good practices', for example in the case of Lithuania.[54] In 2013 an IMF lawyer and economist reflected on their experience in advising and convincing EU governments (eg Greece, Latvia, Lithuania, and Spain) to introduce or modify personal insolvency systems.[55] They identified the need for an appropriate balance between 'maintaining credit discipline' and 'affording financially responsible debtors a fresh start and the need for an adequate institutional infrastructure'. The authors outlined certain 'basic design features for an economically efficient personal insolvency law' from 'early cross-country experience':

— a fresh start for *financially responsible* individuals from the liabilities at the end of the insolvency proceedings (*typically after 3–5 years*);
— *appropriate* filing criteria to make insolvency procedures accessible to individual debtors *while minimising abuse*;
— *automatic and temporary stay on enforcement actions* with adequate safeguards of creditor interests;
— *repayment terms that accurately reflect the debtor's capacity to repay* to ensure an effective fresh start;
— foreign proceedings should be recognised and cross-border cooperation enabled to *avoid bankruptcy tourism*.[56]

individuals as being to 'rehabilitate the debtor by discharging his remaining debts after having repaid the debt for a specified period of time and fulfilled certain requirements, thus enabling him to return to economic life'.

[53] See eg the discussion in Bohle of the different reactions in Central and Eastern Europe to the mortgage crisis and the contrast between Hungary and Estonia. D Bohle, 'Post-Socialist Housing Meets Transnational Finance: Foreign Banks, Mortgage Lending, and the Privatization of Welfare in Hungary and Estonia' (2014) 21(4) *Review of International Political Economy* 913.

[54] IMF, Technical Report Republic of Lithuania (n 52) 5.

[55] Y Liu and C Rosenberg, 'Dealing with Private Debt Distress in the Wake of the European Financial Crisis, A Review of the Economic and Legal Toolbox' IMF WP/13/44. See also M Erbenova, Y Liu, and M Saxegaard, 'Corporate and Household Debt Distress in Latvia: Strengthening the Incentives for a Market-Based approach to Debt Resolution' IMF WP/11/85. This document describes the 2010 Latvian law in the following manner (at 18): 'The new law provides financially responsible individual debtors a fresh start at the end of the insolvency period by discharging their remaining liabilities after the sale of non-exempt assets and meeting the specified repayments requirements.'

[56] Liu and Rosenberg, 'Dealing with Private Debt Distress' (n 55) 15 (emphasis added). In its staff report on Spain in 2013 the IMF suggests also that 'provision should be made for those with no repayment capacity'. IMF Country Report, Staff Document Selected Issues 13/245 (July 2013) at 25.

These are vague, open-textured principles permitting a wide variety of pragmatic solutions. They might prevent the existence of outliers, such as Lithuania's initial 10-year discharge period, but there are many different regimes which could claim to have 'appropriately' balanced the various considerations. Balancing is an inherently political decision-making process made in the face of empirical uncertainty. The reference to an 'economically efficient personal insolvency law' is mere rhetoric without substantially more analysis. 'Cross-country experience' is an inexact source since only modest empirical analyses exist of European insolvency systems. The possibility always for the argument that 'social (or cultural) conditions are different here', mean that these principles provide a starting point for political argument. The leverage of the international experts depends on the nature of their relationship to a state—ranging from the strong influence exercised in conditionality, through technical advice and the annual Article IV monitoring. Success in introducing or modifying measures might depend on the ability to build support within a country, including groups and experts favourable to reform.

The pragmatic development of these principles is illustrated by the cases of Spain, Ireland, Greece, and Cyprus. Spain entered the crisis with a creditor-friendly foreclosure law and no personal insolvency law providing a discharge of debts. Homes could be foreclosed, leaving individuals with no possibility of discharging the balance of the mortgage debt. The *New York Times* published in 2010 a dramatic critique of this phenomenon,[57] and political pressure from within Spain and from the EU resulted in measures to address mortgage arrears.[58] However, the Spanish government, probably influenced by its powerful banking sector,[59] initially refused to introduce a personal insolvency discharge, claiming moral hazard concerns, in particular that reform would damage Spain's good 'payment culture' and pointing to the institutional limitations of the Spanish courts for processing debtors. Spain was not subject to a bailout and conditionality but the IMF attempted to persuade the Spanish government to introduce reform by arguing in 2013 that although international best practices did not exist, 'cross-country experience' suggested the possibility of a law with 'strict entry requirements' which would maintain 'the strong Spanish payment culture'. It repeated this exhortation in 2014, suggesting that an initial long period of good behaviour similar to the German model might be introduced, and subsequently modified as stakeholders became used to the process. Such a framework would be 'in the interests of the

[57] See S Daley, 'In Spain homes are taken but debt stays' *New York Times* (27 October 2010).

[58] See the general discussion of these measures in I Ramsay, 'Two Cheers for Europe: Austerity, Mortgage Foreclosures and Personal Insolvency Policy in the EU' and PG de Cabiedes and MC Gamito, 'Country Report Spain' in H-W Micklitz and I Domurath (eds), *Consumer Debt and Social Exclusion in Europe* (Farnham, Ashgate Publishing, 2015) at 214–17 and 67 respectively. The judgment of the ECJ in Case C-415/11 *Mohamed Aziz v Caixa d'Estalvis de Catalunya* EU:C:2013:164 brought about changes in Spain's mortgage foreclosure law. On political action see eg 'Victims No Longer: Spain's Anti-Eviction Movement', www.opendemocracy.net/opensecurity/carlos-delcl%C3%B3s/victims-no-longer-spain%E2%80%99s-anti-eviction-movement.

[59] See X Vidal-Folch, 'Groupes de pression dans L'Espagne actuelle' (2008) *Pouvoirs* 1 (no 124).

financial sector and preserve Spain's strong payment culture'. Ultimately Spain did introduce a very limited form of personal insolvency discharge (see Box 6.1).[60]

Box 6.1: Spain, the IMF, and the European Semester (2013–2015)

IMF *Spain: Article IV Consultation 2013* Staff Report, July 2013	[G]oing forward, a more comprehensive approach that includes an effective personal insolvency regime with strict eligibility conditions for clearly insolvent people who dispose of their assets, including their houses, to pay their outstanding debts and remain financially responsible over a reasonable period of time (normally 3 to 5 years) to obtain a fresh start. [para 18] **Spanish Authorities' response:** [R]ecent measures adequate … a personal insolvency regime that includes a different solution for mortgages would overburden the courts, could lead to strategic defaults and jeopardize Spain's strong payment culture. [para 19]
IMF Country Report No 13/245 *Spain: 2013 Article IV Consultation—Selected Issues*	Consideration should be given to … introducing a special personal insolvency regime with a fresh start, applying strict conditions in order to maintain the strong Spanish payment culture and ensure financial stability [p 23] … while no international best practices yet exist in this area, key principles for an economically efficient personal insolvency law have emerged from cross-country experience, including *strict entry requirements, discharge of liabilities for financially responsible debtors (typically after 3–5 years) and repayment terms that accurately reflect the debtor's capacity to repay to ensure an effective fresh start only after confirmed satisfactory behavior of the debtor* … [para 6] Insolvent households who do not get relief have a very strong incentive to remain *permanently* in the informal sector. In addition entrepreneurship is harmed by the absence of a fresh start … Finally the risks for financial stability are overplayed as an effective insolvency regime makes the process of recognition of losses that would happen anyway shorter, predictable and thus less costly. [para 9]

[60] I am indebted to discussion, correspondence, and documents from Javier Arias for an account of the development of Spanish law (unpublished on file with author). See also P Gutierrez de Cabiedes and MC Gamito, 'Country Report Spain' in HW Micklitz and I Domurath (eds), *Consumer Debt and Social Exclusion* (Farnham, Ashgate Publishing, 2015) ch 5.

IMF Executive Board Press release, 2 August 2013	The insolvency regime should continue to be improved. A number of Directors encouraged the authorities to consider in future introducing a personal insolvency regime.
EU Council Recommendation 2013 (Spain)	7. … Review insolvency framework for companies and individuals including through limiting personal liability of entrepreneurs and easing second chances for failed businesses. …
	Spanish Law 14 2013 provides the possibility of out of court settlements for individual entrepreneurs.
IMF Country Report, July 2014	Spain could amend its insolvency system to include a framework for natural persons that affords a discharge of unresolved personal debt after liquidation. In line with modern legislation and with other EU countries (e.g. Germany, Ireland, Italy, Latvia) Spain would substantially benefit from a system that provided the opportunity for a full discharge of residual debts not paid off in a liquidation of all non-exempt assets, including one's residence, after a specified number of years of subsequent good faith efforts. [*One of authors of this note was Manfred Balz, architect of the German Insolvency Act of 1994).*] The period of years after which discharge would be recommended while recommended by the European Commission at no more than three years, could be initially set … [at] the point at which creditors would have no overall negative impact on their finances … and at which debtors would still be incentivised to use the insolvency process and use their earning capacity following liquidation of existing assets. The period of best efforts could be reduced over time as stakeholders adapt to the process. [para 19]
Spain: 2014 Article IV Consultation Concluding Statement of the Mission Madrid, 27 May 2014	Debt reduction should also be facilitated by further enhancing the insolvency framework building on the recent improvements, with a focus on helping SMEs, including individual entrepreneurs. In this regard, consideration could be given to introducing a personal insolvency framework that would allow insolvent debtors to have a fresh start after having given up their non-exempt assets and a substantial period of good faith efforts to pay the outstanding debt. Experience in other European countries has shown that such a framework can be designed to be in the interests of the financial sector and preserve Spain's strong payment culture.
	Spanish Law no 1 2015 27 February introduced permitting 5 year repayment plan and proposals for writing off public debts

Spain IMF Staff Report for the 2015 Consultation (2016 12–13)	The recent insolvency reforms are significant steps to help facilitate private sector deleveraging. Consistent with previous staff recommendations, in early 2015 Spain introduced a 'fresh start' for individual entrepreneurs and consumers. The new mechanism allows for a conditional discharge of individuals' residual debt after liquidation of assets in bankruptcy. This could encourage liquidation of nonviable businesses whose debt is inseparable from that of individuals (eg, sole proprietorships) and help households reduce debt to sustainable levels … [para 26] Implemented effectively, the 'fresh start' can encourage demand and entrepreneurial activity in the formal sector, while preserving Spain's strong payment culture. Staff analysis suggests that this could potentially reduce the stock of household debt by around 3–4 percent and the level of corporate debt by about 1–2 percent relative to the baseline, which would contribute to higher private consumption and investment … [para 27] However, there are critical challenges related to implementation, including: Achieving the greatest possible clarity regarding the post-liquidation payment plan and conditions that would lead to a revocation of the fresh start would reduce uncertainty for debtors and limit potential for abuse, ultimately maximizing the positive effects of the reform. [para 28] **Authorities view** The authorities also generally concurred with staff's views on the reforms to the insolvency regime. They agreed with the need to clarify certain key elements in the 'fresh start' reform, and pointed out that Parliament has already approved amendments to do so. … The authorities broadly agreed that the short-term impact of the recent insolvency reforms on banks' earnings was likely to be limited while stressing that the effects on Spain's strong payment culture deserved careful monitoring. [para 30]

Greece and Cyprus provided further opportunities for personal insolvency reform by the troika. Greece introduced a consumer insolvency law in 2010[61] based on the relatively strict German personal insolvency law which requires a mandatory attempt at negotiation and a long period of 'good behaviour'.[62] The Greeks

[61] See Law 3869/2010. The law does not apply to traders. For a recent overview of the current Greek law see G Mentis, 'The Dimensions of the Crisis and the Response of Greek Private Law—A General Overview' in F Ferretti (ed), *Comparative Perspectives of Consumer Over-Indebtedness* (The Hague, Eleven International Publishing, 2016) ch 12.

[62] For an empirical critique of the German law see W Backert, D Brock, G Lechner, and K Maischatz, 'Bankruptcy in Germany: Filing Rates and the People Behind the Numbers' in J Niemi, I Ramsay, and

shortened the period to four years (now three years since 2015 amendments) and also created the possibility for debtors to remain in their residence (subject to limit on value of the home) if they agreed to repay an amount equivalent to 80 per cent of the value of the property over 20 years. The substantive aspects of the law were hardly a debtor's charter but unfortunately Greece did not have an adequate infrastructure (courts, debt advisers, and guidance on standards for negotiation) to administer the legislation and creditors were initially distrustful. The consequences were the predictable failure of the pre-judicial settlement procedure, and with courts becoming overloaded with cases and hearings delayed for years. The government also introduced a moratorium on foreclosure auctions of a debtor's main residence, effective until 2013.

In the face of an increasing number of non-performing loans the IMF concluded by 2012 that the Greek insolvency law was a failure.[63] The general moratorium on auctions was attacked as providing 'blanket protection to borrowers including those who strategically choose not to honor their obligations' and such moratoria contravened 'emerging best practices'. Greece agreed to revise its framework promising that it would preserve 'bank discipline … and minimize moral hazard by targeting borrowers that are in real need',[64] adding that it would 'refrain from supporting any initiative that may undermine the payment culture in Greece'.[65] Greece would end the moratorium, substitute targeted relief for 'vulnerable debtors' and modernise the insolvency act 'in line with best practice in the EU'.[66] However the new Syriza government in 2015 proposed to reintroduce the moratorium while at the same time pursuing 'strategic defaulters'.[67] The subsequent Memorandum of Agreement imposed upon Greece in July 2015 by the EU

W Whitford (eds), *Consumer Credit Debt and Bankruptcy; Comparative and International Perspectives* (Oxford, Hart Publishing, 2009) 288. They note that many debtors have no payment capacity and comment: 'Why should people be kept under financial probation when there is no recognizable output for creditors and there is evidence of poor life quality for debtors.' Even with the 2013 reforms, few debtors will be able to take advantage of the three-year discharge period, which requires individuals to pay 35% of their debts.

[63] See IMF Country Report No 13/153 (2013). 'The existing framework for dealing with household debt—centered around a case-by-case approach applied by the banks, an ineffective insolvency law, and two blanket moratoria on auctions of repossessed assets (de facto preventing property foreclosures)—is deficient.'

[64] Greece, *Letter of Intent MOU*, December 2012, 14–15.

[65] ibid 15.

[66] Greece, *Letter of Intent*, 14 May 2014.

[67] K Hope, 'A Closer Look at Greece's Proposed Reforms' *Financial Times* (24 February 2015). The actual terms of the letter by Greek Finance Minister Varoufakis to the Eurogroup in February 2015 stated: 'Collaborating with the banks' management and the institutions to avoid, in the forthcoming period, auctions of the main residence of households below a certain income threshold, while punishing strategic defaulters, with a view to: (a) maintaining society's support for the government's broad reform program, (b) preventing a further fall in real estate asset prices (that would have an adverse effect on the banks' own portfolio), (c) minimizing the fiscal impact of greater homelessness, and (d) promoting a strong payment culture. Measures will be taken to support the most vulnerable households who are unable to service their loans.'

includes a battery of measures relating to insolvency, with demanding timetables for their implementation. The European Stability Mechanism (ESM) requires:

> reducing the discharge period to 3 years for entrepreneurs in line with the 2014 EC Recommendation; (ii) amendments to the household insolvency law to introduce a time-bound stay on enforcement in line with cross country experience; establish a stricter screening process to deter strategic defaulters from filing under the law, include public creditor claims in the scope of the law providing eligible debtors with a fresh start, tighten the eligibility criteria for protection of the primary residence, and introduce measures to address the large backlog of cases (e.g. increasing the number of judges and judicial staff, prioritization of high value cases, and short-form procedures for debtors with no assets and no income).[68]

The reduction of backlogs through an increase in judges was reiterated in 2016 along with more information and support for debtors including financial literacy.[69] This process of reform will draw on 'independent expertise', external consultants, and 'cross-country experience'.[70]

Cyprus reformed its personal insolvency law in 2015 under the tutelage of the troika. The IMF insisted that reformed foreclosure and insolvency laws should be introduced to address the large number of non-performing loans. The legislation includes the possibility of a repayment plan, a no-income no-asset procedure, and bankruptcy discharge after three years. An insolvency service is created to administer the system. The IMF notes that the new insolvency framework 'draws on some of the best international practices and cross-country experiences'. However substantial local opposition challenged the reform of Cyprus foreclosure system and the IMF withheld a tranche of loans until the legislation was enacted. It criticised 'last minute' parliamentary amendments conferring greater rights on debtors as deviating from 'international norms' and obtained a commitment from the authorities for an immediate review of these provisions. The IMF feared that these rights might 'weaken payment discipline and lead to strategic behaviour by debtors'.[71]

The IMF and troika moved from the absence of best practices in 2010 to 'emerging best practices' in 2013 and 'best international practices' in 2015 justifying the Cyprus reforms. 'Cross-country experience' grounds these practices. A source

[68] Memorandum of Understanding between the European Commission acting on behalf of the European Stability Mechanism and the Hellenic Republic and the Bank of Greece (August, 2015) 18–19, http://ec.europa.eu/economy_finance/assistance_eu_ms/greek_loan_facility/pdf/01_mou_20150811_en.pdf.

[69] European Stability Mechanism, Supplemental Memorandum of Understanding 16/6/2016, http://www.esm.europa.eu/assistance/Greece/index.htm?lang=-en.

[70] Memorandum of Understanding, 2015 (n 68) 15–17. See the critique of the MOU by former Minister of Finance Vanis Varoufakis, https://varoufakis.files.wordpress.com/2015/08/mou-annotated-by-yv.pdf.

[71] See IMF Cyprus, Fifth, Sixth and Seventh Reviews under the Extended Fund Facility: Request for Waiver of non-observance of a performance criterion; and rephrasing of access—Press Release; Staff Report; and Statement by the Executive Director for Cyprus IMF Country Report No 15/155, 11.

in the IMF suggested that the Irish Personal Insolvency Law of 2012 may have become an influential benchmark and Christine Lagarde has referred to the 'exemplary' Irish insolvency law,[72] a view perhaps undermined by the need to reform the law in 2015 to make it more accessible after Ireland was free of the Troika tutelage.

These laws and 'emerging best practices' represent a mixture of policies—a veritable *bricolage*. Some reforms embody potentially progressive ideas such as a swift no-income no-asset procedure, and the inclusion of public creditors in the discharge. Others such as 'stricter screening' procedures—based on concerns about moral hazard—may be costly to implement and deter those in genuine need of a discharge. The Spanish case illustrates the dialogic nature of the process of diffusion of personal insolvency norms and the limits of international bargaining power in this area without clear international indicators and the ever present rhetorical power of the cultural card. Empirical evidence on personal insolvency laws and their effects is limited. The absence of any reliable empirical data on the Greek situation means that no one knows the level of supposed 'strategic defaulters'. The IMF admits that attempts to measure the impact of the Cypriot debt restructuring law are 'speculative'.[73] The technocratic economic discourse of moral hazard, efficiency and 'strategic defaulters', with its associated image of the rational calculating debtor, provide a veneer of science but it is hard not to see this as pragmatic political 'balancing', as the international institutions adapt different solutions to different states, drawing eclectically on comparative experience. And there remains the issues of authority and legitimacy in those cases such as Cyprus where insolvency norms are imposed on a country.

III. European Union Consumer Credit Policy and Personal Insolvency

The EU is committed to the creation of an integrated credit and capital market as part of a 'highly competitive social market economy' that will 'combat social exclusion and discrimination'.[74] The EU contains states with different models of social provisioning and varieties of capitalism.[75] Since the accession of new Member States in Central and Eastern Europe, the EU has a higher Gini co-efficient than the US, a standard measure of inequality. Neo-liberalism undoubtedly influences the development of EU policies[76] and social exclusion is increasingly associated

[72] 'Lagarde: Ireland's bankruptcy laws exemplary' *Irish Examiner* (28 January 2014).

[73] IMF, Cyprus (n 71) 47.

[74] Articles 3, 4 TFEU.

[75] These distinctions may be situated within the four traditional clusters of capitalism in member states: continental social market economy countries, Anglo-Saxon neo-liberal countries, Central and Eastern European countries (neo-liberal), and Nordic (liberal with safety nets) countries.

[76] See eg VA Schmidt and M Thatcher (eds), *Resilient Liberalism in Europe's Political Economy* (Cambridge, Cambridge University Press, 2013). Competition policy was influenced by ordoliberalism

with measures which support market access or greater productivity rather than measures that permit an individual to stand outside the market.[77]

The EU has limited competence in social areas that have traditionally, because of their political and cultural nature, resided with Member States. Social rights at the European level relate primarily to health and safety, discrimination and the rights of migrant workers. Social goods such as social insurance, health care, welfare services, education and housing remain national competences. However, the increased impact of economic rights (such as free movement) on national social rights, the increasing limitations on the ability of states to regulate these effects at the national level[78] and a concern that the EU should have a social face, have resulted in soft forms of governance developing. The perception that attempts to impose uniform solutions would result in strong political opposition has also necessitated such an approach.

Private lawyers in the EU have also debated the meaning of the 'social' in the context of attempts at codification of aspects of private law, and the horizontal effects of human rights law within contract. One influential conceptualisation views personal insolvency law as part of a welfarist 'needs orientation' in private law, recognising the effects of unemployment and illness on an individual's ability to repay.[79]

Individual over-indebtedness and personal insolvency raise both economic and social issues. However EU harmonisation efforts before the financial crisis in 2008 focused on the 'front end' of credit markets in order to facilitate access and competition. The two Consumer Credit Directives of 1987, and the later 2008 Directive, focus primarily on promoting market growth and the 'front end' of credit markets with a nod to responsible lending in the 2008 credit directive. This market development approach neglected the role of insolvency as a ground rule of the single market. Although the 1995 review of the 1987 Directive identified 'the widespread European problem of over-indebtedness', this was bracketed as a social issue best addressed at the national level Thus DG Sanco (the Consumer Protection DG) indicated in 2001 that 'large differences between national social legislation [exist] to cope with this phenomenon [over-indebtedness] … [T]he

a variant of neo-liberalism. D Gerber, *Law and Competition in Twentieth Century Europe: Protecting Prometheus* (Oxford, Oxford University Press, 1998).

[77] See discussion in M Dawson, *New Governance and the Transformation of EU law* (Cambridge, Cambridge University Press, 2011). See also D Schiek, 'The EU's Socio-Economic Model(s) and the Crisi(e)s—Any Perspectives?' in D Schiek (ed), 'The EU Economic and Social Model (n 34).

[78] See eg F Scharpf, 'The European Social Model: Coping with the challenges of diversity' (2002) *Journal of Common Market Studies* 645.

[79] See T Wilhelmsson, 'Varieties of Welfarism in European Contract Law (2004) 10(6) *European Law Journal* 712; Study Group on Social Justice in European Private Law, 'Social Justice in European Contract Law: A Manifesto' (2004) 10(6) *European Law Journal* 653; see also discussion in H Micklitz (ed), *The Many Concepts of Justice in European Private Law* (Cheltenham, Elgar, 2011). For a human rights approach see C Ondersma, 'A Human Rights Framework for Debt Relief' (2014) 36(1) *University of Pennsylvania Journal of International Law* 269.

objective of a Credit directive cannot be to harmonise social legislation, which remain in the field of the national competences'.[80] The 2008 Directive originally included tough 'responsible lending' proposals designed to prevent over-indebtedness. However, after intense lobbying by the financial sector at the national and EU level,[81] it imposed a rather mild requirement on creditors to check debtors' creditworthiness. The absence of a world crisis or a scandal such as bovine spongiform encephalomyelitis (BSE) meant that consumer credit had a relatively low public salience. Consumer choice and credit as 'a lubricant of economic life' were dominant ideas, reflecting the increasing influence of neo-liberalism within the Commission. Ironically, the 2008 Directive was enacted a few months before the collapse of Lehman Brothers in 2008.

During this period, the Commission did subsidise softer initiatives on over-indebtedness under the Open Method of Co-ordination (OMC). The OMC is an approach to governance of social issues in the EU developed after the Lisbon Treaty to provide a 'framework of cooperation' between members for the achievement of common objectives. It establishes objectives, creates indicators, and provides peer review and benchmarks for the development of 'best practices'. It does not envisage the introduction of hard law (such as regulations and directives).[82] A general critique of the 'soft' OMC is that it symbolises the subservient nature of social issues within the EU.[83]

This approach produced modest results in the area of debt adjustment.[84] Several academic reports were published which provided a fairly consistent set of ideas: a repayment plan as a condition of discharge, the possibility of immediate discharge for the hopelessly over-indebted and professional debt counsellors as intermediaries.[85] Studies on over-indebtedness linked it to issues of financial inclusion and access to credit. A central question seemed to be the somewhat elusive search for a European definition of over-indebtedness.[86] The Commission also supported

[80] See T Vissol, 'Updating and Revising the Consumer Credit Directive (87/102)' (2001), http://www.ecri.eu/new/system/files/10+Vissol.pdf.

[81] I discuss this in I Ramsay, 'Changing Policy Paradigms of EU Consumer Credit and Debt Regulation' in D Leczykiewicz and S Weatherill, *Images of the Consumer in EU Law: Legislation, Free Movement and Competition Law* (Oxford, Hart Publishing, 2016) 166–68.

[82] See Art 153(2)(a) TFEU: 'cooperation, promoting exchange of information and best practices, promoting innovative approaches and evaluating experiences'.

[83] In a similar vein consumer policy is critiqued as primarily concerned with ensuring access to markets and consumer choice, rather than protection from the market. See eg discussion in H Micklitz, 'Social Justice and Access Justice in Private Law' in Micklitz (ed), *The Many Concepts of Justice* (n 79).

[84] See D Korczak, *Amnesty of Debts: Amicable Agreements and Statutory Solutions* (Brussels, DG Employment, Social Affairs and Equal Opportunities, 2006).

[85] See eg N Huls, *Overindebtedness of Consumers in the EC Member States: Facts and Search for Solution* (1993) summarised in N Huls, 'Towards a European Approach to Overindebtedness of Consumers' (1993) 16 *Journal of Consumer Policy* 215; Reifner et al, *Consumer Overindebtedness and Consumer Law in the European Union* (EC, 2003).

[86] EU Commission, 'Towards a Common Operational European Definition of Over-indebtedness' DG Employment, Social Affairs and Equal Opportunities; European Commission (2008) 'Financial Services Provision and Prevention of Financial Exclusion' Report prepared for DG Employment, Social Affairs and Equal Opportunities.

non-governmental organisation (NGO) networks such as the European Consumer Debt Network.

In 2007 the Council of Europe published a slightly 'harder' set of recommendations that included both preventive and treatment measures including the discharge of debts as a 'residual remedy' if other measures to write down debt were not possible.[87] The report characterised over-indebtedness as a human rights issue although references to specific human rights were absent from the document. The prevention of social exclusion and a respect for human dignity were organising themes.

Meanwhile, insolvency reform in the EU proceeded without reference to consumers or issues of individual over-indebtedness, focusing on business and corporate insolvency. Attempts at harmonisation of substantive rules foundered on divisions as to the treatment of secured claims and so the 2000 Insolvency Regulation addressed only issues of recognition and jurisdiction, with the objective of preventing forum shopping and ensuring mutual recognition of insolvency proceedings throughout the EU.

IV. EU Personal Insolvency Policy after the Crisis

Several distinct strands of EU policy began to overlap after the crisis. First was the interest in swift and effective insolvency laws as a mechanism of debt deleveraging, freeing up resources for investment and consumption. Second was the increased interest in more liberal insolvency discharge rules in promoting entrepreneurialism. Third, consumer studies increasingly discussed the importance of personal insolvency. An EU-commissioned study in 2014 commented that 'the most commonly reported change by stakeholders in response to over-indebtedness related to legislative steps to make insolvency proceedings more readily available to consumers in financial difficulty'.[88] Fourth, the economic distress of homeowners faced with foreclosure posed the question of the protection of the home in insolvency proceedings. Finally, the absence of a single EU insolvency system potentially raised cross-border investment and credit costs and could result in detrimental forum shopping. These strands raised issues of both consumption and production policy and distinct DGs within the Commission,[89] the EU Parliament, and the ECB, and a cross section of civic society groups. Thus, industry-financed EU think tanks claimed that the resilience in the US economy after the crash reflected the ability of households to quickly deleverage through non-recourse mortgages and

[87] Council of Europe, *Legal Solutions to Debt Problems in Europe.*

[88] See Civic Consulting, *Final Report. The Over-indebtedness of European Households: Updated Mapping of the Situation, Nature and Causes, Effects and Initiatives for Alleviating its Impact* (Brussels, 2014) 13.

[89] Both powerful (DG EC-Fin, Enterprise) and less powerful (Sanco) DGs.

generous bankruptcy law,[90] a position that might be shared by some consumer groups.[91]

V. EU Narratives

A. Promoting Entrepreneurialism Through Personal Insolvency in the EU: The New 'Silver Bullet'?

Fail fast, fail often[92]

The idea that a more liberal discharge procedure will facilitate entrepreneurialism and risk-taking recurs in bankruptcy history. Julian Hoppitt describes an awareness of the value of risk-taking in the development of 18th century English bankruptcy law,[93] William O Douglas noted the role of a liberal discharge in promoting US experimentalism,[94] and the new Labour government at the beginning of the century embraced entrepreneurialism in the 2002 liberalisation of the English discharge procedure.[95] The shortening of the discharge period in Germany from six to three years, introduced in 2014 for individuals able to pay a portion of their debts, is also intended to promote entrepreneurialism.[96] Several European countries have recently introduced special provisions to make it easier for entrepreneurs to fail (Sweden, France and Spain).

Joseph Schumpeter saw a central role for the entrepreneur in the ongoing development of capitalism. For Schumpeter the entrepreneur was the innovator, not

[90] See Daniel Gros, CEPS Commentary, 'Thinking Ahead for Europe', 2 August 2014, http://aei.pitt.edu/53145/1/DG_Transatlantic_Growth_Gap.pdf. 'European officials are right to promote structural reforms of EU countries' labour and product markets. But they should also focus on overhauling and accelerating bankruptcy procedures, so that losses can be recognised more quickly and over-indebted households can start afresh, rather than being shackled for years.'

[91] See Financial Services Users Group, Position Paper (2013) A sentiment endorsed by DG Justice. See 'Insolvency law in Europe—Giving People and businesses a second chance', Věra Jourová, Commissioner for Justice, Consumers and Gender Equality (speech at conference 'Insolvency Law in Europe: current trends and future perspectives' Jurmala, Latvia, 23 April 2015).

[92] See the interesting discussion of the international spread of this supposedly Silicon Valley mantra by John Donohue in 'Fail fast, fail often, fail everywhere' *The New Yorker* (31 May 2015).

[93] See J Hoppitt, *Risk and Failure in English Business 1700–1800* (Cambridge, Cambridge University Press, 1987) 23.

[94] WO Douglas, 'Bankruptcy', *Encyclopedia of the Social Sciences* (London, Macmillan Publishing Co, 1937).

[95] The Insolvency Service Annual Report 2014–15 states at the outset that '[e]ntrepreneurialism and a drive for business growth will be accompanied by financial failures as well as successes'.

[96] Frank Fossen quotes the German Minister of Justice who states that the 'reform of insolvency law is one of the most important projects in business law' and that 'those who exhibit the entrepreneurial spirit deserve legal protection that encourages them in their decision to depart into self-employment'. F Fossen, 'Personal Bankruptcy Law, Wealth, and Entrepreneurship—Evidence from the Introduction of a 'Fresh Start' Policy' (2013) 16(1) *American Law and Economics Review* 269, 274, quoting Leutheusser-Schnarrenberger.

necessarily the inventor or capitalist, but simply the person 'doing … new things or the doing of things that are already being done in a new way'.[97] Schumpeter used the phrase 'creative destruction' to describe how the entrepreneur contributed both to the instability and renewal of capitalism through new methods of production, distribution and so on. A successful entrepreneur might stimulate a host of imitators, thus creating booms that inevitably crashed. He differed from Marx who viewed the inevitable reductions in profits through capitalist competition as leading to its ultimate destruction. Schumpeter recognised that only a few entrepreneurs could succeed and so the high returns to an individual must be balanced against the negative returns to the many who failed.

Writing in the 1940s, Schumpeter thought that with the rise of the large management-controlled corporation, entrepreneurialism was in decline. However, by the late 1990s Manuel Castells was describing the resurgence of self-employment in the new informational economy.[98] Teresa Sullivan, Jay Lawrence Westbrook, and Elizabeth Warren documented the renewal of interest in the connection between entrepreneurialism and bankruptcy in their study of 1981 bankrupts. They noted the conventional wisdom of that era to be the gradual disappearance of self-employment with the rise of large corporations. They found, however, a significant tranche of self-employed individual bankrupts and concluded that more 'systematic attention to the problems of small business should be placed on the agenda of bankruptcy policymakers'.[99] By the 2000s, Schumpeter was being rediscovered by the *New York Times* as the prophet of the bust and boom of the Internet Age.[100]

The EU Lisbon Treaty promised to make the EU the most competitive region in the world and a central aspect of EU policy since 2000 has been the promotion of entrepreneurialism. A series of reports by national experts drawn from Ministries of Justice and the Economy coordinated by DG Enterprise investigated the extent to which EU legal systems provided a fresh start for entrepreneurs at that time. This report established indicators and best practice. Further reports followed in 2007[101] and 2008 when 'A Small Business Act' for Europe requested that Member

[97] J Schumpeter, 'The Creative Response in Economic History' (1947) VII(2) *The Journal of Economic History* 149, 151.

[98] See M Castells, *The Information Age: Economy Culture and Society: The Rise of the Network Society*, (Oxford, Blackwell, 1998) vol 1, 221.

[99] T Sullivan, E Warren, and J Westbrook, *As We Forgive Our Debtors* (Oxford, Oxford University Press, 1989) 121.

[100] Sharon Reier, 'Half a Century Later, Economist's "Creative Destruction" Theory is Apt for the Internet Age: Schumpeter: The Prophet of Bust and Boom' *Your Money* (10 June 2000).

[101] Communication from the Commission to the Council, The European Parliament, The European Economic and Social Committee and the Committee of the Regions, *Overcoming the Stigma of Business Failure—For a Second Chance Policy Implementing the Lisbon Partnership for Growth and Jobs* COM (2007) 284 final, http://eur-lex.europa.eu/LexUriServ/LexUriServ.do?uri=COM:2007:0584:FIN:en:PDF. The report notes for example how 'the death of companies can be compatible with economic dynamism'. It refers also to an OECD study which suggests that '[t]here is reason to believe that increasing global competition is forcing entrepreneurs to react more rapidly and more flexibly, even by closing their business and opening another one. The data confirm a high correlation between entry and exit rates in both the EU and the US, suggesting a continuous process of creative destruction by which low productivity firms exit the market and are replaced by new ones.'

States ensure that 'honest entrepreneurs' should quickly get a second chance. The 2007 report reads like a homage to Schumpeter, with references to the 'continuous process of creative destruction' in both the US and the EU. A study in 2011 claimed that only 4–6 per cent of bankruptcies in the EU were fraudulent, but that 49 per cent of entrepreneurs in a Eurobarometer study mentioned that the major risk of starting a business was the possibility of going bankrupt.[102] The EU 2020 vision[103] promotes both restructuring and 'liberal non-stigmatising' bankruptcy provisions, reducing disabilities on undischarged bankrupts, and with a discharge period of three years or less to facilitate risk-taking by small businesses. The most recent proposals on a European Capital Market identify divergent individual insolvency laws as a barrier to young entrepreneurs.[104] The 2014 Commission 'recommendation' (a form of soft model law)[105] from DG Justice proposed a 'second chance' for 'honest entrepreneurs' with an automatic discharge after no longer than three years.[106] In 2016 this recommendation was included in a proposal for a directive on insolvency. Although the proposal is aimed at entrepreneurs, the Commission recognizes that over-indebtedness of natural persons is a major economic and social problem and member states are invited to 'extend the application of the discharge principles … to natural persons who are not entrepreneurs. … [h]elping consumers back into the economic spending cycle is an important part of good functioning markets and retail financial services.'[107] This economic rationale

[102] Flash Eurobarometer No 283 'Entrepreneurship in the EU and Beyond', http://ec.europa.eu/public_opinion/flash/fl_283_en.pdf.

[103] 'The Entrepreneurship Action Plan is a blueprint for decisive action to unleash Europe's entrepreneurial potential, to remove existing obstacles and to revolutionise the culture of entrepreneurship in Europe.' See Entrepreneurship Action Plan, Re-Igniting the Entrepreneurial Spirit in Europe (COM (2012) 795 Final) at 17–18. Principle 2 of the 'Small Business Act' refers to ensuring that 'honest entrepreneurs who have faced bankruptcy quickly get a second chance'. Communication from the Commission to the Council, the European Parliament, the European Economic and Social Committee and the Committee of the Regions, *'Think Small First' A Small Business Act for Europe* SEC(2008) 2101.

[104] 'The Recommendation also requests Member States to ensure that honest bankrupt entrepreneurs can have a second start after a maximum of three years from a first failure. This will ensure that young entrepreneurs are not discouraged from innovating by the risk of failure, and that they can return to the productive economy with the experience they have gained from a first failure. Evidence shows that second starters are 40% more successful than first starters.' Commission Staff Working Document, 'Initial reflections on the obstacles to the development of deep and integrated EU capital markets' accompanying the document Green Paper, *Building a Capital Markets Union* COM(2015) 63 final, 20.

[105] See Art 288 TFEU. For a summary of this form of soft law see D Chalmers, G Monti, and G Davies, *European Union Law* 2nd edn (Cambridge, Cambridge University Press) 102.

[106] See Commission Recommendation on a New Approach to Business Failure and Insolvency C(2014) 1500. See Recital 20 'The effects of bankruptcy, in particular the social stigma, legal consequences and the on-going inability to pay off debts constitute important disincentives for entrepreneurs seeking to set up a business or have a second chance, even if evidence shows that entrepreneurs who have gone bankrupt have more chance to be successful the second time. Steps should therefore be taken to reduce the negative effects of bankruptcy on entrepreneurs, by making provisions for a full discharge of debts after a maximum period of time.'

[107] 'Proposal for a Directive on preventive restructuring' (n 6) 4, 14, Recital 15. The Commission indicates at 14: 'The Commission will continue to look into how Member States have reformed their

underlines the market rather than social dimension of insolvency relief, evoking the US linking of insolvency relief to the open credit society.

Intellectual support exists for this EU narrative. A widely cited econometric study does indicate a correlation over time between the severity of the bankruptcy discharge and levels of self-employment,[108] which is used in the study as a proxy for entrepreneurship. The study does not, however, comment on the quality or innovative nature of the self-employment that will be encouraged. Another study suggests no connection between insolvency and innovative entrepreneurship.[109] The Insolvency Service in England and Wales found no connection between the liberalised discharge procedures in 2002 and business start-ups (used as a proxy for entrepreneurialism).[110]

A more forgiving bankruptcy law for entrepreneurs may have effects on credit granting, interest rates and collateral requirements. In US states with high homestead exemptions more homeowners are likely to own a business, but may pay higher interest rates for credit.[111] Frank Fossen claims that the introduction of the 1999 German Insolvency Act encouraged less wealthy individuals to become entrepreneurs, thus suggesting that the insurance effects of bankruptcy outweighed the potentially higher costs of borrowing.[112]

Studying the effects of personal insolvency law on entrepreneurialism throws up the difficulties of identifying entrepreneurs. Self-employment is itself a category which ranges from the 'very self-sufficient to extremely vulnerable'.[113] It may

national frameworks and monitor how they implement this specific second chance provision in the proposal, so as to review the situation of consumer over-indebtedness.'

[108] See J Armour and D Cumming, 'Bankruptcy and Entrepreneurship' (2008) 10(2) *American Law and Economics Review* 303.

[109] D Primo and W Green, 'Bankruptcy Law and Entrepreneurship' (2011) 1(2) *Entrepreneurship Research Journal* Issue 5. This study used two measures, self-employment and different levels of venture capital within a state. The latter was intended to capture the 'innovative' nature of entrepreneurialism. See R Lawless, 'Striking Out on their Own; The Self-Employed in Bankruptcy' in K Porter (ed), *Broke: How Debt Bankrupts the Middle Class* (Stanford, 2012) ch 6.

[110] See The Insolvency Service, *Enterprise Act 2002—The Personal Insolvency Provisions: Final Evaluation Report November 2007* (London, Insolvency Service, 2007) 41–42 citing to statistical analysis conducted by DBIS.

[111] See W Fan and M White, 'Personal Bankruptcy and the Level of Entrepreneurial Activity' (2003) 46(2) *Journal of Law and Economics* 543; J Berkowitz and M White, 'Bankruptcy and Small Firms Access to Credit' (2004) 35(1) *RAND Journal of Economics* 69. A Mathur, 'Does the US Bankruptcy Code Provide a Fresh Start to Entrepreneurs?' (2013) 37(11) *Journal of Banking and Finance* 4198 (finding that access to credit and reasonably priced credit are persisting problems for bankrupt entrepreneurs).

[112] Fossen, 'Personal Bankruptcy Law' (n 96). Fossen describes the German Insolvency Code of 1999 as introducing a 'fresh start'. Most commentators would not describe the original seven-year repayment plan in the 1999 Act as a condition of discharge, a 'fresh start', so that the findings deserve further scrutiny. For the harrowing experience of a German entrepreneur's experience of the German Insolvency Act 1999 see A Koark, *Back to Start and Nevertheless Successful*, EUI Working Paper EUI Working Papers Law 2011/09 LAW 2011/09 Consumer Bankruptcy in Europe Different Paths for Debtors and Creditors.

[113] M Westerveld, 'The "New" Self-Employed: An Issue for Social Policy' (2012) 14(3) *European Journal of Social Security* 15, 19, referring to the analysis by M D'Amours and S Crespo, 'The Dimensions of Heterogeneity Among Own Account Self-Employed: Elements for a Typology' (2009) 59(3) *Industrial Relations* 459. See Guy Standing, *The Precariat: The New Dangerous Class* (London,

include individuals who were formerly employed and are in precarious positions with low incomes and few social protections. The OECD, for example, defines it primarily in a manner similar to Schumpeter,[114] but others stress the 'risk-taking' nature of entrepreneurialism.[115] Many small and medium-sized enterprises (SMEs) throughout Europe are unincorporated,[116] and their owners may use their homes as security for business borrowing and personal credit cards for business purposes. It thus becomes harder to separate consumer and business debts, and the business and personal consequences of insolvency.

US bankruptcy law is the inspiration for European policymakers wishing to promote entrepreneurialism through bankruptcy. 'Fail fast, fail cheap and move on' is a mantra associated with Silicon Valley but sociolegal study of bankrupt entrepreneurs in the US does not always provide an optimistic picture of individuals 'bouncing back' in business.[117] Bob Lawless notes the mythology in the US of the founders of Google who financed their business initially through 'all of our credit cards and our friends' credit cards and our parents' credit cards'.[118] He cites Scott Shane's book *The Illusions of Entrepreneurship*[119] to demonstrate the difference between the myths of small business start-ups and the reality. Most small businesses fail, only a few are established in high-tech industries and they contribute only a modest number of jobs. A more forgiving bankruptcy law is certainly justifiable on humanitarian grounds but the evidence is still unclear on its contribution to economic growth through entrepreneurialism. A strong welfare state may also promote risk taking, an argument sometimes made in relation to the growth of small enterprises in Sweden.

One might also question the distinction between the risk-taking entrepreneur and others. Individuals are increasingly being encouraged to be responsible risk takers, investing in education or training, and managing their financial future in

Bloomsbury, 2011). The EC Directive defines an entrepreneur simply as 'a natural person exercising a trade, business, craft or profession' (n 6) Art 2(13).

[114] The OECD defines entrepreneurs for the purpose of the OECD-Eurostat Entrepreneurship Indicators Programme as 'those persons (business owners) who seek to generate value, through the creation or expansion of economic activity, by identifying and exploiting new processes or markets'. *The Missing Entrepreneurs: Policies for Inclusive Entrepreneurship in Europe* OECD/EU (2013) 18.

[115] M Mazzucato, *The Entrepreneurial State: Debunking Public v Private Sector Myths* (London, Anthem Press, 2013), notes at 58 that 'entrepreneurship, like growth, is one of the least well understood topics in economics' and contrasts Frank Knight's view of entrepreneurship 'risk taking' with Schumpeter's idea of product innovation. Mazzucato argues that for Knight 'the behaviour of the entrepreneur is that of a person willing to put his or her career and financial security on the line and take risks in the name of an idea, spending time as well as capital on an uncertain venture'. Ibid at 58.

[116] See W Bergthaler, K Kang, Y Liu, and D Monaghan, 'Tackling Small and Medium Sized Enterprise Problem Loans in Europe' (Washington, IMF, 2015) 6.

[117] See Lawless, 'Striking Out on their Own': The Self-Employed in Bankruptcy' in K Porter (ed) *Broke: How Debt Bankrupts the Middle Class* (Palo Alto, Stanford Univ Press, 2012) ch 6.

[118] Ibid.

[119] S Shane, *The Illusions of Entrepreneurship* (New Haven and London, Yale University Press, 2008).

an increasingly financialised culture.[120] The concept of the 'entrepreneur of the self' who must develop a biography against a background of recurring economic crises and volatility suggests that any sharp distinction between the entrepreneur and the consumer is porous.[121]

The strength of a narrative is not based solely on its empirical truth but the narrative of entrepreneurialism and risk-taking has become an international paradigm linking to neo-liberal conceptions of the 'entrepreneur' of the self and ordoliberal celebration of the entrepreneur driving innovation and change.

B. Financial and Social Inclusion

A leitmotif in EU documents on consumer over-indebtedness is the need for insolvency and debt adjustment procedures to prevent financial and social exclusion.[122] European documents authored by French experts or politicians adopt this concept. The Council of Europe recommendations in 2007 in its proposals on debt adjustment indicates that it should 'encourage effective financial and social inclusion of over-indebted individuals and families, in particular by promoting their access to the labour market'.[123] The EU Economic and Social Committee in 2014 identified the avoidance of social exclusion as an objective of debt adjustment programmes.[124] This report proposed a directive which would require Member States to provide free debt adjustment procedures, a moratorium on claims on the opening of proceedings, the ability to keep the main residence and 'the possibility of cancelling debts in the most burdensome situations and the obligation to leave an over-indebted person enough to live on decently day-to-day, the aim being to reintegrate the consumer into economic and social life quickly'.[125] Member states' legislation on personal insolvency should 'find a solution that will enable households to avoid social exclusion and where possible to pay off their debts as far as their means will allow'.[126]

[120] See N Fligstein and A Goldstein, 'The Emergence of a Finance Culture in American Households, 1998–2007' (2015) *Socio-Economic Review* 1.

[121] But media discourse may still reflect the distinction between entrepreneurs and consumers describing how the former 'bounce back from bankruptcy'. See 'Bouncing back from bankruptcy' *The Guardian* (29 October 2012).

[122] See eg Communication from the Commission to the European Parliament, the Council, The European Economic and Social Committee of the Regions The European Platform against Poverty and Social Exclusion: *A European Framework for Social and Territorial Cohesion* COM/2010/0758 final 1. 'The Commission recognises that 'the most vulnerable people in our societies have borne much of the impact of the economic crisis [and that] the situation of those earning the lowest amount has continued to deteriorate and they now face a greater risk of indebtedness and insolvency'.

[123] Council of Europe, Recommendation CM/Rec (2007) 8 of the Committee of Ministers to member states on legal solutions to debt problems.

[124] Opinion of the European Economic and Social Committee on Consumer protection and appropriate treatment of over-indebtedness to prevent social exclusion (exploratory opinion), Rapporteur-general: Reine-Claude Mader [2014] OJ C 311/38.

[125] Ibid.

[126] Ibid at 5.1.

Financial and social inclusion may be influential ideas in the EU narrative on consumer over-indebtedness,[127] but I noted in chapter 1 that financial inclusion is a concept compatible with a wide range of policies ranging from a swift fresh start to a period of good behaviour or the requirement of credit counselling so that an individual can be re-integrated. An insolvency discharge may be an opportunity for a 'hand up' (rather than a 'hand out') to being a responsibilized consumer of credit, compatible with the conception of social policy as contributing to market objectives. The limited, and sometimes poorly co-ordinated national social initiatives associated with personal insolvency as exemplified by Sweden and France, and the increased prominence of financial literacy as part of insolvency treatment underline this conception of insolvency as increasingly linked to market objectives.

The amelioration of social exclusion may also be justified by the right to dignity and self respect and, indeed, the Council of Europe in its 2007 report linked bankruptcy discharge to the 'right to dignity and self respect'. Human rights discourse has not, however, been influential in discussions of insolvency, although it has seeped into discussions on protection of the home in the wake of the financial crisis.

VI. Bankruptcy Tourism, Regulatory Competition, and Regulatory Learning[128]

'Mr Kray's client list includes doctors, pharmacists and lawyers and even a high-flying management consultant with debts of £16 million.'[129]

The differences in discharge periods between European systems has encouraged a modest 'bankruptcy tourism'. Debtors in strict bankruptcy regimes with long discharge periods may decide to move their COMI (centre of main interests) to a more liberal regime (generally England or Alsace Lorraine).[130] England and Wales

[127] See eg the Civic Consulting Study carried out for the Consumer Directorate in 2014 (n 88), which notes at 11 that 'according to stakeholders' financial exclusion was a highly rated consequence of over-indebtedness.'

[128] For other analyses of bankruptcy tourism see I Fannon, 'Bankruptcy Tourism—Why and How?' (2013) 26(6) *Insolvency Intelligence* 85; T Hoffman, 'The Phenomenon of Consumer Insolvency Tourism and its Challenges to European Legislation' (2012) 35(4) *Journal of Consumer Policy* 461; A Walters and A Smith, 'Bankruptcy Tourism under the EC Regulation on Insolvency Proceedings: A View from England and Wales' (2009) 19(3) *International Insolvency Review* 210.

[129] 'Manager of an agency specializing in assisting Germans to declare bankruptcy in England and Wales', *Daily Mail* (23 September 2009), http://www.dailymail.co.uk/news/article-1215506/Britain-bust-Bankruptcy-tourists-flock-UK-advantage-lax-insolvency-laws.html.

[130] Insolvency jurisdiction within the EU is determined by an individual's COMI at the time of the opening of the proceedings. Until 2017 this was determined by the EU Council Regulation (EC) No 1346/2000 of 29 May 2000 on insolvency proceedings OJ L 160. A new, reformed regulation takes effect in mid 2017. Regulation (EU) 2015/848 of the European Parliament and of the Council of 20 May 2015 on Insolvency Proceedings (recast) [2015] OJ L 141/19. Under Art 3(1) of the Regulation an individual's COMI will either be their habitual residence or the place where an individual conducts the administration of their main interests on a regular basis.

is an attractive jurisdiction for debtors because of the swift discharge, straightforward access to the insolvency procedure and absence of any requirement to notify creditors in advance of filing.[131]

German and Austrian professionals and small business persons represented the initial wave of tourists, followed during and after the financial crisis by a small number of high-profile Irish debtors and a trickle of debtors from the Baltic states and Poland. Firms sprang up to advise potential Germans, Irish or other nationals on how to establish a COMI in the UK. The Irish bankrupts included several entrepreneurs whose property businesses collapsed when the Irish property bubble burst.[132] These individuals had usually signed personal guarantees for their property companies. They were attempting to escape Ireland's draconian bankruptcy laws with a discharge period of 12 years, and were often being pursued by the Irish Bank, which had become the 'bad bank' by taking over the toxic assets of the Irish banks. These individuals could be depicted as the risk-taking entrepreneurs championed by EU policymakers although some media constructed them as the 'business elite' fleeing the ship, being pursued by an outraged government that had bailed out the banks.[133] Although England is a more liberal jurisdiction than Ireland they would still be subject to income repayment undertakings and be required to relinquish substantial property. They would not emerge unscathed.

European law on forum shopping as embodied in the 2000 EC Insolvency Regulation[134] addressed primarily corporate insolvency, providing no definition of a COMI for individual jurisdiction beyond a presumption that a COMI was the place where an individual conducted the administration of his interests on a regular basis.[135] The English courts developed guidelines that attempted to balance the freedom of an individual to relocate at a time when insolvency threatens with the principle that the COMI should be objectively ascertainable to third parties and have some permanence. The courts decided that the issue is determined at the time when insolvency proceedings are opened but that the judges could take into

[131] England and Wales historically had very liberal jurisdiction rules with only the requirement that an individual be present in England on the day of the petition See s 265 of the Insolvency Act 1986. However, the court always had a broad discretion to dismiss a petition if there was an absence of connection with England and Wales. For a recent discussion of the factors taken into account in exercising this discretion see the decision of Register Baister in *Re Kekhman* (2014) generally approved by Morgan J on appeal. See *JSC Bank of Moscow v Kekhman and others* [2015] EWHC 396 (Ch) dealing with a former Russian millionaire businessman petitioning for bankruptcy in England and Wales.

[132] Eg lawyer and property developer Brian O'Donnel owing the Bank of Ireland €71 million, John Fleming owing €1 billion, Paddy Shovlin owing €280 million, Dermot O'Leary and Reg Tuthill €100 million, Sean Quinn owing €2.8 billion and Ivan Yates, owner of a failed bookmaker. See discussion in Fannon, 'Bankruptcy Tourism' (n 128). See also H Vallender, H Allemand, S Baister, P Kuglanz, H Mahijsen, B O'Neill, E Collins, and S Potamitis, 'A Minimum Standard for Debt Discharge in Europe' (2013) *Insolvency Intelligence* 97, footnote 2.

[133] See eg H McDonald, 'Irish Dodge Debts Through UK Bankruptcy Tourism' *The Guardian* (27 May 2012).

[134] Council Regulation (EC) No 1346/2000.

[135] See Recital 13, Council Regulation (EC) No 1346/2000. An earlier report had suggested that for non-professionals the COMI was 'the habitual residence'.

account historical facts.[136] This invited, therefore, a heavily fact-specific analysis of indicia of change. The English courts gradually became tougher in policing this tourism, requiring greater evidence to substantiate a change in a COMI.[137] The Official Receiver in England was not enthusiastic about administering such bankruptcies. It has changed its practices to ensure greater investigation of bankruptcy tourism[138] and closed down several companies offering pre-packaged advice to German nationals on how to take advantage of England's liberal bankruptcy laws.

Table 6.1: Bankruptcy Tourism in England and Wales, 2008–13

	2008	2009	2010	2011	2012	2013
Austria	8	11	1	5	4	2
Belgium	0	0	0	0	1	0
Estonia	0	0	0	1	1	0
France	0	0	0	1	1	4
Germany	43	107	103	141	131	63
Ireland	0	1	4	20	42	34
Italy	0	0	0	0	0	0
Latvia	0	0	0	8	10	9
Lithuania	0	0	0	0	6	10
Netherlands	0	0	0	0	2	0
Poland	0	0	1	4	7	9
Slovenia	0	0	1	0	0	0
Spain	0	0	0	1	1	2

Source: The Insolvency Service, freedom of information (FOI) request. The data describe bankruptcies where the Official Receiver has noted: 'The debtor is a foreign national who appears to have been resident in the UK for a period of less than 12 months, and all or most of the debts disclosed are owed to creditors based outside the UK.' Only a small percentage of these cases would result in an annulment of the bankruptcy.

[136] See *Shierson v Clive Vlieland Boddy* [2005] EWCA Civ 974.

[137] See eg *Re Eichler (A Bankrupt) (No 2); Steinhardt v Eichler* [2011] BPIR 1293 annulling a bankruptcy order made by the same registrar in 2007. For other bankruptcy tourist cases see eg *Schrade v Sparkasse Ludenchild* [2014] EWHC 1049 (ch); *Sparkasse Hilden Ratiyen Velbert v Benk* [2012] EWHC 342 (Ch); *Re Hagemeister (a bankrupt)* [2010] BPIR 1093; *Official Receiver v Mitterfellner* [2009] BPIR 1075; *O'Donnell v Bank of Ireland* [2012] EWHC 2432 (Ch); *Irish Bank Resolution Corp'n v Quinn* [2012] BCC 608.

[138] Modifications were made to the Technical Manual in 2010 with more guidance on the steps to take when dealing with foreign nationals. For example there are separate guidelines on Germany:

> 'When dealing with the affairs of a bankrupt with a connection with Germany, the official receiver should be concerned to establish that the order ought to have been made in England and Wales.
>
> 43.1.3 Germans seeking protection of the courts of England and Wales

Table 6.1 indicates the relatively small number of cases of potential bankruptcy tourists, although the data may be an underestimate.[139] Bankruptcy tourism is, however, of symbolic significance in documenting the impact of freedom of movement on the resources of other countries, in this case the costs of court time and regulators. The importance of freedom of movement as a principle in the context of insolvency was recognised by the European Court of Justice (ECJ) in *Ulf Kazimierz Radziejewski v Kronofogdemyndighten*.[140] This case concerned a Swede living and working in Belgium who wished to file for debt restructuring in Sweden but was refused by the Stockholm KFM because he was not resident in Sweden. The Court held that the Swedish residence requirement infringed his right to freedom of movement under Art 45 TFEU. Freedom of movement implies that individuals should be free to move to another jurisdiction to improve their economic situation, which might include shedding debt and achieving an early rehabilitation.

The arguments for controls on bankruptcy tourism concern the costs generated for creditors who must appear in a foreign jurisdiction and the higher costs for the relevant jurisdiction in administering such a bankruptcy. Creditors might adjust to the possibility of bankruptcy tourism in the granting and pricing of credit. However, moving jurisdiction to take advantage of more liberal insolvency laws is only practicable for affluent debtors, engendering a sense of unfairness for ordinary debtors unable to obtain similar access. This may have animated Irish hostility to their bankruptcy tourists.

Bankruptcy tourism also highlights contrasting English judicial approaches to business and individual insolvency. The English courts have a favourable approach to corporations moving their COMI in order to take advantage of English

> The Service has experienced a rise in the number of bankruptcy petitions presented by German nationals stating that their COMI is, at the date of the presentation of the petition, England and Wales. Typically, it appears that the individuals have been resident in England and Wales for less than 12 months, and there is a significant minority where it appears that there has been no actual change of COMI from Germany and the presentation of the petition is a sham to take advantage of more favourable insolvency legislation.' …
>
> 43.1.5 Creditors
>
> The official receiver should obtain evidence that the bankrupt has informed his/her creditors of his/her move to the UK—including the date of that notice.
>
> The official receiver may also consider making enquiries of the bankrupt's creditors as to when they were advised of the move to the UK, and also to ask them if they have any information to suggest that the bankrupt is living or working outside the UK.'

www.insolvencydirect.bis.gov.uk/technicalmanual/Ch37-48/chapter43/Chapter%2043-1/Part%201/Part%201.htm.

[139] The data must be treated with care. They were collected by official receivers during the interviews with debtors after bankruptcy. Changes in numbers might be accounted for by more dismissals of bankruptcy petitions by registrars. Anecdotal information provided to me by experienced practitioners suggest that these data understate the total number of potential tourists.

[140] See Case C-461/11 *Ulf Kazimierz Radziejewski v Kronofogdemyndighten i Stockholm*. In this case the debtor's business went bankrupt in 1996. He had been subject to an earning attachment order by the KFM since 1997(!). He worked in Belgium for a Swedish employer and in 2011 applied to KFM for debt relief and was refused because he did not have a registered residence in Sweden. The ECJ held the Swedish residence requirement to infringe his right to freedom of movement under Art 45 TFEU.

restructuring laws, a position supported by the UK government.[141] This approach maintains London as an attractive centre for business rescue and supports the lucrative insolvency and restructuring industry. The *Guardian* was more forthright, describing London as being at risk of becoming a 'bankruptcy brothel'.[142] This regulatory competition to be the the most liberal and debtor-friendly restructuring regime, has undoubtedly had an impact on other jurisdictions, driving increasing convergence of approaches to business restructuring. In contrast, England is reluctant to become a destination for individual business or consumer debtors. The difference between individual and corporate insolvency law approaches cannot be justified solely on the basis that in business restructuring all parties are made better off (or at least not disadvantaged). Resort to the English procedures may permit a 'cramdown' of certain groups of creditors. The distinction between 'good' and 'bad' forum shopping is not easy to draw, involving a cost-benefit analysis and value judgements.[143]

Bankruptcy tourism has highlighted the restrictive nature of individual countries' laws, such as the long waiting period for discharge in Germany and Ireland. The Irish government pressed for action at EU level to provide a common solution and the issue was raised during negotiations on reform of the EC Insolvency Regulation.[144] Poland was concerned that although individuals might have genuinely moved to England, they might still have significant creditors in Poland who

[141] See *Re Hellas Telecommunications (Luxembourg) II* [2010] BCC 295. (Company moved to London three and a half months before insolvency proceedings.) A 'Scheme of Arrangement', a technique used for restructuring companies in London, is not included within the EC Insolvency Regulation and provides a liberal basis for jurisdiction, to attract foreign companies to use London as a site for restructuring.

[142] See Elena Moya, 'London Risks Becoming "Brothel" for Bankruptcy Tourists' *The Guardian* (31 January 2010). The author comments: 'Richard Nevins, a restructuring partner at the law firm Cadwalader in London, said the main benefit for bankruptcy tourists is that it allows firms to get rid of certain types of troublesome creditors. Companies such as Greece's Wind Hellas, a telecoms operator, and Germany's car parts maker Schefenacker briefly moved their headquarters to the UK to undergo a British administration procedure. Businesses need only be resident here for a few weeks, have a UK address, and pay the lawyers' fees. "It's like Nevada becoming the divorce capital of the US," said Nevins, "and I don't think we've seen the last of it."'

[143] See *Kekhman* (n 131) where in a recent case concerning a Russian millionaire the courts were willing to take into account the absence of an individual bankruptcy procedure in Russia and that English law might fill lacunae in foreign laws recognising the importance of financial rehabilitation for this individual as a modern objective of bankruptcy law. But they seemed less willing to recognise the 12-year Irish bankruptcy discharge period as a lacuna.

[144] 'We want to avoid a situation where someone can shop around for where is the most lenient form of insolvency legislation and try and take advantage of that … That is why it is important there should be a European approach', Eamon Gilmore, Deputy Prime Minister Ireland, quoted in J Smyth, 'Couple fail to overturn bankruptcy ruling' *Financial Times* (6 March 2013). See also J Smyth, 'Dublin pushes for insolvency overhaul' *Financial Times* (6 July 2012). According to Alan Shatter, Ireland Minister for Justice: 'The very essence of having a common market is that you need to have common rules with regard to bankruptcy legislation and not rules which appear to be in conflict with each other and can provide incentives for people to engage in bankruptcy tourism.' See 'Shatter asks Britain to crack down on light touch bankruptcy tourism' *Irish Examiner* (4 February 2013) www.irishexaminer.com/ireland/shatter-asks-britain-to-crack-down-on-light-touch-bankruptcy-tourism-221574.html.

would be disadvantaged by the English one-year discharge rather than five years in Poland. Several Member States proposed a 'look back' or 'suspect' period where a COMI move would be ignored. Since this could have impacted on the restructuring industry in London,[145] the UK government formed alliances with other Member States to limit this proposal. As a consequence, the 2015 regulation uses rebuttable presumptions rather than bright-line rules.[146]

Several states (for example, France) continue to exclude their consumer schemes from the scope of the regulation and the UK excludes Debt Relief Orders (DROs).[147] The justifications for this exclusion are that DROs do not provide a distribution for creditors, and the fee and process are not designed to deal with the complexity of cross-border cases or the costs of determining a COMI.[148] The Insolvency Service may also fear the increased costs of administering these insolvencies. Yet this will disadvantage a Polish worker who obtains a DRO and may still be subject to action by Polish creditors on return to Poland. The absence of consumer debtor representation in the negotiations (either through states or groups) on the revised regulation is reflected therefore in this particular outcome.

The proposed EU Directive acknowledges both the potentially high costs of relocation to another jurisdiction for an overindebted entrepreneur in a jurisdiction with a long discharge period and also the costs of such relocation for creditors.[149] The baseline requirement of a discharge period no longer than three years illustrates the possibility of 'regulatory learning'[150] from bankruptcy tourism while leaving Member States free to introduce a more generous discharge.

VII. Towards a European Paradigm?

Most federal states locate bankruptcy within the federal jurisdiction. One of the first legislative acts of a united Germany in the nineteenth century was the creation

[145] In particular, on schemes of arrangement. The UK succeeded in having them excluded from the regulation.

[146] The recast regulation presumes in the absence of proof to the contrary that a non-trader's COMI is her habitual residence. However, individuals do not have the benefit of this presumption where they have moved to another Member State within six months of the opening of insolvency proceedings. A similar three-month presumption applies to moving an individual's principal place of business or registered office See Regulation (EU) 2015/848 (n 130) art 3(1).

[147] These are not included in Annex A, and Recital 16 of the recast regulation indicates that the regulation should not apply to proceedings where 'debt of a natural person of very low income and very low asset value are written off, provided that this type of proceedings never makes provision for payment to creditors'.

[148] Email from Insolvency Service, 11/04/15.

[149] Proposal for a Directive of the European Parliament and of the Council on preventive restructuring frameworks, second chance and measures to increase the efficiency of restructuring, insolvency and discharge procedures (n 6) Recital 4.

[150] See S Deakin, 'Legal Diversity and Regulatory Competition: Which Model for Europe?' (2006) 12 *European Law Journal* 440.

of a uniform Bankruptcy Act. The EU Commission has proposed a harmonisation that would provide minimum standards, reducing the differences between systems while strengthening weaker systems.[151] The narrative underpinning these recommendations is primarily economic—promoting economic demand, encouraging entrepreneurship and investment. Legal justification is sought in Articles 53 and 114 of the Treaty, which address respectively freedom of establishment of the self employed and harmonisation of rules to address distortions of competition within the single market. This latter justification is harder in the context of individual debtors since only a modest amount of cross-border household credit exists and was probably one reason for not including consumers within the mandatory three-year limit.[152] The 'social' aspects of debt are hardly mentioned in the Inception Impact Statement of 2016 although the European Parliament has pressed the European Commission to consider issues of insolvency as they affect individuals. Consumer insolvency reforms are therefore riding on the coat-tails of business insolvency reforms, a spillover effect of business reform.

This chapter suggests that an emerging European paradigm of individual insolvency does exist which includes the primacy of a repayment plan where possible with perhaps the possibility in law or practice of a swift discharge for the no-income no-asset debtor. Having said that, substantial differences exist between individual insolvency systems in terms of access criteria, institutional structure, discharge periods and debts that are excepted from discharge. Access criteria in developed systems vary from the relatively liberal English criteria to the strict Swedish criteria. Tax debts are excepted from discharge in some jurisdictions but not others, or under special conditions.[153] Some systems with long repayment periods seem to have fewer exceptions to discharge.[154] These differences do not represent deep cultural differences between countries, but more often interest group influence, or the political compromises of their enactment which may become difficult to change over time, as in the case of Sweden. The trader/non-trader distinction remains significant in several European countries (for example, France and Spain) with a distinction in treatment for consumption and production debt. This might suggest a barrier to harmonisation of laws in this area. However a legitimacy issue exists for any attempt to provide differential treatment for traders and consumers. Facilitating restructuring and a swift fresh start for entrepreneurs in an era of increasing inequality and austerity may be harder to justify if ordinary consumers must struggle with longer repayment periods or greater hurdles to a fresh start.

[151] See Inception Impact Statement, March 2016, 8.

[152] The Commission notes that because of limited cross-border lending the problem should be addressed first at the local level. Directive of the European Parliament and of the Council on preventive restructuring frameworks, second chance and measures to increase the efficiency of restructuring, insolvency and discharge procedures (n 6) 15.

[153] Eg in Germany tax debts are excepted if the debtor has been convicted of a tax crime.

[154] See the interesting discussion of this phenomenon in T Linna, 'Consumer Insolvency: The Linkage between the Fresh Start, Collective Proceedings and the Access to Debt Adjustment' (2015) 38 *Journal of Consumer Policy* 357.

The modest number of empirical studies of the law in action in Europe paint an often problematic picture of long delays for individuals in obtaining professional assistance or access to relief and individuals at the mercy of bureaucrats.[155] They also indicate,[156] as noted above, that many individuals have no repayment capacity. These are the individuals using the *rétablissement personnel* in France, the large numbers of *Nullinsolvenz* in Germany and Sweden, and bankrupts and those with DROs in England and Wales. The great majority of this group are renters, not homeowners. Preliminary research in England and Wales indicates that almost two-thirds of debtors in this group are female[157] and many are sole parents. The majority are unemployed. They usually have debts to financial institutions including credit cards but also debts to central and local state creditors and utilities.[158] Debt relief for this group highlights the overlaps with issues of social policy and housing provision, dependent on the particular form of national welfare systems, suggesting possible difficulties in developing a common European approach to this group.

Home ownership is an important economic and social institution in the EU, with an average of 70 per cent home ownership.[159] During the eurozone crisis a battery of initiatives developed to address mortgage debt overhang including moratoria on foreclosures, writing down of principal, protocols for identifying individuals at risk of foreclosure, and state transfer payments for mortgage interest payments. The ECJ stimulated reform of Spanish foreclosure law through its decision in *Aziz*,[160] which hinted at the human rights dimensions of protection

[155] See eg J Heuer, 'Social Inclusion and Exclusion in European Consumer Bankruptcy Systems' (on file with author) and chs 4 and 5 above.

[156] See review in I Ramsay, 'Between Neo-Liberalism and the Social Market: Approaches to Debt Adjustment and Consumer Insolvency in the EU' (2012) 35(4) *Journal of Consumer Policy* 421 and discussion in ch 1 section III.B.

[157] See Insolvency Service, 'DROS—Initial Evaluation Report' (London, Insolvency Service, 2010) 9 noting that 63% of debtors are female. Also in France where 59% of debtors on *rétablissement personnel* are female Bank of France, 'Household Over-indebtedness: 2014 Typological Survey (Paris, Bank of France, 2015) 17, https://www.banque-france.fr/fileadmin/user_upload/banque_de_france/La_Banque_de_France/Enqu%C3%AAte-typologique-EN.pdf.

[158] An early survey by the Insolvency Service noted that the profile of debtors accessing the DRO system was primarily 'low income, predominantly unemployed individuals with an average of six creditors; over 53% of debt was owed to banks, building societies and credit card companies'. See Insolvency Service, 'DROS—Initial Evaluation Report' (n 157) 3. More informal data since the recession suggest that public creditors may now be more significant. See eg A Pardo, J Lane, P Lane, and D Hertzberg, *Citizens Advice: Unsecured and Insecure?* (2015), which argues that over the past five years there has been a significant shift in problems 'away from mainstream credit issues towards problems with arrears on council tax, rent and energy bills. Five years ago, credit cards were the main debt issue we saw. Now council tax arrears top the list.'

[159] I discuss this topic at greater length in Ramsay, 'Two Cheers for Europe' (n 58) 204–12.

[160] See Case C-415-11 *Mohamed Aziz v Caixa d'Estalvas de Catalunya* EU:C:2013:164. For a commentary see H Micklitz and N Reich, 'The Court and Sleeping Beauty: The Revival of the Unfair Contract Terms Directive (UCTD)' (2014) 51(3) *Common Market Law Review* 771 See the later direct reference by Advocate General Wahl in Case C-482/12 *Peter Macinský, Eva Macinská v Getfin sro, Financreal sro* [2014] OJ C 184/22, para 82: '[W]here the property concerned by the procedure at issue is the

for the home. One issue for European insolvency reform is the extent to which the home should be protected in insolvency to protect against social exclusion and ensure a fresh start. Chapter 2 discussed the significance of the homestead exemption in the US in contributing to entrepreneurialism and maintaining economic stability, but also the failure to include cramdown provisions in Chapter 13 after the Great Recession. Addressing these issues poses a political challenge for the EU, given the existing differences between Member States in protection for the home. Mortgage debt represents the largest share of household debt in many Member States, constituting a significant aspect of banks' lending portfolios. The EU mortgage directive of 2014 included some hortatory measures on foreclosure, under pressure from the European Parliament, and the European Banking Authority may develop principles related to foreclosure which provide minimum standards for a cross-border market in residential mortgages.

The issues in the Europeanisation of personal insolvency are primarily political not cultural. Preferential treatment for certain creditors, such as public authorities or taxes, reflects political preferences and the influence of interest groups. The institutional structures of personal insolvency reflect contingency and path dependency. A primary argument against increased harmonisation is the absence of substantial empirical studies of European systems, the relative novelty of many systems, and the need for further regulatory learning. Such an approach would not prevent the establishment of minimum standards and principles.

VIII. Conclusion

The 2008 crisis transformed household debt from a peripheral aspect of the financial system to an issue for the international financial system. There was, however, no authoritative international policy script on individual insolvency, traditionally viewed as a national matter, subject to local cultural, social and political influences. The new narrative promoted by the IMF and World Bank underlined a set of utilitarian arguments in favour of more liberal discharge procedures for individual insolvency, a category including both business and consumer debt. These arguments clashed with central bank concerns about 'moral hazard' and in some cases governments unwilling to take the political risks of introducing a personal

consumer's home, there must be specific guarantees. Failure to provide such guarantees may prove problematic from a fundamental rights perspective. Indeed, the loss of a family home is one of the most extreme forms of interference with the rights of the consumer. As respect for the home is a right guaranteed under Article 7 of the Charter of Fundamental Rights of the European Union, in the light of which Directive 93/13 must be interpreted, any person at risk of an interference of this magnitude should be able to have the proportionality of such a measure reviewed by an independent judicial body.' See also *Rousk v Sweden* App no 27183/04 (ECtHR, 25 October 2013 final) (lack of effective procedural safeguards against repossession and sale by Swedish tax authorities was violation of Art 8 of the Convention for the Protection of Human Rights and Fundamental Freedoms).

insolvency discharge, a position that may have reflected partly the influence of financial interests in these countries. The narrative of promoting entrepreneurialism now drives EU reforms with consumers benefiting though a spillover effect. The difficulty of separating entrepreneurs from consumers creates potential for further reforms. The concept of a three-year maximum discharge period with perhaps a swifter discharge for the no-income no-asset debtor is a nascent European paradigm. The concept of financial inclusion in the dominant economic narrative is that of a hand-up to individuals to re-enter the market rather than a social narrative which views counselling and debt repayment schemes as necessary to the reintegration of individuals to society.

7

Conclusion: The Future of Personal Insolvency in the Twenty-First Century

This book has documented the interests and narratives in the development of personal insolvency at the beginning of the twenty-first century in the US and three European states and the emerging international narrative of personal insolvency. This chapter draws some conclusions on the different interests and contemporary narratives concerning the role of personal insolvency and the discharge of debts. It also addresses the role and objectives of personal insolvency.

I. Influential Interest Groups

Financial interests influence credit and personal insolvency policy in both public and private fora, through politics and the market. Financial institutions are often long-term repeat players.[1] They can play for rules[2] by influencing formal legislation, informal bargaining within a policy community and seeking favourable precedents. They influence the law in action as significant creditors in most personal insolvencies, in some cases undercutting legislative policy such as the fresh start. The practices of finance companies in the US before 1978[3] and those of the English banks in relation to individual voluntary arrangements in the mid 2000s[4] are examples of their influence on the law in action. In Sweden, the oligopolistic nature of the banks gives them a significant veto over changes to the restructuring system. In France, financial interests operate partly through the Ministry of Finance but also are represented on the over-indebtedness commissions and they monitor the performance of commissions.[5]

[1] M Galanter 'Why the "Haves" Come out Ahead: Speculations on the Limits of Legal Change' (1974) 9 *Law & Society Review* 95.

[2] ibid 100.

[3] See above, ch 2 section III.

[4] See above, ch 3.

[5] See above, ch 4 section V, note 92.

Finance capital is not just another interest group. Charles Lindblom referred once to the 'privileged position of business'.[6] By this, he meant that business does not need to openly press its case on a continuing basis, because governments are very sensitive to the extent to which economic success, and their electoral success, depends on business. Active criticisms of business are disapproved of, so conventional wisdom tends to reinforce this privileged position.[7] Lindblom's conclusion might be applied to the case of finance capital. Governments are concerned about the potential impact of individual debt write-down on the availability of finance and bank capital. This is particularly the case during a recession, when the importance of supporting bank recapitalisation trumps the writing down of household debt. The concern that credit will become more difficult to obtain if personal insolvency is liberalised is a recurring trope in the US, England and Sweden. Whatever the empirical validity of this trope (and the actual effects are often exaggerated as in the $400 bankruptcy tax), it retains a significant influence on decision-making notwithstanding the sustained critiques of the financial industry in many countries since the Great Recession of 2008.

The introduction of a 'no-income no-asset procedure' is acceptable because the effects on credit granting are assumed to be minimal, although even here controls exist to prevent moral hazard. The general body of consumers, who depend on continuing access to credit, may be unlikely to support the liberalisation of individual insolvency if it brings the possibility of reduced access to credit, and may be susceptible to claims that they should not pay for the 'irresponsibility' of other consumers. Politicians are, therefore, hesitant to introduce easily accessible bankruptcy procedures that are not fenced in by significant restrictions on entry and controls to deter the irresponsible debtor. However, because these controls often render the system inaccessible to many, with a consequent low take up, modifications are often made to the legislation in order to increase accessibility.[8] This process does suggest that financial interests are not all powerful and that to retain legitimacy governments must respond to initial negative feedback on legislation. This results in a settling of the legislation over time.

Government departments are significant players in European states. For example, ministries of justice in the UK, France, and Sweden wish to reduce the public costs of operating the court system. They worry about courts becoming overloaded with small debt cases that are viewed as primarily administrative rather than legal in nature, representing situations where individual settlement should

[6] See C Lindblom, *Politics and Markets: The World's Political-Economic Systems* (New York, Basic Books, 1977).

[7] Wolfgang Streeck argues that international finance capital and the bond markets are a special political constituency. He describes the rise in the importance of bondholder creditors to a second 'constituency' of the modern state. W Streeck, *Buying Time: The Delayed Crisis of Democratic Capitalism* (London, Verso Books, 2014) 79.

[8] This occurred in Poland in 2014, which modified its 2009 law to abolish the requirement of social force majeure as an entry requirement. Ireland modified its 2012 law in 2015 in the face of a poor take-up by individuals. This repeats the earlier experience in France. See ch 4 section III.

be encouraged. Judges support this position, which sometimes reflects a lack of interest in 'petty cases'. In an era of austerity, however, states are reluctant to invest substantial public resources in the administration of debt relief. The UK solves this problem through harnessing the public and private 'over-indebtedness industry'. The UK's administrative DRO attempts to reduce the costs of all participants in the debt resolution process. France increasingly seeks to download the work of the Bank of France to social partners. In the recent Hedborg report Sweden recognises the challenge of providing adequate support for debtors. The US is an exception here, where the specialised bankruptcy judiciary and bar resist separate administrative processing, or at least administrative processing not supervised by the judiciary.

Individual debtors or bankrupts rarely form their own interest groups, and so do not participate directly in the policy-making process. When their interests are represented it is therefore usually through other groups, such as general consumer groups, government agencies or intermediaries. In the last category the role of lawyers and judges in the US in portraying debtors and debtors' interests has been influential in shaping US bankruptcy law. Although these groups may be sympathetic to the over-indebted their policy prescriptions will partly reflect their own ideological or pecuniary interests. Thus debt counsellors may view greater counselling as the solution for debtors and some may believe that individuals should not be able to simply 'walk away' from their debts without some behaviour modification. In the US the lawyer-dominated 1970s Bankruptcy Commission believed that a modified Chapter 13 was the optimal solution for most debtors. Individual bankrupts may also benefit from the sidewind or spillover effects of policies aimed at other groups, such as business bankrupts.

II. Contemporary Narratives of Personal Insolvency

Personal insolvency, defined as a swift discharge of debts in return for giving up non-exempt property, is increasingly a suppressed political alternative as a general remedy for over-indebtedness in Europe. An immediate discharge of debts is reserved for the deserving poor—individuals with no significant income and no assets, and with a limited level of debt.[9] This preference is clear in recent Irish,[10] English, and Scottish reforms.[11] The policy preference is for repayment plans as a

[9] Ronald Mann makes the useful point that 'no-income no-assets' is a misnomer. The remedy is designed for the poor who can accumulate limited debts rather than individuals with no income at the time of filing for relief. See R Mann, 'Making Sense of Nation-Level Bankruptcy Filing Rates' in J Niemi, I Ramsay, and W Whitford (eds), *Consumer Credit, Debt and Bankruptcy* (Oxford, Hart Publishing, 2009) 243.

[10] See Personal Insolvency Act 2012.

[11] See Bankruptcy and Insolvency Scotland Reform Act 2014.

primary remedy, often over a period of five years. Figure 3.1and 4.3 in chapters 3 and 4 respectively indicate these trends in England and France. France reserves complete relief for the 'irremediably compromised', who generally fit the profile of a low income, low asset debtor. Other countries do not formally recognize this category. Debtors with no repayment capacity are given a zero-repayment plan but must still wait five (Sweden) or potentially six (Germany) years for a discharge. England and Wales does in theory provide a relatively swift discharge in bankruptcy as a general remedy, but influential narratives construct it as a last resort, little interest-group support exists for bankruptcy as a general remedy and professional intermediaries have limited interest in promoting it. The suppression of 'straight bankruptcy' relief as a general remedy has been reinforced by the work of the international agencies in Europe that promote a modified German model of bankruptcy for individuals with the addition more recently of the 'no-income no-asset procedure'. Straight bankruptcy discharge under Chapter 7 remains an important remedy for the over-indebted in the US and to that extent it remains an exception.

The dominant international discourse of entrepreneurialism, promoting an early discharge to stimulate risk-taking, may provide a sidewind of benefits to consumers in those countries that do not retain the trader/non-trader distinction. The three-year norm for discharge of entrepreneurs in the EU Directive might be extended to consumers. The historical shadow of the trader/non-trader distinction continues, however, to influence reforms in countries such as Sweden, France, and Spain where more liberal bankruptcy provisions were initially restricted to 'entrepreneurs'.

European reforms of personal insolvency law have reflected not only the influence of ideas but also a pragmatic 'muddling through', adapting existing laws with borrowings and transplants from other states.[12] Sweden has borrowed from both Denmark and England, and England borrowed from New Zealand to develop the DRO. States rarely adopt foreign models *tout court* so that significant differences may develop even between closely related jurisdictions, such as Scotland and England and Wales. France stumbled into a new regime for consumers with an experimental Act of 1989 and the unique idea of harnessing the Bank of France to act as administrator. French reformers subsequently referred to many foreign countries in the 2003 reforms, but fitted the introduction of a personal insolvency law within the form, if not the name, of a French concept: *faillite civile*. There is therefore a contingency here in the manner which different states address similar problems that may have long-term effects, as in the case of the distinct French institutional structure of debt relief.

Contemporary European and US narratives about personal insolvency do not differ fundamentally. Both emphasise balancing the fresh start and personal

[12] Reminiscent of Alan Watson's original thesis in *Legal Transplants: An Approach to Comparative Law* (Edinburgh, Edinburgh University Press, 1974).

responsibility, ensuring re-entry to the market but demonstrating concern for moral hazard and upholding the idea of 'can pay should pay' while recognising the need for a relatively swift discharge for those with no repayment capacity or significant assets.

III. Technocracy and Democracy in Personal Insolvency Reform

Personal insolvency law reform raises both technical legal questions and significant economic and social issues. Distributional issues are often secreted in technical detail. The structure of the process of reform is therefore important. Delegation of agenda setting and policy development to stakeholder groups can draw on the knowledge and experience of insiders. Such committees or consultations can identify a consensus that reduces parliamentary time for consideration of more contentious issues. Much personal insolvency policy-making has taken this form of 'quiet politics',[13] which permits insiders to have a substantial influence on the development of policies which have low political salience. 'Quiet politics' in bankruptcy is not necessarily either progressive or regressive. In the US bankruptcy policy was steered by insiders until 1978 with a 'mildly pro-debtor' approach. The transformation of bankruptcy politics into a more public and partisan form resulted in the less debtor-friendly Bankruptcy Abuse Prevention and Consumer Protection Act (BAPCPA) of 2005.[14] In England and Wales, the composition of the insiders on individual voluntary arrangement (IVA) committees and their preferences have steered policy in a more creditor-friendly direction. This delegation to insiders may also result in a process that leads to a policy stalemate or equilibrium. The costs of government intervention to break the impasse are perceived to be high. Crises such as the Great Recession or moral panics over credit card debt can create public pressure for change but the opportunity for radical change may not last as the initial public interest wanes and insiders are able to exert influence over the all-important details of policy implementation. Dramatic change can be sometimes brought about by an 'outsider'. In France, the politician Jean Borloo transformed the French debt adjustment law into an insolvency regime. But even apparently decisive changes prompted by broader public objectives, such as the liberalisation of the English bankruptcy discharge in 2002, may be much less dramatic in their

[13] P Culpepper, *Quiet Politics and Business Power: Corporate Control in Europe and Japan* (Cambridge, Cambridge University Press, 2011).

[14] Legal scholars in the US generally lament the 'politicisation' of bankruptcy policy since the 1970s when expertise—as represented by elite lawyers and academics—was subordinated to an interest group politics dominated by lobbying and money. A general theme in critiques of the BAPCPA is not only that the Congressional process was captured by creditor interests, but that the dominance of politicians and interest groups resulted in badly drafted and at times incomprehensible legislation.

long-term impact given the influence over time of the over-indebtedness industry and financial institutions.

The concept of 'evidence based policy' has become an influential idea but systematic empirical evidence of the impact and effects of personal insolvency law remains modest outside the US. Empirical data are important because they can challenge influential narratives which may be promoted by insiders or professionals involved in the insolvency system. Its absence may often mean that personal insolvency law reforms are exercises in accidental wisdom with unintended consequences. Even systematic reforms such as the US Bankruptcy Reform Act 1978 lacked systematic knowledge of the impact of a centrepiece of reform, the revised and expanded Chapter 13. English reforms from Cork[15] onwards have rarely been based on systematic empirical knowledge of the operation of the individual insolvency system, and the current system reflects a mixture of contingency and the influence of government ministries, financial institutions, and intermediaries, with occasional external interventions when insolvency policy is linked to wider economic goals such as the link to entrepreneurialism in the Enterprise Act 2002.

IV. The Limits of Individual Insolvency?

A major objective of personal insolvency law is the 'fresh start' associated with a discharge of debts. The World Bank Report on the Treatment of the Insolvency of Natural Persons identified several objectives for personal insolvency and a bankruptcy discharge: relief of hardship, increased productivity, promotion of entrepreneurialism, reduced externalities in terms of costs to communities, health care, and family, incentives for responsible lending, and ensuring more accurate accounting. The report appealed also to underlying ideas of the prevention of financial and social exclusion.

A fundamental question is whether in practice the above objectives are attained by personal insolvency systems. Surprisingly few studies exist on the longitudinal effects of personal insolvency. Some US studies argue that many individuals do not achieve a 'fresh start' and that bankrupt households are likely to experience renewed financial difficulties and continue to use expensive sources of credit such as payday loans. Katherine Porter and Deborah Thorne found that one year after bankruptcy 25 per cent of debtors were struggling to pay routine bills and 33 per cent had a similar financial situation to that when they filed bankruptcy.[16] Bankruptcy was insufficient therefore to provide relief for one in three debtors.

[15] See above, ch 3.

[16] 'We found that just one year post-bankruptcy, one in four debtors was struggling to pay routine bills, and one in three debtors reported an overall financial situation similar to, or worse than, when that debtor filed bankruptcy. Our analysis of these data demonstrates that steady and sufficient income is the key to improved post-bankruptcy financial health. Factors that cause household income to decline, such as unemployment and underemployment, illness or injury, and old age, undermine the chances of financial recovery. These data reveal the limitations of bankruptcy as a social safety net

Porter also concluded that Chapter 13 often failed to protect homeowners from foreclosure.[17] Han and Li conclude that 'bankruptcy households are more likely to experience renewed financial difficulties, accumulate much less wealth and use expensive credit sources, such as payday loans. Moreover financial hardship persists even more than ten years after the filings.'[18] This less than sanguine view contrasts with a recent study[19] that analysed the subsequent earnings, mortality and home foreclosure experience of individuals filing for Chapter 13 bankruptcy between 1992 and 2005. Using essentially a randomised methodology[20] the authors found that over the first five post-filing years those granted bankruptcy were significantly better off financially in terms of income than those refused bankruptcy protection. They had a significantly lower five-year mortality rate and five-year home foreclosure rate. The difference between the two groups was represented by the significant deterioration in those who did not obtain bankruptcy protection, that is, bankruptcy mitigated the effects of the financial downturn for the individual preceding bankruptcy. Bankruptcy protection increased incentives to continue to work since it protected against wage garnishment[21] and contributed to economic stability[22] because individuals had less incentive to go underground or to move state to avoid wage garnishment. Economic stability was enhanced by protecting against immediate home foreclosure through the stay on enforcement.

These findings are of interest to European policymakers because the study was of Chapter 13, the repayment option and the dominant norm in European countries. It was also pre-BAPCPA, when the repayment period was normally three years rather than five years. The generally longer period of repayment in European systems and the lack of protection for homes might not result in as extensive benefits for debtors.

The limited number of European studies suggest that a significant number of individuals continue to face debt problems after debt adjustment.[23] In England,

and highlight the fragile economic situations of American families. We conclude that bankruptcy is an incomplete tool to rehabilitate those in financial distress.' K Porter and D Thorne, 'The Failure of Bankruptcy's Fresh Start' (2006) 92(1) *Cornell Law Review* 67.

[17] See K Porter, 'The Pretend Solution: An Empirical Study of Bankruptcy' (2011) 90 *Texas Law Review* 104.

[18] See S Han and W Li, 'Household Borrowing after Personal Bankruptcy' (2011) 43 *Journal of Money Credit and Banking* 491, 514.

[19] W Dobbie and J Song, 'Debt Relief and Debtor Outcomes: Measuring the Effects of Consumer Bankruptcy Protection' (2015) 105(3) *American Economic Review* 1272.

[20] Bankruptcy files are randomly assigned to judges who vary in their rates of granting bankruptcy protection. The authors were therefore able to look at individuals at the margin who might randomly be confirmed or rejected.

[21] The authors tested this by analysing the effects in states with different wage garnishment laws.

[22] Tested through analysis of probability of individual working in the same industry, and on probability of worker in a baseline county.

[23] See eg the study by R Ahlström, S Edström and M Savemark, 'Is Debt Relief Rehabilitative? An Evaluation of Debt Relieved Persons' Health, Life Quality and Personal Finances Three Years after Conducted Debt Relief' 2014:15 (Stockholm, The Swedish Consumer Agency, 2014) and studies in Finland cited by T Linna, 'Consumer Insolvency: The Linkage Between the Fresh Start, Collective Proceedings, and the Access to Debt Adjustment' (2015) 38 *Journal of Consumer Policy* 357, 371–72.

studies of the debt relief order (DRO) indicate that it does provide significant short-term benefits but we know little about its long-term effects. These studies suggest that further research is desirable on the limits of insolvency in addressing structural issues associated with unemployment and low income, and the interaction of debt relief with housing and welfare policies.

The above studies generally conceptualise individual insolvency as part of a social safety net. It may be a second-best solution filling in holes in the welfare system but it performs a useful function. Susanne Soederberg argues, however, that bankruptcy is a disciplinary mechanism of social control within neo-liberal governance which individualises responsibility, neutralising collective responses to debt and defusing political conflict.[24] Soederberg argues that capital increasingly exploits workers through the credit system, a form of secondary exploitation which substitutes high-cost credit for stagnant wages but fails to address the continuing problem of falling profits and productivity. Just as workfare imposes labour market discipline on the unemployed so 'debtfare' imposes the market discipline of high-cost credit on the poor. This 'debtfare' for the poor is one component of the neo-liberal state[25] which plays both a coercive and legitimating role in these developments. Thus the extension of credit to the poor is normalised through the rhetoric of the 'democratisation of credit', 'consumer protection', and 'financial inclusion'. Bankruptcy law must mediate the contradictions in the system by both disciplining debtors and legitimating the system. Individuals are therefore responsibilised through the bankruptcy process, giving them a second chance at being responsible users of credit. Her paradigm is US bankruptcy law and she views the US developments since 1978 through this critical lens, with BAPCPA as an 'integral part of the debtfare state' through its 'intrusive and humiliating means test', its removal of the right of choice for debtors between Chapter 7 and 13, and its disciplining mechanism of debt counselling legitimating the idea that resort to bankruptcy was caused by individual failures.[26]

Soederberg provides little systematic empirical data to support her arguments concerning the role of personal insolvency law and her picture of the demographics of bankruptcy in the US is not consistent with the empirical studies of Sullivan, Warren, and Westbrook which characterise bankruptcy as a middle-class phenomenon—one that may affect a broad cross-section of the population.[27] Whether individuals experience personal insolvency as a disciplining and 'humiliating' experience is however an important research question. Stigma has always

[24] S Soederberg, *Debtfare States and the Poverty Industry—Money, discipline and the surplus population* (Abingdon, Routledge, 2014).

[25] Soederberg identifies monetarism, corporate welfarism, and workfarism as the other components. Ibid 52–65.

[26] Ibid, 86–90.

[27] T Sullivan, E Warren, and JL Westbrook, *As We Forgive Our Debtors: Bankruptcy and Consumer Credit in America* (New York, Oxford University Press, 1989); TA Sullivan, E Warren, and JL Westbrook, *The Fragile Middle Class: Americans in Debt* (New Haven, Yale University Press, 2000).

been an aspect of bankruptcy[28] but the limited studies of the 2005 US reforms such as mandatory debt counselling indicate that counselling has little impact on debtors, with many simply believing that it is a waste of time either because their bankruptcy was caused by external events or because the information provided was not of assistance.[29] This does not deny the potentially symbolic significance of counselling, but does suggest that individuals do not necessarily 'buy in' to neoliberal ideas that bankruptcy is caused by individual failure.

Soederberg highlights, however, the need to think carefully about the potential role of personal insolvency as a 'safety net' and whether it individualises collective problems, defusing political conflict and demands for more collective responses to debt problems. In Spain, the absence of a way out through bankruptcy for debtors trapped with mortgage debt sparked the growth of a political movement. The Platform of Mortgage Victims (Plataforma de Afectados por la Hipoteca) formed in 2009 mobilised for legislative change, and many public demonstrations took place against the background of the high level of distress caused by foreclosures.

Soederberg highlights also the social control role of personal insolvency law which may often be most significant in triggering non-legal sanctions, such as an adverse credit score. Credit scoring and credit reports are increasingly a sorting and disciplining measure and a major concern for individuals contemplating bankruptcy is its effect on a credit rating.[30] A personal insolvency note on a credit file may have a significant impact on an individual's life. Soederberg's analysis also draws attention to the fact that the fresh start for many of the 'surplus population' may simply mean re-entry to a credit market of high costs and exploitation, euphemistically described as financial inclusion.

A crude distinction might be drawn between legal processes which 'do things to people' (for example, the criminal process) and those which provide individuals with resources and are intended to empower them (for example, the introduction of small claims courts). Personal insolvency law straddles this dichotomy and often results in the framing of a complex law that attempts to balance these objectives.

The rise of personal insolvency law in Europe and elsewhere has tracked the rise of neo-liberalism as a dominant world idea and technology of governance. The increases in household credit and debt within economies along with an increase in inequality in many countries are two salient aspects of neo-liberalism. Since the rich save more than they spend as a percentage of their income, economic growth depends on increased spending by middle to lower-income individuals, financed by credit. But this model of the economy seems to lead to continuing crises and problems of debt overhang. Personal insolvency law of some form is therefore an inevitable aspect of such an economy. The particulars of this form will, I have

[28] For a very useful recent review see P Ali, L O'Brien, and I M Ramsay, 'Short of a Few Quid: Bankruptcy Stigma in Contemporary Australia' (2015) 38(4) *New South Wales Law Journal* 1575.

[29] MD Sousa, 'Just Punch My Bankruptcy Ticket: A Qualitative Study of Mandatory Debtor Financial Education' (2013) 97 *Marquette Law Review* 391.

[30] Bankruptcy may remain on a credit record for 10 years in the US, six years in the UK.

argued, depend partly on the role of interest groups, contingency and the ability of groups to promote successfully one of the limited number of tropes in the personal insolvency toolkit. A liberal insolvency discharge is one method of sustaining the debt economy, even if individual financial institutions view it as not being in their short-term interests. A more challenging question is whether there may be too much household credit in the economy?[31]

[31] See eg A Turner, *Between Debt and the Devil: Money, Credit and Fixing Global Finance* (Princeton, Princeton University Press, 2016).

INDEX

www.ingramcontent.com/pod-product-compliance
Ingram Content Group UK Ltd.
Pitfield, Milton Keynes, MK11 3LW, UK
UKHW020141290926
15471UKWH00004B/638

9 781509 932177